Harvard's Quixotic
Pursuit of a New Science

Harvard's Quixotic Pursuit of a New Science

The Rise and Fall of the Department of Social Relations

Patrick L. Schmidt

ROWMAN & LITTLEFIELD
Lanham • Boulder • New York • London

Published by Rowman & Littlefield
An imprint of The Rowman & Littlefield Publishing Group, Inc.
4501 Forbes Boulevard, Suite 200, Lanham, Maryland 20706
www.rowman.com

86-90 Paul Street, London EC2A 4NE

British Library Cataloguing in Publication Information Available

Library of Congress Cataloging-in-Publication Data

Names: Schmidt, Patrick L., author.
Title: Harvard's quixotic pursuit of a new science : the rise and fall of
  the department of social relations / Patrick L. Schmidt.
Description: Lanham : Rowman & Littlefield, [2022] | Includes
  bibliographical references and index.
Identifiers: LCCN 2022001700 (print) | LCCN 2022001701 (ebook) | ISBN
  9781538168288 (cloth) | ISBN 9781538168295 (paperback) | ISBN
  9781538168301 (ebook)
Subjects: LCSH: Sociology—Study and teaching—United States. | Harvard
  University. | Parsons, Talcott, 1902–1979.
Classification: LCC HM577 .S36 2022 (print) | LCC HM577 (ebook) | DDC
  301.071/173—dc23/eng/20220120
LC record available at https://lccn.loc.gov/2022001700
LC ebook record available at https://lccn.loc.gov/2022001701

♾️™ The paper used in this publication meets the minimum requirements of American National Standard for Information Sciences—Permanence of Paper for Printed Library Materials, ANSI/NISO Z39.48-1992.

In honor of David Riesman and E. L. "Pat" Pattullo

In the meantime a very big scientific development has been rapidly gathering force—what our group tried, however, inadequately to formulate as the growth of a "basic social science." I will stake my whole professional reputation on the statement that it is one of the really great movements of modern scientific thought, comparable for instance, to the development of Biology in the last third of the 19th Century.

—Talcott Parsons to Paul H. Buck, dean,
Harvard University, April 3, 1944

Contents

Preface

The starting point for this book is my undergraduate honors thesis at Harvard University, "Towards a History of the Department of Social Relations, Harvard University, 1946–1972." I have drawn on that earlier work and the interviews supporting it. Through that experience, I interviewed many key players and observers in the department's narrative, such as Talcott Parsons, Henry Murray, George Homans, David McClelland, and B. F. Skinner. The book is in part an intellectual history, describing the fierce fights from the 1920s to the early 1940s over what constituted the new and developing disciplines of psychology and sociology at Harvard, as well as the less volatile debates over the direction of anthropology. I examined the failure of Social Relations, once established, to provide a theoretical integration of its constituent disciplines. I also described the broader intellectual shifts in academia—at Harvard and beyond—as theories and approaches fell in and out of favor among scholars in the behavioral sciences.

My work is an institutional history, however, and thus is broader in scope than an examination of the theoretical debates in the behavioral sciences that gave rise to the department. The intellectual issues are extremely important, of course, but they are not the full story. I also examined the other factors that affected the rise and fall of the Social Relations Department: the egos, the academic politics, the practical problems in mounting a large department with disparate disciplines, and the scandals that rocked an already shaky department. I relied largely on primary sources, although I also benefited from superb secondary sources regarding the formation of the department and its early years. I based some of the book's narrative on the correspondence of faculty members, using direct quotes to let them tell the story in their own words at critical junctures.

Acknowledgments

I first wrote about the history of the Department of Social Relations for my undergraduate honors thesis when I was a senior at Harvard College. Many of the faculty members and administrators involved in the department, including two of its founders, Talcott Parsons and Henry Murray, were still active at the university and were willing to be interviewed for the project. A classmate, Julia Moore, also had decided independently that this was a good topic for a thesis, so our respective advisors agreed to let us conduct the interviews together and write our essays separately. We had a wonderful time interviewing twenty-eight faculty members and administrators, who generously gave us a great deal of their time, in some cases more than one interview session. The result in my case was "Towards a History of the Department of Social Relations, Harvard University, 1946–1972," which relied on statements from the interviews as well as traditional documentary research materials.

I received a congratulatory letter from Professor David Riesman, one of our interviewees, who had been a member of the faculty of Social Relations, moving to the Department of Sociology upon its dissolution. Professor Riesman was not on my thesis committee, but he took an interest in what I had produced. He not only read the thesis, but he sent the letter (four pages, single spaced), encouraging me to publish it and offering numerous observations if I chose to do so. "You have done an extraordinary piece of work, and I think it should be published. . . . You have worked with scrupulousness and care, and have produced a document of lasting value. . . . If you do have a chance, as I very much hope, to do further work on it, I would have a number of comments and suggestions to offer. Let me just say a few things in the meantime." I was surprised and honored. For an undergraduate, this was heady stuff to have the author of the classic work on American character, *The Lonely Crowd*, and a major public intellectual of the twentieth century say such kind words. So, what did I do? Nothing. Callow youth. I had just graduated and was moving to Washington, DC, for work, and I had no time or appetite for further scholarly pursuits.

I had forgotten about the letter until I came across it in 2009. My mother had kept it in a large manila envelope along with my report cards, photos, and other memorabilia, dating from kindergarten onward. When she died, the envelope made its way to me. I found Professor Riesman's letter and thought what an extraordinary gesture it was for him to take the time to write me, a mere undergraduate, in such detail. I decided on the spot that I was going to write the department's history, even though it would be only a sporadic effort because I was busy with my international legal practice. When I began my research, I was encouraged to discover that several books and journal articles that discussed the department's founding had cited my thesis, even though it was only available in the Harvard University Archives.

Much information on the department has become available since I wrote my thesis, allowing me to expand and to transform that short essay into this book. Nearly all the key players are no longer with us, and their correspondence and files have in most cases become available in the Harvard University Archives. The letters of Talcott Parsons, Gordon Allport, and Jerome Bruner are particularly rich in details about the department. In addition, faculty members Gordon Allport, George Homans, Jerome Bruner, and Timothy Leary published autobiographies that discussed, at least in part, the department. A biography of Henry Murray described his isolation in the Psychology Department and his subsequent time in Social Relations. Notable PhDs in Social Relations—Arthur Vidich, Norman Birnbaum, David Schneider, and Clifford Geertz—also have written about the early years of the department when they were graduate students. In 2015, I was fortunate to have interviewed Norman Birnbaum, who had strong and colorful views on the department's disunity. Howard Gardner, both an undergraduate and graduate student in the latter years of Social Relations, has published a blog and a memoir, *A Synthesizing Mind*, discussing in part his experience as a graduate student and the lifelong influence on his work of the interdisciplinary approach and ethos of the Social Relations Department and faculty members Jerome Bruner, Erik Erikson, and David Riesman. These books—and the Birnbaum interview—provided me with a variety of viewpoints on the department from faculty and students.

I feel a deep personal connection to this topic. Working on my senior essay was the highlight of my undergraduate years. It was a thrill interviewing these giants of the twentieth-century behavioral sciences. And for three years, I had a work-study job in the Social Relations Library, the last physical vestige of the Department of Social Relations after its demise. From behind the checkout desk, I could observe the lobby of William James Hall and the comings and goings of the remaining faculty members of Social Relations (now on the faculty of the successor Department of Psychology and Social Relations), as well as B. F. Skinner, who had disapproved of the work of the social and clinical psychologists since he was a graduate student in Psychology at Harvard in the late 1920s.

I am grateful to many people for their assistance and support in the writing of this book. I owe a great deal to E. L. "Pat" Pattullo, who encouraged me to pursue the history of the Social Relations Department as my thesis topic and who served as my advisor. I enjoyed an independent study course I had designed my junior year on the history of science that examined the evolution of Psychology at Harvard, so I was already aware of, and intrigued by, the Social Relations experiment. He had been the director of the Center for the Behavioral Sciences, and he was knowledgeable about Social Relations and its decline. Pat first had been my freshman advisor at Harvard, and I think it may be unique for a Harvard student to have had the same person as both freshman advisor and senior thesis advisor. He also was a great friend. Of course, I owe a large debt to David Riesman, as I already described. I would not have written the book without his encouragement. I am grateful to my late mother, Jeanne Schmidt, for safekeeping his letter to me, just one of the countless things, big and small, that she did for me.

Many friends helped with the book in various ways. I thank Dan Sorensen for reading a completed draft of the manuscript. He kept me moving forward with his incisive editorial comments and his good humor. I am grateful to Bill Sorensen for recommending that I consult his brother Dan and for encouraging me throughout the book project. Ellen Devine also reviewed a draft and offered many helpful comments, along with her reassurance that this was a story worth telling. I benefited from the support and goodwill of many other friends along the way, some even harking back to the writing of my thesis: Hedy Behbehani, Taher Behbehani, Robertico Croes, Tad Devine, Natasha Giddens, Ann Hodgman, Neda Khalili, Janie Kim, Tamera Luzzatto, Dean Overman, Elizabeth Reinhardt, Andy Schulman, Cliff Sloan, Anne Sontag Karch, Cy Vance, Lorna Potter Walker, and Ned Walker.

I mentioned my interview of Norman Birnbaum, and I am grateful to him for being so generous with his time. Jonathan Sisk, Mary Wheelehan, Kate Powers, and Sarah Sichina at Rowman & Littlefield provided helpful advice and guidance. Howard Brick, Andrew Jewett, Scott McLemee, Lawrence Nichols, and Ben Railton read two chapters of the manuscript for Rowman & Littlefield and made numerous valuable suggestions for improving my approach. I am indebted to Juliana Kuipers, the collection development curator/archivist at the Harvard University Archives, and the entire staff there for their indefatigable efforts in helping me with my research. I also am grateful to Susan Gilman, the librarian for Tozzer Library at Harvard University, for her assistance. I wish to acknowledge Zachary Leary, who graciously granted me permission to quote from Timothy Leary's *Flashbacks: An Autobiography.* I am grateful to Jamie Cohen-Cole for allowing me to quote from *The Open Mind: Cold War Politics and the Sciences of Human Nature.* I deeply appreciate Joel Isaac and his exhaustive research on the Carnegie Project on Theory as described in *Working Knowledge: Making the Human Sciences from Parsons to Kuhn.* I would also like to thank Gary A. Fine for permission to quote from his unpublished paper on the dissolution of the Department of Social Relations. Finally, I wish to thank Whitley Bruner for granting me permission to quote from the letters of his late father Jerome Bruner, who cared deeply about the position of psychology at Harvard and who wrote eloquently on the topic.

1

Psychoanalytic Thought Arrives at Harvard

Roiling the Disciplines

For educated persons today it is easy to forget how fresh and radical Freud seemed in the 1930s or how much controversy he inspired.

—George Homans

The psychoanalysts are inclined to consider the academic psychologists curious fellows in no way concerned with those real problems which they as psychotherapists have to meet. The psychologists, on the other hand, are inclined to look on the psychoanalysts as "mystics" or "cultists."

—J. F. Brown

On January 29, 1946, the Faculty of Arts and Sciences at Harvard University voted to create a new department.[1] It was a daring experiment by a conservative institution: integrating social anthropology, sociology, social psychology, and clinical psychology into a single department, leaving two diminished departments, Psychology and Anthropology, in its wake. No other university had such a department. At Harvard it had been years in the making, following turbulent infighting in the affected departments and reflecting wider movements in the social sciences before and after World War II. The faculty approved the new department at 5:30 p.m., but the years of germination and conflict left one important detail overlooked.[2] What should Harvard call it? According to one witness, "six p.m. was the sacred hour of adjournment for faculty meetings," so an undignified scramble ensued to find a suitable name.[3] The accurate but "suffocating" name was not in contention: the Department of

Sociology, Social Psychology, Clinical Psychology and Social Anthropology.[4] Someone suggested the Department of *Human Relations*, which
captured the spirit of the venture, but the faculty vetoed it immediately
because rival Yale already had an Institute of Human Relations. The name
also appeared to infringe on the Harvard Business School because human
relations was an area of study there.[5] The clock was ticking. The faculty
grew restless. Finally, at 5:59, someone proposed "Social Relations," and
because the faculty wanted to go home, they approved the name without
debate.[6]

This new band marched at the head of what David Riesman—the
renowned sociologist, keen observer of higher education, and himself
a member of the Social Relations Department—termed "the academic
procession." Its life—and death—was witnessed by all.[7] Throughout its
history, Social Relations boasted a faculty of some of the most important
scholars in American social science of the twentieth century and produced graduates who would also become notable scholars. Alongside
the academic accolades, however, scandals divided the faculty and cast
the department in an unfavorable light, not just at Harvard but nationally and even internationally. Social Relations is notorious for faculty
such as Timothy Leary and Richard Alpert (reborn as Ram Dass), who
researched the effects of psilocybin on students, and Henry Murray, who
traumatized undergraduate Ted Kaczynski (later the Unabomber) in a
three-year-long abusive psychological experiment. The 1960s zeitgeist
roiled the department beyond the Leary-Alpert scandal. The radical Students for a Democratic Society infiltrated the teaching staff of the department's largest course in 1968, promoting a political agenda with farcical
academic standards and igniting a bitter controversy in Social Relations
and throughout the Harvard community.

The idea for Social Relations was hatched in the 1930s. Scorned by
traditional interests in their Harvard departments, rising faculty stars
in anthropology, sociology, and psychology fled their antagonists, seeking to create not merely a new department but a new social science. The
refugees were Talcott Parsons, Gordon Allport, Henry Murray, and Clyde
Kluckhohn—supported administratively by Dean Paul Buck. They promised an interdisciplinary science that would supplant the elder social
sciences of history, government, and economics in the ability to explain
human behavior. An audacious aspiration, critics found it as imperious
as it was implausible. Inspired by the new and controversial works of
Sigmund Freud and Carl Jung, the group met clandestinely to plot the
bold venture, giving their efforts a conspiratorial air. They called themselves the "Levellers" in recognition of the many levels they believed the
study of behavior required. Their big break came when their vision was
legitimized by interdisciplinary research during World War II conducted

by the Research Branch of the War Department and the Foreign Morale Analysis Division of the Office of War Information. Government agencies employed teams of clinical and social psychologists, cultural anthropologists, and sociologists to study issues important to the war effort, such as assessing the morale of the Japanese, as well as the spirit of our own troops.

Some of the Levellers and other early members of the Social Relations Department had worked in these wartime research efforts. Such collaboration under urgent conditions led to a productive exchange of concepts and methodologies across the established disciplines. This teamwork had a lasting effect on the participants, many of whom were determined to deepen and institutionalize the exchange after the war ended. Already moving toward an interdisciplinary focus before the war, the founders of Social Relations now had concrete experience of collaborating with scholars of other disciplines. They also had a grandiose confidence that they could study—and solve—any social problem by employing methodologies from their constituent disciplines. Indeed, sociologist Talcott Parsons, the intellectual ringleader of the group, believed it was possible, drawing on these disparate disciplines, to develop a single theory to explain human behavior.

The expectations for the social sciences ran high in postwar America, and Harvard's Social Relations Department was at the epicenter of the enthusiasm. As historian David Engerman explained: "The lofty aspiration to apply social science to improve society has long been a part of American life, but in few moments, and in few places, was that aspiration as fervently held as at Harvard in the 1940s."[8] David McClelland, an early member of Social Relations and later its chairman, recalled, "We had a wonderful time . . . dreaming dreams about how to foster basic science in a way that would also contribute to human progress."[9] Only twenty-five years later, however, many at Harvard dismissed the Department of Social Relations as the Department of "Residual" or "Remnant" Relations.[10] Clinical psychology and sociology had left the fold; the latter was reestablished in its own department, while the former was abandoned after many setbacks.[11] Social anthropology returned to its old home in the Peabody Museum and the Department of Anthropology.[12] The remaining subdisciplines of Social Relations (developmental, social, and personality psychology) reunited with the Psychology Department (which was then dominated by experimental psychologists) to form the Department of Psychology and Social Relations.[13] In 1986—forty years after the founding of Social Relations—Harvard shortened the name to the Department to Psychology, removing the last official vestige of Social Relations.[14]

In the lead-up to the formation of Social Relations, and throughout its existence, faculty and administration were preoccupied—even obsessed at times—with whether Harvard was forging a new trail in the behavioral sciences or falling behind other universities. The loss, and even the threatened defection, of a leading scholar to another university over disagreements about the proper scope and direction of a discipline served as a catalyst for change on more than one occasion. Harvard is unquestionably a leader in academia, but it is necessarily, if clandestinely, a follower of academic fashion as well.[15] The interplay of two forces created the Department of Social Relations. A positive force was the founders' dream of creating a new interdisciplinary social science. There also was a negative force that pushed them out of their original departments. Four of the five founding faculty members felt such hostility—personal and professional—within their own departments that they simply needed to escape: Henry Murray (Psychology), Gordon Allport (Psychology), Clyde Kluckhohn (Anthropology), and Talcott Parsons (Sociology). These professors clashed with the established faculty in their departments. The disputes were neither arcane nor petty. Rather, they were profound conflicts about the direction and definition of their disciplines, and they were especially intense in the Psychology and Sociology Departments:

> Between 1935 and 1945, members of the Psychology and Sociology Departments could not agree on what did and did not count as belonging to their fields. In psychology, the faculty were barely on speaking terms. They divided on every possible issue that bore on the nature of the discipline and department. So deeply ran the disagreements that psychologists could not agree on what constituted fact, experiment or the "general" core of their field.[16]

The fighting was highly personal. George Homans, a member of the Sociology Department and later of Social Relations, bellowed that "Social Relations was a department built on personality conflicts—hate!"[17] The irony, of course, is that the social sciences focused on understanding human behavior were decidedly unsocial when it came to relations between and among its own faculty members. By creating the Department of Social Relations, the founders were able to escape their adversaries in their original departments. At the same time, a legitimate and bold academic vision—the unification of their interests and disciplines in a new, interdisciplinary department—beckoned them. The origins of Social Relations trace back to the 1930s. The complex and varied forces that led to the formation of Social Relations continued to influence its evolution as a department as well as its ultimate demise. Its history is replete with recurring debates over the proper theoretical focus and core intellectual identity of the department. To be sure, it is a story of a single department, but it must begin with a brief look at each of the three departments whose problems, personalities, and parochialism contributed to its rise.

ANTHROPOLOGY: A DEPARTMENT
STEEPED IN ARCHAEOLOGY

Of the departments partially or wholly subsumed under Social Relations, Anthropology was the oldest. Anthropology began at Harvard with the establishment of the Peabody Museum and the creation of the Peabody Professorship of American Archaeology and Ethnology.[18] The museum thrived, becoming part of the university in 1897. Even earlier, in 1890, a Division of American Archaeology and Ethnology was formed, and anthropology courses were added in 1894.[19] In recognition of the expanding academic territory covered by this division, Harvard changed the name to the Department of Anthropology.[20] The 1890s launched a series of archaeological and ethnological expeditions, and the department began instruction in physical anthropology.[21] The first social anthropologist at Harvard, Lloyd Warner, found himself in a department in the tradition of archaeological and physical anthropology. Both he and his area of interest were newcomers to the department. Warner did not stay long at Harvard, departing for the University of Chicago.

Clyde Kluckhohn took his place. As the only social anthropologist in a decidedly archaeological department, he too felt overwhelmed.[22] His primary interests were even farther removed from the central focus of the department than those of Warner.[23] Psychoanalysis and Freudian psychology only recently had been introduced in the United States, but Kluckhohn, who had undergone analysis in Germany, was an acolyte.[24] He applied psychoanalytic theory to his fieldwork with the Navajo Indians.[25] It was groundbreaking work, but the senior faculty in the Department of Anthropology viewed it with alarm, deeming it dubious and unscientific.[26] Kluckhohn, in turn, had no interest in the traditional "stones and bones" physical anthropology of his colleagues and was unpopular in the department.[27]

Kluckhohn did not have to look far, however, to find colleagues outside of the department who shared his interest in psychoanalysis.[28] He befriended Henry Murray of the Psychology Department, who had undergone a "life-altering experience with Karl Gustav Jung" and later became a charter member of the Boston Psychoanalytic Society.[29] Kluckhohn found another like-minded colleague in Talcott Parsons of the Sociology Department, who was also fascinated with the new and controversial theory. These young faculty members frequently discussed the potential applicability of psychoanalysis to their respective disciplines. But sympathetic colleagues outside of his discipline made Kluckhohn no happier with the situation within his own department, which continued to inhibit his approach to anthropology.[30]

PSYCHOLOGY: A DEEPLY DIVIDED DEPARTMENT

Henry Murray in the Psychology Department—the second department to be subsumed partially into Social Relations—felt similarly stifled. He arrived at Harvard in 1926 as an assistant professor and director of the recently established Psychological Clinic, made possible by a gift of $125,000 from Morton Prince, a prominent Boston psychiatrist. As associate professor of abnormal and dynamic psychology, Prince had directed the project for the last two years of his life.[31] Upon his death, Murray became the director. Many department members regarded the clinic as a "stepchild" of the Psychology Department.[32] Critics suggested that Prince had "purchased" his professorship with his $125,000 gift of the clinic.[33] Worse, the clinic lacked perpetual funding, and Murray lacked a permanent appointment; it was a tenuous existence at Harvard for both.

Despite having read widely in the field, Murray conceded that he lacked the relevant academic background: "No man more ignorant of textbook knowledge was ever admitted to a department of psychology."[34] Indeed, as an undergraduate at Harvard, he avoided the subject, having been repulsed by the experimental approach in the only psychology class he ever sampled: "At college a bud of interest in psychology was nipped by the chill of Professor Munsterberg's approach. In the middle of his second lecture, I began looking for the nearest exit."[35] What cemented Murray's fascination and lifelong dedication to psychoanalysis—or what he called "depth psychology"—was his visit with Jung in 1925. Murray credited Jung's book *Psychological Types* as "what started me off in earnest toward psychology."[36] And Murray was mesmerized when he later visited Jung in Zurich: "The 'great flood gates of the wonder world swung open' and I saw things that my philosophy had never dreamt of."[37] Nothing had prepared him for the meeting: "In 1925, however, I had no scales to weigh out Dr. Jung, the first full-blooded, spherical—and Goethean, I should say—intelligence I had ever met, the man whom the judicious Prinzhorn called the 'ripest fruit on the tree of psycho-analytical knowledge.' We talked for hours, sailing down the lake and smoking before the hearth of his Faustian retreat."[38]

At Harvard, Murray confronted a department with traditional interests hostile to his own. The source of the hostility was rooted in history. Psychology instruction at Harvard began in 1875 in the Department of Philosophy with a graduate course taught by William James. Undergraduate instruction started in 1876.[39] James reportedly quipped that "the first lecture in psychology that I ever heard was the first I ever gave."[40] From the outset, James sought to establish psychology as a scientific discipline apart from philosophy. In 1892, Harvard established the Psychological Laboratory, and James recruited Hugo Munsterberg from Germany to direct its operation.[41] But in Munsterberg, James got more science than he expected, and he grew disillusioned with the German's approach to psychology, seeing it as "cold" problem-centered scientism.[42] He believed Munsterberg's purely experimental approach to psychology "lost sight of the human dimension" and "was both misdirected and meaningless."[43] Disappointed, he abandoned the discipline, exchanging his professorship of psychology for that of philosophy.[44]

James left psychology at Harvard completely in the hands of Munsterberg, who made significant advances in the new field, just not in the direction James desired. Munsterberg acquired space for laboratories in Emerson Hall and brought in new faculty to teach psychology, including R. M. Yerkes, who pioneered research in animal behavior at Harvard.[45] Munsterberg died in 1916, but psychology was not without a guiding force for long. The arrival of E. G. Boring in 1922 heralded the beginning of a new era.[46] Boring assumed leadership of the laboratory, the primary focus of the psychologists.[47] Despite Munsterberg's success, psychology had remained in the Philosophy Department, although it did gain separate course listing in 1913.[48] Boring was strongly committed to an experimental approach and considered the "rescuing of psychology from these philosophers" to be his mission.[49] While James, at least initially, had sought to free psychology from philosophy intellectually, Boring concentrated on an administrative emancipation. And Boring succeeded in strengthening the discipline in numerous ways. Harvard expanded the psychology facilities further in 1929 when the laboratory acquired an annex on the top floor of Boylston Hall. It was not until 1935, however, that he sensed that success was at hand: "After twelve years my mission at Harvard was still unfulfilled. We were then a de jure Psychological Laboratory in a de facto Department of Psychology in a de jure Department of Philosophy and Psychology in a Faculty of Arts and Sciences. Lowell would have kept it thus, but Conant under my constant pressure created change."[50]

James B. Conant succeeded A. Lawrence Lowell as president of Harvard University in 1933, and he set in motion the changes sought by Boring.[51] Conant approved a visiting committee's report to the Board of Overseers of Harvard College that psychology be made a separate department from philosophy.[52] The committee pointed out "that the philosophers, in voting upon questions arising in relation to psychology, find themselves passing on subjects that they do not understand, and that psychologists in their turn are placed in a similar position."[53]

With great deference to the wishes of the department members, the committee stated: "If lay opinion may be ventured, this desire [for separation] seems well based. Very few people seem to care for both Philosophy and Psychology, the Psychologists of the present day seem to be by nature scientific, with a bias toward things that can be proved and measured, the Philosophers to be dedicated to the study of external verities."[54]

The committee's recommendation soon became reality. In 1934, Harvard established the Department of Psychology, with Boring as its chairman.[55] According to Boring, he had been "acting as chairman without authority for a dozen years," but he still bristled that the new department remained part of a Division of Philosophy and Psychology.[56] Two years later, however, he rejoiced in removing the final administrative influence of philosophy on psychology: "I moved that the Faculty abolish all divisions in order to leave the departments autonomous, except those departments that asked for divisional amalgamation, and that motion passed. Now at long last we had access to the Dean without a philosopher as intermediary. My mission was accomplished."[57]

Boring's crusade to rid psychology of philosophy institutionally triumphed, but fellow psychology professor S. S. Stevens had a more aggressive agenda. He wanted to purge the study of psychology of any nonscientific contagion. Stevens—an experimental psychologist—sought to suppress psychologists from studying mental processes immune to precise empirical measurement, not only at Harvard but in the discipline at large.[58] He cofounded the Psychology Roundtable, a highly influential and select group of young psychologists, who were dedicated to experimental research.[59] The roundtable founders recoiled at the so-called "scientific work" being presented at the American Psychological Association, and they felt compelled to establish "an exclusive community designed to separate the good from the bad psychologists."[60] From that position, Stevens could, on an institutional basis, extend his mission to purify "scientific experimental psychology from that which he deemed had failed to reach the standard of true science."[61]

EXPERIMENTAL PSYCHOLOGISTS
DOMINATE THE DEPARTMENT

In the 1930s, behaviorism—one branch of experimental psychology—dominated the field of psychology, enabling Stevens to operate from a position of great strength.[62] He promoted a movement within experimental psychology known as operationism, which he believed would bring even greater scientific rigor to the field. Like experimental psychologists, behavioral psychologists believed the world could only be understood through empirical investigation of "visible and measurable behavior."[63] Thus, they excluded from psychology the study of any mental processes that could not be observed. Their focus of inquiry was "on organisms learning by rote or trial-and-error," and they viewed behavior "as a series of stimulus-response reflexes chained one after the other."[64]

For them, there was no room in psychology for studying insight, will, intuition, motivation, phobias, creative thinking, reverie, and any number of other mental processes. Both at Harvard and in his role as founder of the Psychological Roundtable, Stevens pursued a policy of exclusion that "drove the study of emotions, personality, and indeed, all higher mental processes out of psychology's inner sanctum."[65] If behavioral psychologists, and their brethren in experimental and operationist psychology, were not interested in higher mental processes, what were they studying in order to explain human behavior? Stevens, for his part, studied how actual physical sounds, as measured by decibels, compared with the "psychological loudness" of sounds or how the loudness was experienced.[66] At Harvard, he directed the Psycho-Acoustic Laboratory.

Stevens's contempt for the study of personality or mental processes permeated the Psychology Department, including the graduate students and researchers such as B. F. Skinner. For Skinner, the only valid subject for psychological inquiry was the effect that the environment had on a subject, i.e., how an organism learned through "random trial and error and the association of particular behavioral responses with a reward or other stimulus."[67] Because the mind and its processes are not visible and measurable, he viewed any attempt to speak or write about them as "nonsense."[68] It was said he feigned deafness if a colleague said anything with a "mentalistic language."[69] Indeed, he dismissed all social sciences as unreliable: "I don't believe we have any principles in political science or in economics that can be trusted."[70] Although Skinner was only a graduate student and researcher in the 1930s and not yet on the faculty, his views reflected the rigid, unwelcoming attitude of the Psychology Department toward the study of mental processes.

EXPERIMENTAL PSYCHOLOGISTS
DISPARAGE MURRAY'S WORK

Thus, Henry Murray was isolated in a department built around the laboratory and populated by strong-willed men dedicated to experimental psychology and inimical to any other strand of psychology.[71]

His psychoanalytic approach to human behavior clearly did not fit their mold.[72] His colleagues scorned him because he was not scientific.[73] Murray, in turn, ridiculed their narrow focus:

> At first I was taken aback, having vaguely expected that most academic psychologists would be interested in Man functioning in his environment.

But not at all: almost everyone was nailed down to some piece of apparatus, measuring a small segment of the nervous system as if it were isolated from the entrails. I was in the position, let us imagine, of a medical student who suddenly discovers that all his instructors are eye, ear, nose and throat specialists.[74]

The Psychology Department did not consider his interests in problems of motivation and emotion worthy of study: "[My interests] were not susceptible to exact experimental validation, a standard that rules out geology, paleontology, anthropology, embryology, most of medicine, sociology and divine astronomy. If my chief aim had been to 'work with the greatest scientific precision' I would never have quit electrolytes and gas."[75] Ironically, Murray was no stranger to hard science, and his cre-

Figure 1.1.   Henry A. Murray, 1962. HUP Murray, Henry (3), olvwork188005. Harvard University Archives.

dentials in this regard surpassed those of his detractors. Not only had he graduated from Columbia Medical School, completing a residency in surgery, but he also had a PhD in biochemistry from Cambridge University.[76]

Murray's colleagues denigrated his work with human subjects; he was not a "real psychologist," merely a "literary" or "applied psychologist."[77] Murray counterattacked his scientifically oriented antagonists: "[They were] obsessed by anxious aims to climb the social scale of scientists and join the elect of this day's God at any cost. What else could account for their putting manners (appliances and statistics) so far ahead of ends (importance of the problems studied)? No matter how trivial the conclusions, if his coefficients were reliable, an experimenter was deemed pure and sanctified."[78] Throughout his life, Murray displayed his disdain for experimental psychologists. Years later, he addressed the august American Psychological Association on "The Personality and Career of Satan."[79] He chided the audience for its "immaculate Scientism" and argued instead for drawing upon many areas of humanistic learning such as biblical studies, church history, and medieval philosophy.[80]

Boring and others disparaged at every opportunity the research conducted under Murray's supervision at the Psychological Clinic and the quality of Murray's teaching; nothing was off-limits or too petty. The unwritten policy at Harvard required new assistant professors to be tough teachers. Murray's detractors saw his popularity with students as proof of insufficient rigor.[81] Graduate student Jerome Bruner, for example, found him to be charismatic and inspiring: "To hear Murray diagnose the stories that people made up in response to the pictures of his Thematic Apperception Test, was, I thought, like reading Henry James."[82] On a substantive level, the biotropic psychologists criticized the validity of Murray's research methods, especially his use of hypnosis. The Yale Institute of Human Relations had recently been forced to cease using hypnosis in its research, so suspicion about the safety of hypnosis was in the air. In 1931, a Radcliffe student alleged that she had been the victim of sexual advances while in a hypnotic trance induced by a graduate student conducting research at the clinic. After that incident, Boring forbade Murray to use hypnosis in research with students as subjects.[83]

Murray's work on psychoanalysis also collided with the conservative tenor of Harvard and Boston.[84] It was a highly controversial theory (and imported from Europe, therefore immediately suspect) that elevated the study of sexuality. This was all too much for many proper Bostonians to absorb. Murray responded publicly to the controversy. He wrote a piece for the student newspaper, the *Harvard Crimson*, to counter the rumors and speculation regarding the activity of the Psychological Clinic and its focus on abnormal psychology, including "sex and other so-called Freudian material."[85] He mocked the American university—including

Harvard—in that period as a "coolbed of conservatism" where "our professors are by nature prudent, our students docile."[86] He said the "bon
petit diable" (good little devil) of abnormal psychology raised suspicion
precisely because it forces people to confront the "blue print of the mental underworld" and to "recoil."[87] He asked rhetorically why Harvard
should allow the study of abnormal psychology at all if it was so deviant:
"If this is true, how is it that a university first fashioned by high church-
men should admit this troublesome child within its august portals?"[88]

Harvard sociologist George Homans, the definition of a Boston Brah-
min (a nephew of Henry Adams raised in the self-described "better side"
of the Back Bay and a Harvard graduate), recalled how shocking psychoanalysis was at the time. In 1988, he wrote that, "for educated persons
today it is easy to forget how fresh and radical Freud seemed in the 1930s
or how much controversy he inspired."[89] One of the first Americans to
practice psychoanalysis—and the leading American-born "conduit" for
introducing the controversial theory into American academic psychology—was Henry Murray.[90] Harvard was ground zero for the controversy.

The battle between psychoanalysts and academic psychologists was
more than a parochial Harvard matter. It was one front in a larger struggle about the direction of American psychology. At Harvard, the conflict
was particularly intense because the Psychological Clinic was affiliated
with the college and not the medical school.[91] This was a requirement
of Morton Prince, the Boston psychiatrist who made the gift of the clinic
to Harvard and became its first director.[92] This was atypical at the time:
elsewhere the only contact the adherents of psychoanalysis had with
academia was confined to the medical schools of universities.[93] Psychoanalysis was sometimes taught in the neuropsychiatric departments of
medical schools, but never in any academic department of psychology, or
at least not as a routine part of the curriculum for either undergraduates
or graduates.[94] Psychoanalysts had no choice but to develop their own
training centers outside the universities.

According to J. F. Brown, a historian of psychology in the 1930s and
1940s, both psychoanalysis and psychology suffered from the split, resulting in "an academic psychology which is precise but sterile, and a
psychoanalysis which is badly in need of scientific criticism but vital and
fruitful."[95] Murray was not alone in his frustration with academic psychologists, and as Brown observed, the result was a counterproductive
stalemate.

> The outcome of this state of affairs is most unfortunate. The psychoanalysts
> are inclined to consider the academic psychologists curious fellows in no
> way concerned with those real problems which they as psychotherapists
> have to meet. The psychologists, on the other hand, are inclined to look on

the psychoanalysts as "mystics" or "cultists." Nothing is gained by either side and the resulting disdain and suspicion are mutual.[96]

Murray described this divide vividly in a 1935 article titled "Psychology and the University" in which he asserted, "If psychology is defined as the science which describes people and explains why they perceive, feel, think, and act as they do . . . no science of the kind exists."[97] He criticized academic psychologists as "encrusted specialists" from whose "web of activity consideration of man as a human being has somehow escaped"—the "vestal virgins of unusable truth."[98] For Murray, academic psychology was essentially worthless, contributing, "practically nothing to the knowledge of human nature."[99]

He had kinder words for Freud and psychoanalysts, who he believed were on the right track but needed more training in fundamental science, greater discipline, and less hostility to research.[100] He labeled Freud "a strange genius who made some of the shrewdest guesses that have ever been recorded."[101] Murray summarized the problem: "Academic psychologists are looking critically at the wrong things. Psychoanalysts are looking with reeling brains at the right things."[102]

The derision of psychoanalysis within the Psychology Department acquired an even sharper edge in 1937 with a new addition to the faculty: Karl Lashley, a renowned psychologist of animal behavior.[103] His appointment was the result of President Conant's search to find "the best psychologist in the world" and bring him to Harvard.[104] In the search, Harvard had also considered Sigmund Freud and Carl Jung.[105] Although those two names resonate more today than Lashley, especially with generalists, many in the field indeed considered Lashley at the time to be the world's best psychologist.[106]

Boring supported bringing Lashley to Harvard, hoping he would strengthen the department's focus on experimental and empirical psychology, but Boring got far more than he expected. Lashley so stridently and dogmatically championed empirical psychology that he annoyed nearly everyone. Colleagues found Lashley to be "narrow minded to the point of irrationality when discussing points of view that differed from his own."[107] He even questioned the scientific basis of Boring's work—who himself was a devout experimentalist.[108] Predictably, Lashley considered Murray's focus on psychoanalysis to be a disgrace. According to B. F. Skinner, who viewed the ferment from his perch as a graduate student, Lashley was contemptuous of Murray's work and furious that Harvard tolerated his approach.[109] Lashley joined strict experimentalist S. S. Stevens in his opposition to Murray and his methods.[110] Though Boring also disapproved of Murray's approach, he remained less overtly critical. Boring, Lashley, and Stevens, along with another experimentally minded colleague, J. G. Beebe-Center, comprised what Boring called the "biotropic" side of the department stacked against Murray.[111]

MURRAY'S ALLY: GORDON ALLPORT

The "sociotropic" or social side of psychology was made up of Murray, Robert White, and Gordon Allport.[112] White, a junior staff member, was interested in personality psychology and worked in the clinic with Murray. Allport, a senior member of the department, worked both in personality and social psychology.[113] Allport believed he had much in common with Murray, joking, "Our fields of interest lie so close together that by unspoken agreement we allow a 'narcissism of slight differences' to keep us in a state of friendly separation."[114] By necessity, the two men united in standing up to the experimental psychologists, but there was more than a *slight* difference in their theories and personal styles.[115] Jerome Bruner, a graduate student and later a fellow faculty member, summarized: "If Murray stood for Freud, Jung and the night view of human nature, Gordon Allport's was the day view."[116] Murray had an intuitive, enthusiastic, and impulsive approach to work, and he was largely pessimistic about human nature.[117] Allport, on the other hand, was formal and controlled in his style, with a boundless optimism for improving the human condition.[118] Bruner found them "a curious pair of respectful allies in that hardnosed environment" of the Department of Psychology.[119]

Allport and Murray diverged on a central point, however. Allport did not share Murray's admiration for psychoanalysis. As a newly minted Harvard PhD in psychology, Allport traveled to Europe on a fellowship and arranged to meet Freud in Vienna. Although he did not consider himself anti-Freudian, Allport's meeting with Freud convinced him that psychoanalysis had "excesses" and was unduly focused on unconscious motives.[120] Allport often told the story, attributing to it psychological significance: "It had the character of a traumatic developmental episode."[121] The meeting began awkwardly. Freud sat stone silent. Perplexed and uncomfortable, Allport sought to break the ice by recounting his observation of a little boy on the streetcar ride to Freud's office.[122] During the ride, the boy repeatedly told his mother he did not want to sit on a "dirty seat" and "next to a dirty man."[123] To Allport, the boy's fear of dirt seemed highly unusual and might spark a conversation with the taciturn great man. Freud finally spoke: "And was that little boy you?"[124] Allport was "flabbergasted" and changed the subject.[125] Freud's finding of an unconscious motive in the recounting of his observation led Allport to conclude that psychoanalysis focused too much, and too soon, on a deep probing of the unconscious rather than first giving "full recognition to manifest motives."[126]

Murray thought his friend Allport "was done with Freud before he went there," because he "doesn't like anything to do with sex and so forth and so forth and the unconsciousness."[127] He noted Allport's comfort with the conscious over the unconscious: "He's all for the consciousness. It's interesting he thought of consciousness as large and the unconscious as a little bit of a thing down there, and Freud thought the consciousness was a little thing up there, the unconscious the iceberg below."[128] Murray also believed Allport was annoyed because Freud had "hit him right on the head, right on the nose."[129]

> It was a very clever thing [of Freud] to say, because that's just what Allport is. I mean, he is a very fastidious person, he is very clean himself. He isn't compulsive, or he isn't neurotic or anything like that. But he is just very strong on the side of gentility and being very clean and his desk was always perfect and so forth and so forth, and all his correspondence [was orderly] and so forth.[130]

Allport's explanation for the episode—as told by his wife many years later—was that Freud rarely saw anyone other than patients, and absentmindedly he had mistaken Allport for one.[131] In that context, Freud's question to Allport was simply an attempt to help him with a perceived obsession.[132] Whatever the genesis of Allport's dislike of psychoanalysis, he decided not to incorporate it in his research. Instead, he began a lifelong study of personality and its manifest aspects.

Allport suffered less scorn from his Harvard colleagues than Murray.[133] He was familiar with biotropic methodology, having received his doctorate in psychology at Harvard as well as having published several papers on imagery and memory.[134] From 1924 to 1926, while serving as a professor in Harvard's Department of Social Ethics, Allport had assisted Boring in the teaching of Psychology 1, thus gaining greater familiarity with experimental psychology.[135] Nonetheless, Allport differed greatly from the biotropes, particularly in his concern for social ethics and values. A consuming interest in Gestalt or humanistic psychology, sparked by his studies in Germany under such teachers as William Stern and Eduard Spranger, drew Allport out of the mainstream of American psychology of the time.[136] This exposure led him to focus on personalistic psychology, the study of the whole person rather than isolated traits, which became a hallmark of his later work.[137] Despite his sympathy for Murray's work and sharing with him the sociotrope labeling by Boring, Allport's varied and undogmatic approach to psychology made him more acceptable to the biotropes, so much so that he became chairman of the department in 1937 with the blessing of Boring.[138] Allport's eclectic approach to

Figure 1.2. Gordon W. Allport, 1964. HUP Allport, Gordon W. (14), olvwork278613. Harvard University Archives.

psychology also did not impede his career beyond Harvard. In 1939, the American Psychology Association elected him its president.[139] And in 1951, his peers voted him the second most influential force in the history of personality theory—Freud came in first.[140]

MURRAY'S TENURE REVIEW: A FLASH POINT

Preceding Allport's ascension to the chairmanship of the department, however, was an internal tumult from 1936 to 1937 that crystallized in a highly personal way the marked divisions between the biotropes and sociotropes: the promotion and tenure review of Henry Murray.[141] Murray and his brand of psychology vexed Boring and the biotropes; furthermore, he was in the unenviable position of depending on them for the advancement of his career. Under normal circumstances, this would have been a straightforward assessment of an assistant professor's scholarship. In Murray's case, however, it was nothing less than a referendum on "the disciplinary acceptability of psychoanalysis, and on which view of psychology would dominate at Harvard."[142]

Boring and Lashley rejected psychoanalysis as a theory. Each had undergone analysis and found it lacking, so Murray's interest in it troubled them.[143] They also questioned Murray's holistic research methods because they deviated from those used in the physical sciences and by the biotropes of the Psychology Department. For Boring and Lashley, this was no simple scholarly squabble about theory and methods. They viewed it as an existential threat to the newly independent Department of Psychology, which they conceded needed shoring up because its erstwhile promoter, Harvard president James B. Conant, thought it lacked academic rigor.[144] To combat Conant's perception, and in keeping with their own experimental moorings, Boring and Lashley sought to minimize Murray. To them, Murray's emphasis on psychoanalysis risked moving the study of psychology at Harvard in the wrong direction.[145] After extricating psychology from the philosophers, Boring was not about to see his department veer off into an equally unscientific area of inquiry.

As a junior professor in this controversial and fledgling field, Murray was at a distinct disadvantage. His tenuous predicament was, as Triplet stated, "complicated by the fact that he stood at the fringe of a discipline that was itself at the fringe of acceptance."[146] There were personality clashes as well. Boring, a Quaker from a family of modest means, had a plain style and resented the charismatic and worldly Murray, whom he regarded as an impudent playboy who did not hide his affinity for the "good life."[147] And Murray had the wealth to pursue such a life; born into an affluent New York family, he married Josephine Rantoul, an heiress to a large family fortune. Murray—and Prince, the director of the Psychological Clinic—also irked Boring by sporting white lab coats to flaunt their standing as medical doctors: a status Boring lacked.[148]

The young professor was in an unenviable situation, but he was supremely confident in himself and in his nascent field. He was a tough target and not about to capitulate to the experimental psychologists. A *New York Times* review of a book by Murray would gush about him decades later:

> In writing about Henry Murray it is nearly impossible to avoid falling into clichés. A Renaissance man. A legendary figure. One of the pioneers of contemporary psychology. And so on. They are all true. What is most dazzling about the man and the career is his extraordinary versatility, the protean nature of his talents and achievements. . . . Not since William James has there been a psychologist so versatile, nor has anyone else written with equal verve and boldness.[149]

The battle over Murray's tenure was set. On December 9, 1936, President Conant appointed an ad hoc committee to decide Murray's fate.[150] The committee, as might be expected, became deadlocked. Concluding that the decision required a value judgment on the merits of personality research, the committee left the decision to Conant. This was bad news for Murray because Conant, a brilliant research chemist and thus a "hard scientist," was known for his distrust of psychoanalysis; Murray suspected he wanted to move the clinic to the medical school.[151] And Conant's brother-in-law, Billy Bridges, had committed suicide while undergoing psychoanalysis, which Murray believed prejudiced Conant against his work.[152]

Conant's committee evaluated the unpublished manuscript of Murray's *Explorations in Personality* detailing his research at the clinic (which would be published a year later, eventually becoming a classic of American psychology). The deliberations were confidential, but Murray later learned that Allport had compared him to Harvard's revered humanistic psychologist William James.[153] The committee liked the comparison, except for Lashley, who protested that James had done "more harm to psychology than any man that ever lived."[154] At Harvard such a declaration was "blasphemy . . . explicable only as the *faux-pas* of a hotheaded newcomer" to Cambridge such as Lashley.[155] Conant stormed from the room in anger.[156]

Allport and Lashley each sent a letter to Conant pressing his case. Allport wrote, "The chief merit . . . [of Murray's work] is that it pushes forward the frontiers of research in the psychology of personality. Nowhere else in the literature will one find in a single study such breadth of perspective, so many ingenious methods, and such intensive treatment of individual life."[157] Allport acknowledged the criticism of personality psychology as a new field, but he argued that Murray was propelling the discipline to a higher, more serious level: "It must be borne in mind that Murray is working in an almost virgin territory where chicanery and system-making have always prevailed. He brings a more critical mind to his subject than did Charcot, Prince, Freud or Jung."[158] Allport pleaded to preserve the strain of sociotropic psychology at Harvard and to link Murray's work with that of William James, decrying the narrowness of biotropic psychology: "I earnestly hope that you will not now permit the humanistic tradition in psychology at Harvard to be imperiled and destroyed. The critical standards of the 'exact sciences,' admirable in their own right, are not catholic enough in outlook to serve as the norm for the newer science of the human mind."[159] Lashley, in turn, attacked the validity of Murray's research methods:

> I am impressed . . . by the failure to meet satisfactorily any one of the . . . objective checks . . . by what I can interpret only as a sort of intellectual dis-

honesty where statistical tests for reliability are used and then glossed over as of little importance when they do not show the desired reliability, and by the supercilious attitude which Murray and his students show towards the available methods of validating their results.[160]

President Conant received these alternating salvos with no resolution in sight. The situation deteriorated even further. Allport threatened to resign if Murray did not receive tenure and a promotion, and Lashley threatened to resign unless Murray was terminated immediately.[161] Boring sought to break the deadlock by suggesting that Murray not receive tenure, but rather be promoted to associate professor with two five-year appointments, giving him the chance to demonstrate the validity of his work.[162] Satisfying neither Allport nor Lashley, the compromise had another flaw: if Murray did not have tenure, the clinic could not receive university funds to supplement its endowment. Conant, however, sought—and received—assurances from the Rockefeller Foundation that it would provide long-term financial support to the clinic notwithstanding Murray's lack of tenure.[163] Having finessed the financial angle, Conant agreed to the compromise and announced his decision on March 17, 1937.[164]

Allport and Lashley both blinked; neither resigned. Allport accepted the decision and stayed at Harvard. Lashley also remained, but only after demanding a special research professorship that allowed him to sever any responsibility to, or contact with, the Department of Psychology.[165] Outside of Harvard, observers viewed the compromise as a victory for Murray and the clinic, and Murray received numerous congratulatory letters.[166] After all, the clinic survived. The solution assured the publication of Murray's *Explorations in Personality* and the continued existence of a training ground for the next generation of American psychologists dedicated to psychoanalysis and humanistic psychology.[167] In short, it provided psychoanalysis a refuge in an otherwise antagonistic American academy, and thus played no small part in the course of the history of American psychology.[168] Donald MacKinnon, Murray's first graduate student, told his mentor that "a discontinuation of the Clinic would have been a blow to every center of teaching and research in dynamic psychology while its continuation is a boon to every such center. . . . Every psychologist owes you a profound debt of gratitude."[169]

For the moment, Conant prevailed in papering over the department's identity crisis. Personal and professional tensions remained, simmering and eventually acting as a catalyst in the creation of the Department of Social Relations. Allport continued to worry about the direction of the department, which he believed was willfully ignoring the new movements in psychology. Experimental and behavioral psychology still had a stranglehold on the Psychology Department at Harvard. Arguments over methods, requirements, curriculum, and appropriate thesis subjects raged. The faculty could not agree on what constituted the discipline of psychology and were hardly speaking to one another.[170]

ALLPORT STRIKES BACK

In 1939, three years after the bruising battle over Murray's tenure, Allport launched a public counterattack on experimental psychology and, not so indirectly, on his colleagues E. G. Boring, S. S. Stevens, and Karl Lashley. As president of the American Psychological Association, Allport used his presidential address to rail against "operationism"—Stevens's brand (and Boring's to a degree as well) of experimental psychology—as a "ritual of method" unconnected with daily life.[171] Operationism posited that only replicable physical "operations" constitute science, and that which could not be measured was not suitable for science. Stevens's philosophy thus excluded the work of Allport and Murray from the "science" of psychology, which of course was essentially the same argument Lashley had made against granting tenure to Murray.

The speech is a revealing display of Allport's pent-up frustration about Harvard's parochial problems in psychology as well as of prevailing national trends. It is unlikely that many in the audience knew the extent of the brutal clash over the identity of the discipline at Harvard. Allport proceeded to review fifty years of psychology, surveying over 1,600 articles in the top fourteen journals of the literature to determine where the discipline had been and where it was headed.[172]

Allport concluded that a divide was developing between applied psychology, dealing with living, social issues, and pure or experimental psychology, dealing with more abstract matters.[173] He believed these groups were "parting ways to some extent—an event which some will deplore and others welcome."[174] In particular, he regretted the recent rise in the number of articles mentioning operationism and the decline in articles on applied psychology and social betterment. Allport lamented psychology's neglect of higher mental processes, such as the speech of human beings, in favor of studies of nonverbal behavior and animal studies. He also expressed concern over a disregard for studies of single cases. Allport concluded his introduction pessimistically, stating, "It also looks as if modern psychology were becoming appreciably unhistorical."[175]

He denigrated operationism, citing it as one of the "waxing and waning fashions of the day."[176] He derided it as "the current watchword of an austere empiricism" and a "magic concept" with a trajectory in the literature that was "onward and upward leading somewhere into the world of tomorrow."[177] To drive that point home, the text of his speech included a cartoon of a man riding a rocket ship of "operationism" into outer space.[178] Allport instead called for a discipline that was broad and inclusive, accepting viewpoints beyond experimental psychology. To him, a narrow exclusionary psychology was shortsighted and undemocratic:

> The desirability of keeping alive diversified investigation and a diversified sense of importance is the generous lesson that democracy teaches us. Now, if ever, must we learn it well and apply it to ourselves. If we rejoice, for example, that present-day psychology is . . . and as our survey has shown— increasingly empirical, mechanistic, quantitative, nomothetic, analytic, and operational, we should also beware of demanding slavish subservience to these presuppositions.[179]

What Allport meant by democracy was the freedom of psychologists of whatever stripe to pursue their individual interests. He theorized that "democracy will ultimately gain by giving each thinker all the space he wants. . . . Each worker may elect, as he pleases, any section or subsection of psychology that he finds suited to his taste and abilities."[180]

Allport refused to concede that nonoperational branches of psychology were not science. Rather, he asserted that psychology—as a science— should be diverse enough to permit contributions by psychologists working in the tradition of William James and Sigmund Freud:

> Why not allow psychology as a science—for science is a broad and beneficent term—to be also rational, teleological, qualitative, idiographic, synoptic, and even non-operational? I mention these antitheses of virtue with deliberation, for the simple reason that great insights of psychology in the past—for example, those of Aristotle, Locke, Fechner, James, Freud—have stemmed from one or more of these unfashionable presuppositions.[181]

To him, Stevens and Boring designed a discipline that was increasingly narrow, accommodating only the true believers among the experimental psychologists and excluding all other psychologists: "Methodism as the sole requirement of science means that all the faithful crowd onto a carpet of prayer, and with their logical shears cut more and more inches off the rug, permitting fewer and fewer aspirants to enjoy status."[182]

Allport warned that psychology was in "danger of becoming a cult" that excluded innovative research in favor of a behaviorist approach.[183] He declared that psychology must "avoid authoritarianism" and instead be judged by whether it helps understand human behavior.[184] Given the then current geopolitical events in Europe with Nazism on the rise, it seemed intentional that Allport described operationism with loaded terms such as "authoritarianism" and "undemocratic."

He also noted a significant increase in the use of animals in psychological research and a change in the nature of the research. Articles on animal psychology had risen from 3.5 percent of all studies in 1888–1889 (studies to determine how "animals as animals" behave) to over 15 percent of studies in 1938 (studies to determine a universal psychology "revealed by all animals from insects to Homo Sapiens.")[185] Allport asserted with alarm that "an increasing number of investigators now pin their faith upon experimentation with animals," with 25 percent of the papers delivered at that year's meetings based on animal research, rising from 11 percent in 1914.[186]

He found the trend in the number and types of animal studies to be disturbing. This was exquisitely awkward because the most prominent scholar in animal studies in the world was Karl Lashley, his nemesis in the Psychology Department. Ratcheting up the tension, Allport mocked the field of study: "A colleague, a good friend of mine, recently challenged me to name a single psychological problem not referable to rats for its solution. Considerably startled, I murmured something, I think, about the psychology of reading disability."[187] At this juncture, Allport celebrated holistic and humanistic psychology, explaining that the study of animals was of limited utility "in a sphere where the culture and peculiar genius of humanity prevail."[188]

> But to my mind came flooding the historic problems of the aesthetic, humorous, religious, and cultural behavior of men. I thought how men build clavichords and cathedrals, how they write books, and how they laugh uproariously at Mickey Mouse; how they plan their lives five, ten, or twenty years ahead; how, by an elaborate metaphysic of their own contrivance, they deny the utility of their own experience, including the utility of the metaphysic that led them to this denial. I thought of poetry and puns, of propaganda and revolution, of stock markets and suicide, and of man's despairing hope for peace. I thought, too, of the elementary fact that human problem-solving, unlike that of the rat, is saturated through and through with verbal function, so that we have no way of knowing whether the delay, the volition, the symbolizing and categorizing typical of human learning are even faintly adumbrated by findings in animal learning.[189]

In 1939, the Psychology Department remained bitterly divided, with the biotropes and sociotropes dueling over the direction of their discipline. It was civil war by the standards of the academy, each side contemptuous of the other's brand of psychology, unable to agree on the most basic contours of the discipline. Allport's broadside against operationism in his American Psychological Association speech undoubtedly deepened the divide. Despite his pessimism about the standing of social psychology against experimental psychology, Allport began to see a rise in the fortunes of his brand of psychology. Several events of the 1930s contributed to this shift. The concept of attitude emerged as an accepted focus for American social psychology.[190] The Depression and the approach of World War II provided social psychologists with a fertile field, and they began research on such issues as wartime industry, unemployment, and national morale.

SOCIOLOGY: A NEW AND FRAGILE DEPARTMENT

Harvard administration and faculty debated the value of yet another young and troubled social science that would form part of Social Relations—sociology. The birth of sociology at Harvard, like that of psychology, suffered a long and difficult labor. It had to detach itself from not one but two departmental parents: Economics and Social Ethics. In the late 1890s, the Economics Department moved from exclusively studying classical economic theory to analyzing contemporary affairs and incorporating courses of sociology.[191] Indeed, sociology at the time was considered a "forward wing of a great advance in economic thinking at Harvard."[192] The Economics Department had an assistant professor of sociology as early as 1893, and in 1901 Thomas Nixon Carver began providing regular instruction in sociology.[193]

Sociology failed to establish a separate identity, however, because most of its early contributions were immediately incorporated into the wider field of economics.[194] Many economists, on the other hand, accused sociologists of attempting to "invade" their field and appropriate their subject matter.[195] Sociology's harshest critics at Harvard regarded it "as an upstart, as unscientific, chaotic, and devoid of unique subject."[196] Sociology at Harvard "had no effective support as the 'master discipline' and little support as a 'separate' but 'equal' discipline."[197] Lacking a distinct focus, sociology at Harvard withered.[198] The discipline's struggle to emerge from economics was not restricted to Harvard; a similar story replayed throughout American and European academic communities.[199]

Such was the relationship of sociology to the Economics Department. But the growing interest in social problems at the turn of the century had led to the establishment of another department that dealt with sociological topics. In 1905, Harvard created the Department of Social Ethics with a substantial gift from Andrew Tredway White. Further support from White reached a sum of almost $300,000, endowing Social Ethics with a financial security that few departments could rival.[200] White's largesse freed the department from any dependency on the university treasury and made it the most financially stable department except for the new School of Architecture.[201]

Academically, however, the department enjoyed less stability. Critics attacked it as an amorphous hybrid somewhere between moral philosophy and sociology. Social Ethics survived largely through the efforts of its faculty founder, Professor Francis Peabody, who parried the criticisms of his department with a combination of persistence and tact.[202] It helped, of course, that he sat on the sizeable stash provided by Andrew Tredway White.[203] Peabody resisted mergers of Social Ethics with other divisions of the university, fearing this would dilute its focus on moral problems of society. He derided sociology, stating that it, "like dirigible ballooning, may easily become a passion for inventive minds, but it is still in great difficulties of balance and steering, and remains for the present very much up in the air."[204]

Peabody sought respectability for Social Ethics by giving it a scientific gloss with such innovations as a Social Museum housed in Emerson Hall.[205] With the retirement of Peabody in 1913, however, the department lost its primary defender. Without any tenured faculty members, Social Ethics stagnated. No one at Harvard knew what to make of the department, what it was doing, or where it belonged organizationally.[206] President Lowell preferred to transfer the department to the Divinity School. But the department's generous benefactor Alfred Tredway White argued that Social Ethics should stay at the college, telling Lowell to "keep in mind the interests of that large body of undergraduates who, as likely to become men of affairs, should realize the fundamentally ethical nature of many of our social problems."[207]

In 1918, Lowell searched for a new leader of Social Ethics. He wanted a "man, rare and difficult to find, who would, by his personality, attainments and reputation, impress the students to an unusual degree."[208] He believed he had found such a "charismatic figure" in Richard C. Cabot, a professor of clinical medicine at the Harvard Medical School. Cabot's service in World War I convinced him that an ethical education was important, telling others that a "non-ethical education was just as apt to be a curse as a blessing."[209] The new chairman of the ailing department assumed his duties in 1920 and initiated an extensive reorganization. His enthusiastic schemes failed, however, when it became apparent that Social Ethics was simply not an academically viable enterprise. Cabot's goal, "to make men better themselves," was not a sufficient rationale.[210]

Although they were social ethicists, the faculty members associated with Cabot maintained other professional identities as well, and soon they departed for more traditional posts. Three instructors (Gordon Allport, Niles Carpenter, and Robert Foerster) left Harvard (Allport only temporarily), while Peabody's successor, James Ford, spent most of his time in Washington as director of Better Homes of America.[211] Their departures suggested that Cabot was failing to revive the department and that it "had no academic future."[212] Social Ethics foundered as it grew further away from the main current of sociological thought, its only claim—albeit a weak one—to academic validity. Sociology in the Economics Department, meanwhile, had dwindled to one faculty member.

President Lowell failed to rejuvenate Social Ethics with the recruitment of Cabot as its chairman, and what support Lowell had offered previously now evaporated. He decided to cut his losses. He told Cabot that Social Ethics by itself was not "a good subject for concentration" (concentration is Harvard's terminology for a major).[213] He believed the department lacked academic rigor, serving as nothing more than a "refuge for students who do not care to work hard."[214] Searching for ways to inject greater discipline in Social Ethics, Lowell looked to an alliance with Sociology, which he thought should be made into "a severe discipline."[215]

Under Lowell's guidance, Harvard sought to unite these fragments of sociology, establishing in 1927 an undergraduate field of concentration in Sociology and Social Ethics. The concentration was presided over by a committee selected by President Lowell: A. M. Schlesinger and E. A. Whitney (History), W. Y. Eliot (Government), E. F. Gay and T. N. Carver (Economics), E. A. Hooton (Anthropology), R. B. Perry—who was the first chairman—and G. W. Allport (Philosophy and Psychology), and R. C. Cabot (Social Ethics).[216] According to Perry, the new concentration would focus on two basic questions linking the newly married disciplines: what is society and what should it be?[217] The former was the province of the more science-oriented sociology, while the latter maintained the link to the strain of moral philosophy embedded in social ethics.

In 1930, Lowell recruited Pitirim Sorokin, a prominent professor of sociology at the University of Minnesota, to fill Harvard's first chair in Sociology.[218] Sorokin was a colorful figure by Harvard's standards: he had been a revolutionary in Russia, acting as secretary to Alexander Kerensky. He was imprisoned and sentenced to death by Lenin, but later exiled. After coming to the United States, he became a prominent scholar at Minnesota for his work on social mobility, rural sociology, and the Russian Revolution. The rationale for the committee arrangement was that neither Sociology nor Social Ethics possessed unique methodologies and therefore should be overseen by members of those disciplines from which they borrowed methods.[219] In addition to guiding the concentration, the committee deliberated on whether Social Ethics should even be continued. Professors Cabot, Allport, Ford, and Perry favored its continuation, while the majority wanted to establish a new Department of Sociology.[220] The arrival of Sorokin as Harvard's first professor of sociology strengthened the voice of this latter faction. Sorokin, a forceful proponent of sociology as an independent discipline, opposed combining Social Ethics and Sociology within a single department.[221] Despite his efforts, however,

Harvard united Social Ethics and Sociology in a Department of Sociology on February 10, 1931, but courses in social ethics disappeared from the department's offerings within a few years.[222]

The events from 1927 to 1931 that led to the ouster of Cabot as chair of Social Ethics and the replacement by Sorokin as chair of a new Department of Sociology were considered odd by at least one prominent observer. Decades later, famed Columbia University sociologist Robert K. Merton, who had been a graduate student in Sociology when Sorokin was at Harvard, recalled it was "a quite implausible event which had a Lowell, then President of Harvard, actually displacing a Cabot with a Russian émigré, Pitirim Sorokin—all this in the course of transforming a venerable Department of Social Ethics into a newfangled Department of Sociology."[223] Commenting on the incongruity of the transition, Merton invoked the well-known ditty about the Boston elite: "And this is good old Boston, The home of the bean and the cod, Where the Lowells talk to the Cabots, And the Cabots talk only to God."[224]

Sorokin was soon joined in the new department by his former colleague from the University of Minnesota, Carle Zimmerman, who had been appointed as a nonpermanent associate professor. Of the department's senior faculty members, only Cabot, Ford, and Sorokin were primarily sociologists; the remainder held joint appointments with other fields. This group, which shared the voting privilege, included E. F. Gay (Economics), W. Y. Eliot (Government), L. J. Henderson (Biology), A. M. Tozzer (Anthropology), A. M. Schlesinger (History), and R. B. Perry and G. W. Allport (Philosophy and Psychology).[225] This meant that, initially, sociologists were a minority in their own department when voting on senior appointments, policy matters, and curriculum.[226]

At last formally independent, Sociology still faced difficulties. It remained small, suffering from an identity crisis. Although Sorokin, now chairman of the new department, was a strong advocate of sociology as a discipline with a unique methodology, some sociologists considered his notions out of touch with current sociological thought.[227] Both he and Zimmerman pursued the study of sociology as philosophy of history.[228] They were not particularly interested in the interface between economics and sociology or in the works of Emile Durkheim and Max Weber, which were capturing the attention of younger sociologists.[229] Their neglect of such major themes influencing sociological thought vexed one hard-charging young faculty member, Talcott Parsons, who had transferred from the Economics Department in 1931, beginning as an instructor and becoming an assistant professor in 1936. He felt that Sociology at Harvard was lagging developments in the field at large. Moreover, he was extremely interested in precisely those areas that held little interest for Sorokin and that Zimmerman disliked.[230] He and Sorokin were on a collision course. Although Sorokin had initially been impressed with Parsons, their relationship soon became highly contentious.[231]

Parsons had received a doctorate in philosophy at Heidelberg for his thesis on "The Concept of Capitalism in the Theories of Max Weber and Werner Sombart."[232] He had also translated Max Weber's essay, "The Protestant Ethic and the Spirit of Capitalism," which was published in 1930, and he played a leading role in introducing Weber to American scholars.[233] After coming to the Economics Department at Harvard, Parsons became interested in formulating a scheme for social theory. But he became restless there, concluding that economics could not accommodate the all-encompassing social theory he had in mind. The Economics Department, in turn, did not hold in high regard his interest in sociology as opposed to the more "technical preoccupations of economics."[234]

Figure 1.3.   Talcott Parsons, circa 1970. UAV 605.295.7p, olvwork499788. Harvard University Archives.

What he envisioned was nothing less than a theory to integrate all social sciences. Indeed, Parsons would become renowned as a grand social theoretician, resolutely, some say obsessively, pursuing an integrative theory—the great white whale to his Captain Ahab. When Parsons died in 1976, Daniel Bell, another leading Harvard sociologist, wrote of him in the *New York Times* with a headline that said simply, "Talcott Parsons: Nobody's Theories Were Bigger."[235]

Early in his academic career, Parsons was shaped by a wide range of disciplines: philosophy, economics, sociology, biology, psychoanalysis, and physiology. He was particularly influenced by his close contacts with the physiologist Lawrence J. Henderson and the economist Edwin F. Gay. Parsons's dissatisfaction with departmental drift in Sociology and his search for an overarching social theory would determine the direction of sociology—and more—at Harvard.

By the late 1930s, the Departments of Psychology and Sociology at Harvard were in turmoil; Anthropology to a lesser extent also had troubles. Young professors intensely interested in new theories and methods chafed under the old guard in their departments, who regarded their interests as unscientific, frivolous, or even dangerous to the established order. The debates over what constituted the disciplines, and what was a suitable topic or method of inquiry, would continue and grow even more contentious.

2

✛

World War II
Changes Everything

Interdisciplinary Research Emerges

In the meantime a very big scientific development has been rapidly
gathering force. . . . Like all really big pioneer movements it is not understood by the majority of the established high priests of social science.

—Talcott Parsons

We feel that in the postwar period the present departmental structure
will suddenly reveal itself to be a total anachronism, entirely inadequate
to meet the need for interdisciplinary research and instruction that the
period of reconstruction will demand.

—Gordon Allport, Clyde Kluckhohn, Henry Murray,
Hobart Mowrer, and Talcott Parsons

Talcott Parsons's pursuit of an all-encompassing social theory led to
the publication in 1937 of *The Structure of Social Action*, in which he as-
similated and developed the ideas of Durkheim, Pareto, and Weber.[1] His
work on sociological theory acquired a new dimension as another emerging body of thought—Freudian psychoanalysis—captivated him. Freud
"proved to be one of the few crucial intellectual experiences of my life,"
he said, leading him to undertake formal training at the Boston Psychoanalytic Institute.[2] Parsons drew upon Freud's motivational categories of
psychoanalysis to help explain the dynamics of social systems.[3] Psychoanalysis brought Parsons into contact with other young faculty members,
Henry Murray of Psychology and Clyde Kluckhohn of Anthropology,
who shared a common interest in the theory.[4] Gordon Allport was drawn
to their discussions because he too shared many of their intellectual

concerns, although notably not psychoanalysis. Hobart Mowrer, a psychologist affiliated with both the Department of Psychology and the Harvard Graduate School of Education, also joined the group.[5]

According to Murray and Parsons, these young nontenured professors wanted to study man as he functions in society.[6] The inability to pursue freely their common interest in their own departments added an emotional dimension to their intellectual bond and lent an air of conspiracy to their meetings, which were held in each other's homes and the Psychological Clinic.[7] They considered their group a kind of "shop club," referring to themselves as the "Levellers" because of the "many levels of on which behavioral phenomena required consideration."[8] Parsons described the group's shared interests in crossing departmental divisions:

> Most important we had come to know each other well and to an unusual degree in a university where departmental lines tend to constitute barriers to communication, we had engaged in many informal discussions of substantive scientific problems with each other, in the course of which the closeness of our interests became ever more obvious, so much so that our membership in different departments seemed increasingly anomalous.[9]

Parsons, Murray, and Kluckhohn first connected as core members of the storied "Harvard Pareto Circle"—a seminar organized by Harvard professor Lawrence J. Henderson in 1932 to examine the work of Vilfredo Pareto, the Italian economist and sociologist.[10] Other regular attendees included Joseph Schumpeter, Crane Brinton, Bernard DeVoto, and Elton Mayo. The Pareto Circle and the Levellers' group were examples of what Joel Isaac termed the "interstitial academy" at Harvard in the interwar period, providing "practitioners of nascent research programs with enclaves in which to exchange ideas and conduct inquiries outside of established departments and curricula."[11] This informal academy provided a "unique space in which hitherto marginal projects in the human sciences were able to come to fruition."[12] Several fields, such as sociology, psychology, cultural anthropology, and social systems theory, among others, began at Harvard as "fugitive professional ventures."[13] Harvard's interstitial academy gave these emerging and sometimes controversial fields the space they needed to gain ever so gradually a legitimate place within the institution.[14]

THE LEVELLERS PROPOSE A NEW DEPARTMENT: DEAN PAUL BUCK EXPRESSES INTEREST

The Levellers soon contemplated uniting their interests formally within the university. Harvard made the first official move in this direction in

1940, establishing an interdepartmental program under the direction of a faculty committee chaired by Parsons—the Committee on Concentration in the Area of Social Science.[15] The program encompassed all six social science disciplines: history, government, economics, sociology, anthropology, and psychology.[16] This new program evolved from a review of the concentration program at Harvard conducted by a committee headed by Professor Charles H. Taylor.[17] His committee recommended a trial program of concentrations broader than those already offered in the physical sciences, humanities, and social sciences.[18] The war effort drew most of the undergraduates away from the college, so the new undergraduate program in the "Area of Social Science" lasted less than two years.[19] Nonetheless, it allowed Parsons, Mowrer, and Kluckhohn to collaborate for the first time as instructors in an interdisciplinary academic structure.[20] Furthermore, the foray forced them to confront a central problem of their interdisciplinary enterprise—the absence of a common vocabulary.[21]

To fill this gap, Parsons, Kluckhohn, John T. Dunlop, M. P. Gilmore, and Overton H. Taylor wrote "Toward a Common Language for the Area of Social Science."[22] Parsons characterized this effort as "a kind of theoretical charter of basic social science."[23] They sought to "build up a single model of human behavior in societies in addition to several separate and specialized abstractions" of the various social sciences.[24] They never published the charter, but the exercise gave the Levellers the opportunity to promulgate a common language for the social sciences, which they characterized as a set of related abstractions that would "at once cut across and unify the prevailing abstractions of the separate disciplines."[25] They proposed a conceptual scheme reducing the abstractions in the social sciences to elementary categories, which could in turn be integrated in a single coherent framework.[26] This was the only way, they concluded, "to talk in the same breath about the phenomena with which anthropology, economics, government, history, psychology and sociology have dealt."[27]

They further asserted that their disciplines were more instrumental in explaining human behavior than history, government, and economics, the strongest and most esteemed of Harvard's social science disciplines. They contended that human behavior, as that takes form between individuals and in groups and institutions, is the domain of psychology, sociology, and anthropology.[28] Such behavior, in turn, becomes "structured into types of activity of peculiar importance," which are the focus of government and economics.[29] These types of activity, with the passage of time, are the province of history. The authors viewed special instances of groups and institutions of history, government, and economics as best understood by and through the "more basic social sciences of psychology, anthropology, and sociology."[30] It was a bold move for the Levellers that had "a strong element of wish fulfillment."[31]

This intrepid approach reflected Parsons's search for a theory of human behavior and his belief that the older social sciences were unsuited to the task. After all, in 1931 he moved from the venerable Department of Economics to the fledgling Department of Sociology, at least in part to continue that search. He believed only sociology, allied with the relevant areas of psychology and anthropology, could produce such a grand social theory. Parsons, Kluckhohn, Murray, Allport, and Mowrer now believed they possessed a framework for pursuing an interdisciplinary agenda. Optimistic that further integration might be possible within the university, they drafted a proposal for a new department that included the sociotropic side of their disciplines: social anthropology, sociology, personality psychology, and social psychology.[32] The idea of an interdisciplinary program was not without precedent. The most notable example was the Yale Institute of Human Relations, where Mowrer studied and subsequently taught.[33] The Levellers adopted it as a general model.[34]

In 1942, the group sent President Conant a proposal to create a broad interdisciplinary Department of Human Relations.[35] Conant ignored it, probably for two reasons.[36] Foremost were Conant's long absences from the university because of his involvement with government agencies during the war.[37] Parsons and others also believed that Conant was hostile toward psychology in general, and humanistic psychology in particular.[38] The group persevered, however, and in the following year they approached newly appointed dean Paul Buck with their idea. Buck was dean of Harvard from 1942 to 1953 and provost from 1945 to 1953.[39] He had considerable influence in the administration during the war because President Conant was out of the picture.

The group asked him to appoint a committee to consider "the improvement of the curriculum and administrative organization within the social sciences, especially within the region of rapidly developing thought that is now embraced by the scattered Departments of Anthropology, Sociology, and Psychology."[40] They explained that other universities, such as Yale and Chicago, had been experimenting with techniques to "solve the same problem," although none was entirely successful or set the precise model for Harvard.[41] Nonetheless, they concluded that these universities have faced the fact that the historical divisions between the disciplines were impediments to advances in the study of the social and psychological development of the individual.[42]

They warned that Harvard must be prepared to move quickly to address the problem after World War II ended: "We feel that in the postwar period the present departmental structure will suddenly reveal itself to be a total anachronism, entirely inadequate to meet the need for interdisciplinary research and instruction that the period of reconstruction will demand."[43] The appeal worked. Dean Buck constituted the five faculty

Figure 2.1. President James B. Conant and Dean Paul H. Buck, Harvard University, circa 1942. HUP Conant, James (62a), olvwork653471. Harvard University Archives.

members as an informal committee authorized to examine the proposal in detail.[44] He kept their expectations in check, however, with the caveat: "I can promise you only the opportunity to explore the problem. You will understand that difficulties will arise in any scheme of reorganization that may be proposed. But I do want you to have confidence in my determination to rebuild and to encourage experimentation toward a more perfect structure of education at Harvard."[45]

The men met several times over the summer of 1943 and forwarded their report to Buck in September.[46] In submitting the report, the group stressed the radical nature of their proposal and the unanimity of their recommendations: "The five of us represent four separate departments of the University, and yet we have found ourselves in unanimous agreement on every major point. This fact, we believe, signifies that the time is ripe for a reconsideration of present departmental boundaries. Our proposals, it would seem, gain validity from the diversity of experience that we draw upon."[47] The report indicted the current setup, warning again that Harvard was unprepared for the postwar period: "[The] present basic structure of the so-called social sciences at Harvard is faulty in its foundation and in its direction, and that unless it is remedied Harvard will not meet its obligation to provide in the future a place where men returning from military service can find the kind of teaching, training and research they will need for the era that lies ahead."[48]

The authors played heavily on the fear—perhaps hoping it would resonate with a dean—that Harvard was falling behind other universities: "Innovation and experimentation in the structure and organization of the social sciences is occurring primarily in the endowed rather than in the State universities. At the present time Harvard is trailing instead of leading in this connection."[49] They also aired the long-simmering grievances the authors had within their own departments.[50] The group listed the defects of excessive departmentalization and "petty rivalries among component disciplines which result in narrowing the student's mind so that in becoming expert in one subject he is ignorant of, or even intolerant toward, related branches of knowledge."[51] And they revealed a defensiveness of their young disciplines vis-à-vis the more well-established departments at Harvard: "More fundamentally, however, we feel that the headstart of History, Government and Economics at Harvard has obscured the fact that underlying these imposing disciplines there is a body of basic social science, which has now matured to a point where it be used [sic] for formal training purposes."[52]

They felt their time had come. They believed their disciplines were emerging from the shadows cast by the Departments of History, Government, and Economics. The Levellers were no longer content, as Isaac described, to live "on the margins of the organizational chart."[53] Their audacious approach asserted that the fields of social and dynamic psychology, social and cultural anthropology, and institutional sociology dealt with the "nucleus of knowledge" that underpinned the other disciplines.[54] They claimed that what was "basic to all the social sciences is *the human individual or personality in the social system* [emphasis in original]."[55] They doubled down on the argument they first made in the 1941 report, "Toward a Common Language for the Area of Social Science." In other words, their disciplines constituted the building block of all other social sciences in the same way that anatomy and physiology formed the nucleus of the biological sciences.[56] The authors further argued that not all social sciences deserved equal weight: "One of the serious misconceptions encouraged by the present form of the departmental organization in this and most other American universities is that each of the departmental 'branches' of social sciences is accorded about the same significance in the total body of science—each is a distinct and sovereign 'science.'"[57]

They divided the social sciences into three groups. The first group—history—was "synthetic," with a "rigor lying mainly in the level of the ascertainment of specific fact."[58] One can only imagine how this bland characterization of history was received by their champion to date, Dean Buck, a Pulitzer Prize–winning historian. The second group included economics and government, which "dealt with the certain peculiar phenomena, usually best observed in highly complex and differentiated societies."[59] The third group—comprised of the authors' own fields—"can be treated as basic to both the others, not in the sense of being more 'important,' or enjoying greater dignity, but in the literal sense of the term: they deal with things which ought to be presupposed by the other disciplines."[60]

The report recommended that the existing Departments of Anthropology, Sociology, and Psychology be dissolved, stating they "are the result of the accidents of historical development rather than divisions of labor corresponding to coherent and well-limited terrains of investigation."[61] More damning language followed: "Indeed, they promote intellectual confusion and friction by the unrealistic juxtaposition of very divergent, though equally legitimate, interests."[62] They argued that the current departments were "specious units" that prevented collaboration in teaching and research; their traditions and barriers inhibited interchange among staff and students as well.[63] The group recommended uniting the three departments in a new Department of Basic Social Science within the Faculty of Arts and Sciences.[64] It was not a wholesale transfer of the three departments, but rather only "those portions . . . which together supply the indispensable foundations for training in all the social sciences," i.e., social anthropology, sociology, social psychology, and the Psychological Clinic.[65] The report recommended reshuffling the social sciences deck at Harvard: Those portions of Psychology, such as physiological psychology, that would not be absorbed into the Basic Social Sciences would go to Human Biology.[66] Archaeology would be taken from Anthropology and moved to History.[67] Physiological anthropology would go to Human Biology, and parts of Sociology not suited for the Basic Social Sciences would find residence in History or Economics.[68]

Payson S. Wild, dean of the graduate school, circulated the document to all faculty members in the social sciences. That same year, the group held two meetings to discuss the report, but no action was taken.[69] Gordon

Allport described the reception of the report: "The memorandum was well received, but the tentative decision was that perhaps a rejuvenated Department of Sociology might be the auspices for such developments as were desirable."[70] The proposal failed to gain traction. The exigencies of the war took two key players from Harvard to Washington. Kluckhohn went to work in the Foreign Morale Analysis Division (FMAD) of the government, and Murray left to help establish the assessment staff of the Office of Strategic Services (OSS), the forerunner of today's Central Intelligence Agency.[71] Hobart Mowrer did not go to Washington but took a teaching job elsewhere.[72] Parsons remained in Cambridge, but he served as a part-time advisor to the Foreign Economic Administration in planning for the postwar reconstruction of Germany.[73] Those who remained on campus faced the disruptions of war, leaving little time for internal politics.[74]

THE RIFT IN PSYCHOLOGY WIDENS: ALLPORT SEEKS ALTERNATIVES

Events within and outside the university soon coalesced to favor the creation of a new department.[75] The first occurred in the Psychology Department, where a permanent appointment was up for grabs. The sociotropes felt that the appointment should be made in personality psychology, specifically Henry Murray, who years earlier had suffered mightily in his tenure review at the hands of the biotropes.[76] The biotropes naturally wanted an additional permanent member from their own ranks.[77] The biotropes prevailed. In March 1944, the permanent appointment went to S. S. Stevens, the strong-willed opponent of sociotropic endeavors, particularly those by Murray and the clinic.[78] For Allport, the die was cast, for Stevens personified the antithesis of the Murray-Allport position.[79] Only five years earlier, Allport in his speech before the American Psychological Association had blasted operationism, with Stevens as its leading practitioner, as an authoritarian fad obsessed with empiricism and unconnected to real-world issues. Psychology at Harvard had taken an extreme and irrevocable step away from social and personality psychology, and Allport now feared for the well-being of his own areas of research in the very department he chaired.[80]

Allport protested to E. G. Boring: "A new Gestalt has been created, within which I and other units of the Department will have to find a new equilibrium."[81] He foresaw the loss of the "rich breadth of subject matter" of psychology to the narrow definition of the discipline adhered to by biotropes Lashley and Stevens. Allport captured the situation: "There is not a single millimeter of overlap between S's [Stevens] science and mine. I fit as well into astronomy or into paleontology as into a Department dominated by Stevens—supported by you and Lashley."[82] He felt that there was no longer a "fundamental willingness to let all candles burn" and that this lack of "minimum homogeneity" would continue to be missing in their generation.[83] He deplored the "methodological scorn" directed at the clinic by Lashley and Stevens, and to some extent by Boring.[84] Allport failed to see how a balanced undergraduate concentration (major) can be provided against such opposition.[85] He summarized the problem with Stevens's appointment: "I don't see where my garden patch can grow. In short, the outlook for a balanced Department is gone, not necessarily because of the imbalance of specialties among its permanent members, but because of the *attitudes* of two of them [emphasis in original]."[86]

Drawing on the themes in his 1939 speech, Allport described the trends in academia that would suffocate in a Psychology Department dominated by biotropes. At Harvard and elsewhere, the social sciences were taking a broader approach. Of course, as one of the authors of the 1943 memorandum to Dean Buck proposing a new Department of Social Sciences, he already had made clear that the separation of anthropology, sociology, and social psychology was artificial. Movements in the social sciences for reorganization directly affected his work, and they conflicted with the narrowing of the Psychology Department. Allport lost all hope, resigned to being carried by the coming wave of reorganization of the social sciences. In his letter to Boring, Allport conceded defeat: "Under the circumstances, I might have worked out my relation to this trend within the Departmental frame, and might have assisted the Clinic in doing so likewise. Things being as they are, I shall not resist a re-departmentalization. On the contrary, I think I should encourage it. As an historical movement it is probably inevitable anyway."[87]

Allport did not have to wait long to ride the currents of change. Later that spring, Dean Buck asked all chairmen to begin planning for postwar developments, and Allport, as chairman of the Psychology Department, encouraged a restructuring.[88] Allport responded citing his worries about the future of Psychology at Harvard and suggesting what might be done.[89] He said Harvard's Department of Psychology was small in comparison to psychology departments in other leading universities. He questioned whether the department could meet future demands on it because of the "rising tide of interest in psychology as a consequence of the war" and the vast diversity within the discipline.[90]

Allport concluded that a reorganization was needed: "The question is whether the future of psychology at Harvard can be as progressive and as significant as the times require unless some radical change of outlook prevails."[91] He proposed two alternatives to Dean Buck: (1) expand the department to add new specialties and develop at least one into "unquestionable pre-eminence," or (2) end the department altogether, moving the biotropes to the Department of Biology and the sociotropes to the Department of Sociology. He acknowledged that the latter alternative was drastic, but he felt that "Harvard might be anticipating correctly a change that will eventually be forced in other institutions as well because of the excessive diversity of the subject matter included within the field."[92] Months later, he recounted this in a letter to Boring, bringing him up to speed on his discussions with Buck:

> Perplexed by the assignment [on postwar planning] I wrote asking the Dean whether I should proceed on the assumption that the Department of Psychology should continue "as is" with no expansion, or whether it could be expanded, or whether some reorganization seemed desirable (such, for example, as joining the Clinic and work in social psychology to the Department-of-Sociology-as-contemplated-for-the-future).[93]

Allport also disclosed that a full year earlier he—along with his fellow Levellers—had submitted a memorandum to the dean suggesting the creation of a new Department of Social Sciences consisting of the "interrelated" parts of anthropology, sociology, and psychology.[94] Apparently, Boring, who had so painstakingly brought into existence an independent Department of Psychology, emancipated from Philosophy, was unaware of Allport's behind-the-scenes maneuvering to restructure it. Now that action was imminent, Allport laid his cards on the table with Boring for the first time. Allport already knew change was forthcoming when he told Boring that Dean Buck wished to convene a meeting with himself, Boring, Stevens, Parsons, and Kluckhohn, but he merely speculated that the topic was the division of the department: "Since Parsons and Kluckhohn are involved, I presume the purpose of the conference initiated by the Dean is to discuss in an exploratory way the desirability of committing fision [sic] in Psychology in order to strengthen the new social-science development. If it is desirable, what's to happen to the remainder of the Department of Psychology?"[95] He cautioned his colleagues that they should prepare accordingly for the conference along these lines and be "shrewd in anticipating the course of psychology *in the future* [emphasis in original]."[96] Allport ended his missive with a vivid image of the current state of the department: "My observation suggests that psychology is now a loose and flapping tent, and that tightening up is somehow necessary."[97]

TALCOTT PARSONS MAKES HIS MOVE

Meanwhile, in the Sociology Department, forces for institutional realignment gathered steam. Allport's speculation about an enlarged Department of Sociology that could accommodate him, Murray, and White seemed more realistic given the agitation by Talcott Parsons for sweeping and expansionary changes in sociology. Parsons's distress about the direction of sociology at Harvard was at its height when Northwestern University offered him the chairmanship of its Department of Sociology.[98] As chairman, Parsons would have a large infusion of funds that Northwestern had recently received to augment its social science programs.[99] The offer was a significant catalyst for change in sociology at Harvard because it gave Parsons leverage to promote a new interdisciplinary department, or at the very least "an enlarged 'super Department of Sociology.'"[100] The latter would add Allport, Kluckhohn, and Murray to the faculty and remove Sorokin as chairman.[101] Parsons wasted no time in making his case to Dean Buck:

> Perhaps you will be willing to regard this more as a personal communication than as an official memo. I think that the essential thing from my point of view is that the offer from Northwestern has brought the whole complex situation here to a head in such a way as to force the crucial question of the future role at Harvard, and particularly in the policy of its administration, of the kind of scientific work with which my own career has been identified. I want to use my own personal case as "pressure" only in the sense of helping the administration to face issues of policy which I feel it will have to face sooner or later anyway.[102]

He admitted that "a large element of my motivation [in accepting the Northwestern offer] would be a protest."[103] Parsons pulled no punches. He intended to put Buck on the spot: "It would be meant to force you to do some explaining as to why I had left Harvard."[104] Parsons sharply criticized Harvard's failure to appreciate the great interdisciplinary movement that was developing in the social sciences beyond Harvard, and he questioned whether Harvard was destined to be merely a follower of innovations led by other universities.[105] He characterized Sociology, Anthropology, and Psychology as "weak departments" in need of rescuing and restructuring so that their socially oriented subdisciplines, properly consolidated, could lead this new movement.[106] After labeling the sociology experiment at Harvard "very badly bungled," he stated that "Sorokin should never have been appointed to lead a great development in the first place," adding, "the administration should never have allowed him to secure a permanency for Zimmerman."[107] Parsons felt that that the Sociology Department, encumbered by these mistakes, was left "to stew in its own juices."[108] Psychology still suffered from its "recent dependence on Philosophy and its internal fracture of subject matter," a polite reference to the war between the biotropes and sociotropes.[109] Parsons dismissed Anthropology as "a kind of exotic side-show of the University," existing in an unfortunate isolation.[110] He hammered the theme that Harvard was missing out on a historical opportunity:

> In the meantime a very big scientific development has been rapidly gathering force—what our group tried, however, [*sic*] inadequately to formulate as the growth of a "basic social science." I will stake my whole professional reputation on the statement that it is one of the really great movements of modern scientific thought, comparable for instance, to the development of Biology in the last third of the 19th Century. Like all really big pioneer movements it is not understood by the majority of the established high priests of social science.[111]

He believed this movement needed a new institutional framework to achieve its potential, and that the "vested interest of those already in the field" was standing in the way.[112]

Parsons again appealed—as he and his coauthors had done in their 1943 report—to Buck's presumed desire not to see Harvard fall behind other universities. He posed the issue as a pivotal moment for Harvard—would it recognize the opportunity and this new direction in academia or simply be a follower and coast along on its "wealth and past prestige"?[113] He summarized, "The essential question to me is whether Harvard is going to seize the opportunity to be a great leader in this movement or is going to move only as it is forced to do so by the competition of other institutions."[114] Parsons also revisited another theme in the 1943 report to Buck: the disciplines of economics and government would soon decline in intellectual importance relative to the new social science that his group represented.[115] To buttress his case, Parsons noted that President Conant also saw the need to develop a social science program at Harvard. According to Parsons, Conant agreed with his assessment of the bungled Sociology Department and remarked, "It's pretty bad when three out of the four permanent members are the wrong people," referring to Sorokin, Zimmerman, and James Ford.[116] Buck believed Sorokin was not up to the job of leading the department, which only strengthened Parsons's lobbying efforts. According to fellow sociology professor George Homans, "Buck did not think much of Sorokin. He preferred Parsons because he was a better administrator and kept his emotions under control."[117] Parsons stated that there was "a great deal of evidence that Paul Buck was very much dissatisfied with the Sorokin situation."[118]

Sorokin's style was emotional, confrontational, and hyperbolic. He described himself as a "wild Jackass always kicking everything about."[119] Using another animal metaphor, he had been described as a "lone wolf" scholar, making no attempt to develop a following of any kind, let alone a school of sociology.[120] Graduate students considered him unapproachable, a cantankerous elder statesman who was "distant, demanding and denigrating of their scholarly endeavors."[121] All of this put Sorokin in stark contrast with the younger Parsons, whose style and scholarship, particularly his drive to take sociology beyond the history of philosophy approach of Sorokin, was a better fit for Harvard and its "institutional ethos" at the time.[122] It was an ethos "aloof and clinical about the conditions of society . . . and objective about the world," which meshed well with Parsons's push to make sociology more scientific.[123] Parsons was also more popular with students and administrators. He maintained informal contacts with students through an Adams House discussion group and conveyed "a certain openness . . . that implied that one's opinions counted for something."[124] Importantly, he also had personal relationships with both President Conant and Dean Buck, and he had established ties with major professional associations.[125]

It was common knowledge that Sorokin and Parsons fought constantly.[126] The origin of the animosity is unknown.[127] Some firsthand observers believed Sorokin was jealous of Parsons's popularity with students; others thought there was little regard for one another's scholarship.[128] Graduate students reported that Sorokin and Zimmerman were "out to get" Parsons, describing him as an "embattled young man."[129] George Homans witnessed the relations between the two, first as a graduate student and later as an instructor in Sociology. He speculated that the reason for the bad blood was simple envy:

> Sorokin's authoritarian tendencies may have been exacerbated by jealousy. For a small and young department, sociology by the 1930s had attracted an unusually large number of able graduate students, persons who were later to become distinguished in the profession. . . . Many of these students wanted to study with Talcott Parsons, who had come to Harvard as an instructor, fresh from Heidelberg and enthusiastic for the work of Max Weber. He did more than anyone else to introduce the work of Weber to American scholars. I have a slight suspicion that Sorokin may have been jealous of Talcott's popularity with the students. At any rate, he was said to have made life administratively unbearable for Talcott.[130]

Against the Sorokin-Parsons battle of wills and the general tumult in Sociology, Parsons's letter to Buck may have been the tipping point. Buck soon offered Parsons a full professorship and chairmanship of Sociology effective July 1, 1944.[131] More important, he told Parsons to plan for a postwar merger of the disciplines of sociology, social and clinical psychology, and social anthropology.[132] Buck had mixed motives in acceding to Parsons's demands.[133] There was a consensus that Sociology was a troubled department, that Sorokin should be replaced as chairman of Sociology, and that Parsons had the credentials and capability to be a full professor and a more effective chairman.[134] The effect of Parsons's threat to leave for

Northwestern unless Harvard moved to integrate the social sciences was only one factor in Buck's decision. Parsons was not yet a full professor, and it seems unlikely that his threat alone would have caused Buck to realign three departments in the social sciences.[135]

Buck also knew how unhappy Allport and Kluckhohn were in the Departments of Psychology and Anthropology, respectively. He was acutely aware of Allport's frustration with the biotropes' de facto control of the Psychology Department and of how Allport, Kluckhohn, and Parsons believed their young disciplines had no room to grow at Harvard, overshadowed by the more established social sciences. Buck described this in a 1944 letter to Boring, forewarning him of a possible reorganization and pledging to support the three discouraged professors:

> Allport has felt frustrated, not merely because of the set-up with the Department of Psychology, but also because he, with Parsons and Kluckhohn, felt that the older social sciences (Economics, Government, and History) were strongly entrenched and hostile to the (at Harvard) newer social sciences of Sociology, Social Psychology and Cultural Anthropology. If steps can be taken to give Allport, Parsons, and Kluckhohn a somewhat brighter goal to work toward, I am sure the situation will change tremendously for the better. I think such steps can be taken. . . . It may be that they can work out their future in some pattern of team work. I sincerely hope so, and I shall do what I can to assist them.[136]

But there was more to Buck's move than simply strengthening Sociology and keeping Allport, Buck, and Kluckhohn happy (he seemed uninterested in Murray's predicament). That move would have been a pedestrian administrative goal of any attentive dean. Rather, Buck genuinely seemed to share the "epistemological values" of the Levellers and the view that higher education would benefit from a broader and more diverse intellectual base.[137] Jamie Cohen-Cole has suggested that Buck's role in guiding the drafting of "General Education in a Free Society" at Harvard showed that his values were aligned with those of Parsons: "Both the general education project and Parsons's vision for the social sciences placed a high value on intellectual breadth achieved through communication."[138]

Buck also thought the new grouping "represented a logical development of scientific thought during the last generation."[139] He believed in the promise of interdisciplinarity, overseeing the creation of another such hybrid department at Harvard in 1946: the Department of Engineering and Applied Physics. He saw the benefit of merging disciplines in the hard sciences as much as in the social sciences, noting that "the most useful man in our laboratories in solving engineering problems under war pressure was the man who was thoroughly grounded in all the basic sciences."[140] For Buck, the creation of Social Relations relied on the same logic: "In the eyes of many members of the Faculty this step was in its own sphere quite as radical as that taken in the field of Engineering Sciences and applied Physics."[141] He fully supported the application in the academy of the problem-based approach that had proven so effective in wartime.

Buck tracked new developments in the field. The following year he would task Parsons to report on interdisciplinary activities at other universities.[142] At a minimum, he had an appreciation of what Parsons and his colleagues hoped to achieve and how it compared with what other institutions were doing in the field.[143] According to David Riesman, Dean Buck understood the dynamics at play better than President Conant, who was "naïve about the need to protect by some sort of tariff boundary the infant industry, as it then was, of what now proudly and imperiously calls itself 'humanistic psychology.'"[144] Riesman believed Conant "preferred a kind of clean desk arrangement out of naivete," leaving it to the "strong-minded and intelligent" Buck to defend the experiment.[145] As a historian, Buck undoubtedly weighed whether his administrative moves were in line with the larger developments in the social sciences and how they would be viewed in the future.

The creation of an enlarged Department of Sociology began with the replacement of Sorokin by Parsons as chairman.[146] Parsons became chairman in 1944, but the department remained divided, and tension continued between Sorokin and Parsons.[147] The small and troubled department needed repair.[148] A visiting committee report of 1944–1945 remarked, "Obviously, the Department should not be allowed to be continued as at present constituted.[149] Changes in the Department of Sociology, however, were already underway in 1945.[150] The death of Professor James Ford opened one position in the department, but Buck managed to make two permanent appointments.[151] George C. Homans, who had previously been a junior member of the department before taking a leave of absence to serve in the navy, received one, and Samuel Stouffer, a sociologist from the University of Chicago who had served as director of the research branch of the Educational and Information Division of the War Department, received the other.[152]

WARTIME RESEARCH: A CATALYST FOR THE NEW BEHAVIORAL SCIENCES

Stouffer's appointment adumbrated developments in the social sciences at Harvard.[153] During World War II, many social scientists became involved in research related to the war effort. Indeed, within the first year of America's entry into the war, 25 percent of all Americans with a graduate degree in psychology were working on the cause, most of them full time and directly for the U.S. government.[154] By the end of the war, approximately 1,700 psychologists worked for the U.S. military.[155] Initially, psychologists hesitated to participate, lacking confidence in their discipline's ability to deliver precise results. According to Gordon Allport, they were reluctant "to advocate policies not based upon 100 percent scientific certainty."[156] In a 1941 journal article titled "Psychological Service for Civilian Morale," he spurred them to action, urging a "bit of boldness" and declaring, "This is no time for feelings of inferiority or for statistical scrupulosity."[157]

Many war-related problems led the government to rely extensively on the social sciences for solutions.[158] Molding of morale and assessing men for covert missions were central concerns. The prevention and treatment of neuropsychiatric disorders was another. Studies of the social and psychological makeup of the enemy was yet another. Even the selling of war bonds was a topic of study.[159] The most important contribution of the social sciences to the war effort was not, however, their degree of involvement, but rather the nature of that involvement.[160] The problems of a nation at war required interdisciplinary collaboration that blurred many of the distinctions that had been so steadfastly upheld by the academy.[161] The military—the consumer of the research—had no interest in departmental or disciplinary distinctions; it simply wanted comprehensive answers utilizing all the disciplines.[162] Its approach was necessarily problem centered, cutting across disciplines.[163] Thus, anthropologists, sociologists, psychiatrists, social psychologists, and clinical psychologists joined forces as what some jokingly referred to as the "chairborne" research unit of the U.S. military.[164]

Disciplinary identities receded as social scientists worked together toward a common goal.[165] They introduced new methods along with novel applications of tried concepts and methodologies.[166] The new techniques of survey research and laboratory experimentation would have important effects on postwar intellectual developments. They also applied anthropological concepts derived from the study of primitive cultures to contemporary societies and broadened biologically based psychology to include developments in social psychology and sociology. These modes of understanding human behavior added a new dimension to economic and political analysis.[167]

Stouffer's work as director of the Research Branch of the War Department in this atmosphere of urgent collaboration was particularly relevant for the group at Harvard.[168] It closely paralleled the approach to the study of man the Levellers had been postulating: an examination of man in relation to his culture and society that drew upon several relevant disciplines.[169] Stouffer described how this collaborative work impressed him: "There are several streams of influence which are converging to develop social psychology and sociology into sciences with conceptual schemes from which, it is hoped, empirically verifiable inferences and predictions can eventually be made."[170] He identified four such streams: (1) the combined dynamic, clinical, and social psychologies; (2) learning theory; (3) social anthropology; and (4) sociology.[171]

Of the combined dynamic, clinical, and social psychologies, Stouffer opined: "Many of the ideas of Freud and his followers may eventually be rejected, but there can be no question as to the tentative utility of many of the concepts of psychoanalysis and of their revolutionary significance in the study of social psychology."[172] He credited this stream as shifting the emphasis in the study of man as a rational person to the study of man as a person who is often unconscious of the real motives for his behavior.[173] He described learning theory, the second stream, as having its roots in early Pavlovian concepts of conditioned response and the theories of reward and punishment, which he believed were undergoing change in response to new data.[174] He further believed that the experimental tradition that students of learning theory were bringing to social psychology was an important advancement.[175] Stouffer added that social psychology would be stunted in its development until it required "experimental verification" as part of its research.[176] The third stream of influence derived from social anthropology, which through studies of nonliterate societies highlighted the "plasticity of the human organism" and the wide variations in human behavior related to learning the values of one's cultural environment.[177] The study of these variations in personality and social behavior provided perspective for studying personality in Western culture.[178] Finally, he credited sociology as contributing to a clearer understanding of the social system apart from the individuals within it.[179] This, then, the "study of man as he functions in society," was precisely the approach that that Parsons and the Levellers had envisaged.[180] Stouffer's pioneering efforts along the same lines and his eventual arrival at Harvard lent a new vigor to their conviction that such a venture was feasible.[181]

The wartime research experience of other social scientists also hastened the movement toward a new department.[182] Indeed, the experiences of the Levellers themselves fortified their original belief in such a move.[183] Clyde Kluckhohn served in the Foreign Morale Analysis Division (FMAD) of the Office of War Information (OWI). He and his wife Florence were among the first anthropologists hired by the OWI.[184] Several government research groups studied morale in general, but the FMAD investigated Japanese morale in particular: why it appeared to be strong, whether it might change, and how a change might be instigated. In short, the OWI wanted to know, "Who are the Japanese?" and "What makes them tick?"[185] The

OWI thought these were cultural rather than psychological questions and thus recruited anthropologists to study—and to manipulate if possible— the morale of Japanese soldiers and civilians.[186] Few of the anthropologists had undertaken any fieldwork in Japan, but the OWI believed they could identify relevant cultural patterns without such experience.[187]

Alexander H. Leighton, a psychiatrist and anthropologist, who was chief of the division, described the full range of topics investigated by the FMAD in connection with Japan. The study focused on "civilian morale and internal social conditions" there, seeking to discover any weaknesses in support of the war effort. FMAD critically assessed the assumption that the populace was "uniformly and effectively mobilized in support of the war."[188] It examined the effects of food shortages, air raids, and disruptions of normal life. The FMAD analyzed how "these hardships affected the capacity for war production and how they might influence the will to resist in the event of Allied invasion of the homeland."[189] It gathered data on tensions between various groups in Japan, such as industrial workers, farmers, women, students, and intellectuals to determine whether any of them showed signs of dissatisfaction with the war. The study was useful not only during the war but also had significance for the postwar occupation and administration of Japan.[190]

Like Stouffer's unit, the FMAD employed a problem-centered approach that drew disciplines and subdisciplines together. The social scientists who established and directed the project brought to bear the research methods of sociology, psychology, social anthropology, and psychiatry. They believed in the utility, indeed the necessity, of using these social sciences to study human behavior. "A basic premise of the research was that social phenomena are susceptible to scientific analysis through formulation of inductive generalizations."[191] Accepting the ability to make valid generalizations about social phenomena from specific instances led these social scientists to enter a new enterprise—prediction. They were charged with the daunting mission of assessing enemy morale and making estimates accordingly.[192] Kluckhohn's experience with the FMAD strengthened his own belief and that of his Harvard cohorts, in much the same way the work of Stouffer had, that their attempts at creating a new department were valid.[193] As noted earlier, Parsons did not leave Harvard, but he assisted the School for Overseas Administration and consulted for the Foreign Economic Administration.[194] He also actively contributed to the postwar planning for Germany, arguing against the Morgenthau plan for its deindustrialization.[195]

Yet another member of the Levellers—Henry Murray—also had defining wartime experiences.[196] In 1942, Murray accepted a senior staff position with Assessment Station S (S for Secret, of course) of the Office of Strategic Services, the precursor of today's CIA.[197] The OSS had become a "magnet for Harvard scholars" after William Langer, a faculty member in history, became the head of its Research and Analysis Branch.[198] Murray's work involved the assessment of men and women for hazardous missions for the OSS, often behind enemy lines.[199] He developed methods to evaluate the personalities of OSS recruits for their fitness as spies and special agents.[200] Few precedents existed for Murray to go on, so he brought into this vacuum the theory and research methods he had developed over the last ten years at the Psychological Clinic at Harvard.[201] The work of the OSS assessment team was the first American attempt to base selection procedures on Gestalt principles by studying the whole person in numerous settings.[202] He helped establish similar assessment programs in California and Washington, and he traveled abroad to assess OSS personnel in the field.[203] He even supervised the testing of Chinese paratroopers for sabotage and intelligence missions behind Japanese lines.[204] The OSS promoted Captain Murray to major and ultimately to lieutenant colonel, and it awarded him the Legion of Merit for his duty.[205] Murray was most proud, however, of his analysis of the personality of Adolf Hitler.[206] He did a brief study in 1940, and the OSS subsequently asked him to expand it to examine Hitler's sources of influence with the German people and to predict his response to defeat. In October 1943, Murray produced the 227-page study, "Analysis of the Personality of Adolph [*sic*] Hitler, with Predictions of His Future Behavior and Suggestions for Dealing with Him Now and after Germany's Surrender."[207] He predicted the Nazi leader's suicide, believing Hitler was compelled to do so as the "last resource of an insulted and unendurable existence."[208]

Diverse specialists populated the OSS staff. Again, the urgency of the war dictated that disciplinary identities melt into the background; interdisciplinary cooperation was now paramount.[209] Although the notion of interdisciplinary work had been in the air before World War II, as indicated by the stirrings at Harvard, the cooperative work among psychologists, sociologists, and cultural anthropologists legitimized the efforts of the Levellers hoping to fuse these three disciplines into a single department.[210] The alliance between the social sciences and government research agencies during World War II affected not only Harvard but the entire academy, setting in motion trends that would occupy the attention of social scientists everywhere.[211] Much of the analysis conducted by the FMAD, for example, was based on assumptions derived from the fields of cultural anthropology, psychology, and psychiatry.[212] Psychiatrists and psychologists began considering the effect of cultural environment—largely the province of anthropologists—on personality. Cultural anthropologists, in turn, became interested in Freudian concepts, most notably psychoanalysis.[213] Out of these hybrid interests emerged the school of "culture and personality."[214] Research in culture and personality had begun in the early 1940s, but only after World War II did it gather force.[215] The pioneering work in this field was done primarily by Bronislaw Malinowski, Margaret Mead, Ruth Benedict, and Gregory Bateson. Benedict's groundbreaking book, *Patterns of Culture*, one of the first studies of national character, is considered the seminal work in the subject.[216] Later research in culture and personality employed even more psychoanalytic theory, especially in the work of Ralph Linton, Abram Kardiner, Cora DuBois, and Clyde Kluckhohn.[217] The efforts of such investigators and the innovative work of the FMAD laid the foundation for the field to flourish after World War II.[218] The Research Branch of the army under the direction of Stouffer pioneered the use of statistical methods to investigate human behavior, a critical contribution to the postwar developments in the social sciences. After the war, the work of the Research Branch was collected and analyzed in the four-volume work *The American Soldier*.[219] This monumental book, more than any other single work, brought the scientific attitude survey into academia.[220] It is a prime example of interdisciplinary work funded by the Carnegie Corporation that had long-lasting results.

World War II transformed psychology in the United States.[221] The discipline made significant contributions to the war effort, gaining recognition and respect. The navy made a glowing assessment of psychology's record during the war: "The application of psychology in selecting and training men, and in guiding the design of weapons so they would fit men, did more to help win this war than any other intellectual activity."[222] The reputation of psychologists "had risen from one of lowly technicians to one of wise consultants and managers," who now enjoyed a newfound public appreciation.[223] Indeed, there were not enough of them to fill the demand in both public and private sectors.[224] The war also emboldened anthropologists, who were exuberant about the postwar prospects for the social sciences based on their military research experiences. Kluckhohn believed the new social sciences had unlimited potential and could have "consequences as revolutionary as those of atomic energy."[225] Margaret Mead thought scholars were positioned to help in "devising new [social and political] forms to keep human beings safe in a narrowing world."[226] There was no shortage of confidence on the part of these leading anthropologists.

As psychologists, anthropologists, and sociologists collaborated on wartime research, they were creating a "new institutional landscape for the human sciences."[227] At least in spirit, it reflected the interdisciplinary approach that Talcott Parsons and his colleagues had been advocating at Harvard since 1940.[228] Joel Isaac characterized the military and civilian entities conducting research during World War II as "the proving ground of the new human sciences."[229] In the beginning, the social scientists believed they would provide data-gathering and advisory services much like economists and sociologists had done for the government during the New Deal, the most recent emergency that brought social scientists into national service.[230] Their new role, however, would surpass the previous alliance between social science and the government as it became clear they were expected to do more than merely provide data and advice.[231] The exigencies of the war required them to engage in the "prediction and control of human behavior," using tools such as those developed by Clyde Kluckhohn and others for studying, predicting, and manipulating morale (domestic and foreign) and by Henry Murray for assessing the fitness of spies for the OSS.[232]

It was logical that Harvard would respond positively to the trends in social science research that had sprung from wartime research because the Levellers had already made interdisciplinary moves along these lines.[233] Responding to this national turn toward collaboration among disciplines, Dean Buck dispatched Talcott Parsons in the spring of 1945 to visit and report on several research facilities that were applying social science techniques to social problems.[234] In addition to the Yale Institute of Human Relations and the Research Branch in the Information and Education Division of the War Department, Parsons visited the Columbia Bureau of Applied Social Science Research, the North Carolina Institute of Social Research, and the Bureau of Agricultural Economics.[235] Parson's findings led him and his collaborators to conclude that a new interdisciplinary department would require research facilities of a sort previously unknown in a university setting.[236]

As the end of World War II approached, several developments in the preceding years converged to set the stage for the creation of the Social Relations Department. The wartime research of the Levellers and other social scientists had reduced the divisions between and among the behavioral sciences, reinforcing their conviction that an institutional grouping of the relevant disciplines was warranted. Indeed, Allport viewed this shared experience as critical to the founding of the Social Relations Department, contending that "in the course of their wartime service most of our staff had lost their strict academic identities."[237] He believed that "a man could be a good social scientist whether or not his main training had been in psychology, sociology, anthropology, statistics, or some other discipline."[238] Of course, the Levellers also had complementary experiences at Harvard in developing an interdisciplinary approach that largely preceded America's entry into the war. At the same time, the conflicts in the Departments of Psychology and Sociology had made life intolerable for Allport, Murray, and Parsons; a headache for the Harvard administration; and a debilitating drag on the day-to-day functioning of the departments. After a false start with President Conant, the Levellers

finally captured the attention and support of Dean Paul Buck for an interdisciplinary department. A strong dean, he had a keen appreciation of
the social sciences, an understanding of the fraught faculty relations in the
relevant departments, and a sympathy for the personal and professional
plight of Parsons and his group.

3

The Founding
of the Department

A Determined Dean Acts

Something had to be done.

—Henry Murray and Talcott Parsons

At Harvard we have weighed the fusion of the social sciences against
the integrity of psychology as a single discipline and have decided in
favor of the former, even while the American Psychological Association
moves in the opposite direction for the fusion of all psychology.

—Gordon W Allport and E. G. Boring

The wartime experiences of the Levellers legitimized their cause to create an interdisciplinary department. Dean Paul Buck took an interest
in these favorable developments in the social sciences. Despite the forces
moving toward a new department, however, obstacles remained.[1] Harvard was considering alternative modes of reorganization, particularly
with the Psychology Department.[2] President James Conant had appointed
an outside committee, headed by Alan Gregg of the Rockefeller Foundation, to review the status of Psychology in the university. A review of the
questions that the committee was charged to investigate reveals that a
structure congenial to Parsons and his group was not one of the options
under consideration.[3]

In the foreword, President Conant posed several core questions:

What different types of professional psychologists should be trained by the
University and in what faculties? What coordination, if any, should we attempt between the work of the psychologists and the psychiatrists in the

different faculties? What instruction in Psychology is a desirable part of the general education of undergraduates or students in our various professional schools? Should we recognize the different types of Psychology by suitable labels on our professorships and separate methods of reviewing permanent appointments, or should we attempt to have an over-all committee on Psychology which would be concerned with new appointments in the whole field?[4]

Neither the report nor its foreword recommended an interdisciplinary enterprise. On the contrary, the report—published in 1947, after unexpected delay—opposed any such fragmentation of Psychology: "The arguments for the separation of social psychology from the rest of psychology must be explained on other grounds than those of logic. . . . One cannot think of the separation of social psychology from psychology as helping the comprehension of human behavior."[5] Thus the report of the Gregg committee rejected anything resembling a Department of Social Relations, particularly if it included social psychology, but its official recommendation against such action came too late.[6] By the fall of 1945, with the rush of new and returning students and with increased lobbying for restructuring the social sciences by Parsons and others, pressures for change grew.[7]

Parsons campaigned for change in the social sciences at Harvard, even if the change only indirectly supported the idea of a new interdisciplinary department. On October 16, 1945, three of the Levellers—Parsons, Allport, and Kluckhohn—joined other faculty members in a letter to President Conant.[8] They asserted that Harvard's social sciences faced a serious challenge from proposed federal legislation to fund research in the social sciences as well as natural sciences.[9] If Harvard refused to participate for fear of jeopardizing its independence, then it would leave the field open to institutions "with possibly lower standards" to command those resources, making it more difficult for Harvard to compete.[10] They argued that Harvard must accept the challenge and participate in the funding, using the monies to set a higher standard of scientific achievement.[11]

The group further warned that the social sciences at Harvard needed reorganization to take full advantage of such funding:

> As at present organized, however, the social sciences at Harvard are exceedingly poorly prepared to live up to the challenge which seems certain to come. Even within the Faculty of Arts and Sciences they are scattered between the six different departments of which we are respectively members, with no overall organization of common research interests, since the present Committee on Research in the Social Sciences is soon to be dissolved.[12]

President Conant took no action, instead referring the letter to Dean Buck. Initially, Buck seemed uninterested as well, telling Parsons his direct approach to President Conant "is one not conducive to the best results."[13]

DEAN PAUL BUCK COMES ON BOARD

After further consideration of the document, including meeting with the group, Buck made a surprising turnabout. Harvard was not ready to establish the sort of broad university council proposed in the report. Rather, he felt it was "far more feasible to start at the other level and begin building up" and to create a new department for the social sciences.[14] Parsons, Allport, and Kluckhohn got more than they had expected. Buck intended to propose a motion to the faculty establishing a new department "to include all the present Department of Sociology, (thus abolishing it as such), Cultural Anthropology, and Social Psychology."[15] He thought it was time for action, and his proposal for a new department had "the virtue of being entirely feasible."[16] Buck also believed he could find funds to establish a laboratory of social sciences as a key part of the department.[17] The laboratory could serve as a hub for receiving funds from the government and private sources, thus remedying one of the deficiencies delineated in the group's warning letter to Conant. Over time, the laboratory could become available for use by faculty from other departments and faculties, but the laboratory would remain in the Department of Social Sciences.[18]

The Levellers rejoiced. After years of being marginalized in their own departments, they now could see the new departmental alignment taking shape. Parsons wrote Buck, "I should like to express to you now my profound gratification that you have seen your way clear to take this step. It is, of course, precisely what I and some of my colleagues have been hoping for a long time."[19] Gordon Allport responded to Buck similarly: "Your communication brought considerable encouragement and satisfaction."[20] Hobart Mowrer wrote to the Dean, saying, "I have just learned of your plan for the establishment of a Department of Social Science and writing to say how deeply pleased I am."[21] He added that the proposal should be useful in fostering cooperation among social scientists with common interests but different formal training.[22] Mowrer, one of the original Levellers, was on the faculty of the Graduate School of Education, however, and he did not join his fellow conspirators in the new department.

Clyde Kluckhohn from Anthropology penned the most effusive response: "You know my views well enough to have some idea how happy and excited your letter of Nov. 14th has made me."[23] He heaped praise on Buck for taking this action, adding, "And I am deeply convinced that time will show that this was not the least wise or important of the many acts of courageous statesmanship that are characterizing your administration."[24] He ended even more ebulliently: "It is wonderful and exhilarating to go with the prospects you have opened for the kind of organizational set-up you sketch in your letter. Thank you."[25] Oddly, he raised an issue with Buck that "is even more crucial in terms of your proposal"—the fate of Kluckhohn's close friend Henry Murray. Perhaps he feared that Murray, frustrated in his long fight against the biotropes, might have been considering leaving Harvard, even though a haven now seemed in the offing. Or, because Buck mentioned only moving social psychology and did not specify clinical psychology as well, Murray's fate may have seemed uncertain to Kluckhohn. He pleaded to Buck, "Harvard cannot afford to let Harry Murray go."[26] He listed the reasons:

> He is easily the most distinguished clinical psychologist in America and probably in the world. This judgment I have heard from leading psychologists of California, Chicago, Yale, and many other American universities. I have heard from responsible psychologists and psychiatrists of Britain that they consider his work the most original and fertile of any American, regardless of psychological field. On the face of it it is ridiculous that at his age (50), with his reputation, his breadth of training and experience, his attraction for students, his publications that Harvard should only now be offering him a permanent appointment and that at the associate professor level. In addition to being a great scientist, he is also a great man. And, as you know better than I, the two do not always go together.[27]

Kluckhohn's concern over Murray's fate was an outlier among the Levellers. No one else mentioned it. Allport, for example, simply assumed clinical psychology was included in the move, replying to Buck, "Your letter does not specify that Clinical, Personnel, and Child Psychology should be considered part of 'Social Psychology' but I should like to assume that you have grouped these subjects together in your own mind."[28]

BORING OBJECTS TO SPLITTING PSYCHOLOGY

Not surprisingly, the reaction from the departments diminished by the plan was less enthusiastic, ranging from begrudging support to outright hostility. Sorokin in Sociology did not favor the move, and in the department's vote on the matter, he abstained.[29] According to Kluckhohn, the chairman of the Anthropology Department, Alfred Tozzer, believed the move was harmful to his department but positive for the university, stating, "Well, this is against the interests of the department of anthropology but since I really admit it is in the interests of the university of the whole

I cannot do otherwise than give it my support."[30] Other members of Anthropology either supported the move or did not oppose it.[31]

Leading the biotropes in Psychology, Boring vociferously objected, accusing Buck of a surprise attack: "You cast a bomb-shell into the Departments of Anthropology, Sociology and Psychology! We must work out the best solution for everybody, but I am not sure that yours is it. I have spent the week-end trying to think out how Allport, Parsons and Kluckhohn can get what they want without the rest of us being sacrificed to their needs."[32] He enclosed a counterproposal. Boring conceded there was a field of common interest among Allport, Parsons, Kluckhohn, and Murray, referring to it as "the nature of the whole individual as he enters into social relations."[33] He said it was "hard to find an acceptable name for this field," as if that were a fatal strike against the plan. He suggested calling the field Social Anthropology, Social Psychology, or even Dynamic Psychology, because these would be fields that include the "psychology of personality" that united the three defectors. Whatever it was to be called, he agreed that Harvard should support it and give these professors "an institutional relation."[34]

Boring called the proposal flawed, arguing that Harvard must have a Department of Psychology that included both "the sociotropic psychology as well as biotropic psychology."[35] On a practical level, Boring noted that graduate students coming to Harvard "will seek training . . . as psychologists, not as social scientists nor as psychobiologists."[36] They will need the "status of psychologist professionally," and that required exposure to the full range of psychology, which they would lack if the components of psychology were split into two departments.[37] He contended that Harvard needed a Department of Sociology "for similar institutional reasons."[38]

Boring's ultimate concern, however, was the Psychology Department losing social psychology and his "friend-enemy" Gordon Allport, as David Riesman had characterized the duo's relationship long before the portmanteau "frenemy" became fashionable.[39] As one of the most renowned psychologists in the world, Allport's loss would be a blow to the department. Boring feared that a Psychology Department lacking social psychology would be placed at a disadvantage with intact psychology departments at other universities. He insisted that his fellow biotropes needed to be familiar with sociotropic psychology. Boring noted plaintively, "I remember how we struggled to get Allport in the Department in 1930 because we could not do without him. The need for him is no less now."[40] Boring expressed no concern, however, over the impending loss of Henry Murray and clinical psychology.

Boring's counterproposal was as weak as it was unwieldy. He proposed that a committee be established to oversee the field.[41] It would include all relevant faculty members of the new field and function like other interdepartmental committees. It would also assume control of the proposed laboratory and undertake departmental functions involving social anthropology.[42] Eventually, the committee might offer a program for the PhD or become a field for undergraduate concentration, but only after faculty approval. He added that Kluckhohn could be transferred to the Department of Psychology if his work is principally psychological.[43] This suggestion was particularly bizarre and tone deaf. Given that psychologists Allport and Murray were miserable in the Department of Psychology, why would cultural anthropologist Kluckhohn, who was aligned intellectually with them, want to join such a hostile environment? Boring pleaded for the status quo, aiming an unusual barb at Buck:

> Instead of tearing apart existing institutions and throwing Harvard out of adjustment with the cultural changes in the country at large, it [the counterproposal] maintains what has been the advantage in the past and provides a matrix in which a new conception can grow. When the work of the Committee begins to overtop the work of its allied departments, it will be time enough to consider adjusting the departments by Procrustes' methods.[44]

Boring hardly endeared himself to the dean by comparing him to a despicable character in Greek mythology. Procrustes was a robber who would invite travelers to spend the night at his home, then tie them to an iron bed and adjust them to the bed either by stretching them to fit it or, if they were too tall, cutting off their legs. Moreover, it was Boring—not Buck—who seemed "out of adjustment," with the changes in the country moving in the direction of interdisciplinary efforts in the behavioral sciences. Buck had been wrestling with the issue for years. Indeed, he had written to Boring the year before, describing the problem and hinting that a realignment might be necessary to satisfy Allport, Parsons, and Kluckhohn. He had researched the matter, dispatching Parsons to observe developments at universities and institutions around the country, and he knew what was intellectually afoot.

Buck wrote to "Mr. Boring," dismissing him tersely. "No, I do not think your proposal meets the problem."[45] He scoffed at Boring's professed surprise at the plan for a new department: "But my (what you call) a bombshell brings what has been smoldering for so long into the open where it can be discussed."[46] He invited Boring to attend a meeting of the relevant departments the following week, curtly stating that he "could make his views known there."[47]

Boring grew increasingly agitated, writing Buck again on the subject, complaining that the new arrangement in Psychology was a threat to his effectiveness at Harvard.[48] He even considered the possibility that Buck was out to get him: "I can perhaps be forgiven the paranoid thought that it might be that you are anxious to pocket me and limit my activities because I seem to be the enemy to progress at Harvard. First, let me defend myself and then get away from personalities."[49] And he worried whether the Psychology Department could continue to be called Psychology, and how the rest of the profession would react. He feared psychology at Harvard would be ridiculed:

> The right name for the Department of Residue is INDIVIDUAL PSYCHOLOGY, but it would get us laughed at if used. Physiological Psychology is impossible, and whoever gave you that advice had his mind on something else. General Psychology is just as bad. You are going to find, I think, that you must call the Residue PSYCHOLOGY or do something that will seem ridiculous to the profession.[50]

Professor J. G. Beebe-Center of Psychology also argued against the move, although more calmly, telling Buck that psychology cannot be divided into independent parts.[51] He explained that psychology involves the functions (conscious or behavioral) of an organism and a basic characteristic of these functions is their inter-relation.[52] These conditions precluded separating the components of psychology.[53] He prophesized that any attempt along these lines was bound to fail: "The inclusion of Social Psychology in a Department of Social Science would sooner or later result in either the absorption of all of psychology in the new Department of Social Science, or in the return of social psychology to the Department of Psychology."[54] Beebe-Center further told Buck that he agreed that "something needs to be done"—the phrase seemingly on many lips at the time—because of the divergence of interests among the members of the Department of Psychology.[55] He suggested two alternatives, either placing all of psychology in a new Department of Social Science or creating a "Committee on Social Sciences" to represent the interests of social psychology, sociology, and cultural anthropology.[56]

Dean Buck brushed aside all criticisms and counterproposals.[57] He seized control of the situation, moving quickly to promote his proposal.[58] He hosted a meeting of all faculty members on term or permanent appointment to the Departments of Anthropology, Psychology, and Sociology.[59] They voted to appoint a committee to draw up a plan for a department comprised of the sociotropic elements of Anthropology, Psychology, and Sociology.[60] The committee consisted of the chairman and one other member of each of these disciplines.[61] Talcott Parsons served as chairman and, along with Carl Zimmerman, represented Sociology. A. M. Tozzer and Donald Scott represented Anthropology, while E. G. Boring and Gordon Allport served on behalf of the Psychology Department.[62] The committee submitted its plan to each of the three departments separately. Each department involved approved the plan, and it was sent on to the faculty.[63] The plan and its subsequent approval caused consternation within the three departments.[64] Much argument and lobbying accompanied its approval.[65]

Paul Buck applied his considerable leverage as dean to force its approval, for he felt that "something had to be done," according to Parsons and Murray.[66] On January 29, 1946, something indeed was done when the faculty voted to establish a Department of Social Relations.[67] The new department would incorporate the existing Department of Sociology, the fields of social and clinical psychology as offered in the existing Department of Psychology, and the field of social anthropology as offered in the existing Department of Anthropology.[68]

The faculty authorized the department to offer a field of concentration in social relations to undergraduates and to recommend candidates for the bachelor's degree with or without honors. Social Relations would give instruction leading to the AM and PhD degrees and recommend candidates for these degrees, with the following subjects recognized for the PhD: sociology, social psychology, clinical psychology, and social anthropology. The plan further abolished the present concentration in the area of social science as well as the Committee on Concentration in the Area of Social Science.[69]

During the faculty meeting, an amendment was proposed to delete "clinical psychology" from the higher degree offerings, but it was defeated. The faculty also rejected the establishment of a PhD degree in social relations, permitting degrees only in the constituent fields of the department.[70] The only remaining issue was the name of the new department, a matter that had been totally overlooked. Gordon Allport described the hasty resolution:

> Six p.m. was the sacred hour of adjournment for faculty meetings. At a meeting in January 1946 the faculty authorized the formation of the new department but at 5:30 p.m. had not yet christened it. The name Human Relations was suggested, but that would never do because Yale already had an institute by that name. It would be too suffocating to call it the Department of Sociology, Social Psychology, Clinical Psychology and Social Anthropology although that is what it was. At about 5:59 p.m. someone proposed "Social Relations" and owing to the lateness of the hour the name was adopted without debate.[71]

On February 1, 1946, Harvard issued a press release announcing the news and explaining the rationale for, and the scope of, the new department:

> Experience during the war indicated that attempts to segregate fields of study in human relations raised undesirable barriers. Delving into and cooperating with other departments, the Department of Social Relations will

include studies of man's culture and his theories of art, science, technology, philosophy, religion, ethics and law; of man as a social being, with emphasis on examination of entire cultures as working units; and of the mind of man and his conscious and behavioral adjustments to the exigencies of life. The new arrangement represents a synthesis, believed to be unique, of work formerly distributed between the Departments of Anthropology, Psychology and Sociology, which hitherto, under American educational systems, have had little effective relationship with one another.[72]

BORING AND ALLPORT EXPLAIN THE "DRASTIC MOVE"

This was big news in the academy. Allport acknowledged that it "was a drastic move for Harvard and startled that portion of the academic world which watches changes in Harvard's educational policies."[73] He and Boring, insistent that their colleagues throughout the country should be informed of the event, cowrote an article in the *American Psychologist* later that spring announcing the change in departmental structure at Harvard.[74] After years of fighting over the direction of the Department of Psychology, Allport and Boring collaborated in explaining the reasons for the division of the Psychology Department and the creation of the Department of Social Relations.[75]

Boring, who vehemently opposed the "tearing apart" of Psychology and the loss of Allport to Psychology, had no change of heart, but he was willing to put a positive spin on it for the public.[76] In his 1961 biography, he wrote of the rupture of Psychology to form Social Relations: "I was doubtful, but these human naturalists were sure. I gave in when one of them, like the Prince of Wales before Stanley Baldwin, pleaded with me for the right to marry for love."[77] A colorful image, but his permission was not needed. Dean Buck pushed the move through regardless.

In the article, Allport and Boring cited the influence of historical developments on the "inherent logic of subject-matter" of academic departments. Each of the relevant departments—Anthropology, Psychology, and Sociology—had followed its own trajectory, and despite being "closely linked in much of their subject-matter," had little to do with one another until now.[78] Over the previous ten years, rigid departmental lines had been challenged by an evolving "synthesis of socio-cultural and psychological sciences."[79] They asserted that the union was "widely recognized within the academic world in spite of the fact that there is no commonly accepted name to designate the synthesis."[80] Harvard established the Department of Social Relations to more precisely characterize this "emerging discipline" as "[dealing] not only with the body of fact and theory traditionally recognized as the subject-matter of sociology, but also with that portion of psychological science that treats the individual within the social system, and that portion of anthropological science that is particularly relevant to the social and cultural patterns of literate societies."[81]

They credited World War II as having accelerated the "fusion of research activities" in this new field, obliterating the already deteriorating distinctions among social scientists studying the same fundamental problems.[82] They noted that the first crack in the theoretical walls separating these disciplines had appeared nearly twenty years earlier with the emergence of the area of study known as "culture and personality."[83] Since then, many other topics of concern had arisen that cut across the narrow fields of specialization in traditional departments: "community analysis, attitude assessment, the process of socialization in childhood and youth, the study of group conflict and prejudice, factors in national and institutional morale, the nature of institutional behavior, aspects of communication and propaganda, ethnic and national differences and similarities, problems of social and mental adjustment of the individual in his social situation."[84] These topics were merely a sample of what they saw as a trend in the basic social sciences.[85] They believed that new common problems confronting these disciplines required new skills and tools. Social Relations would thus be accompanied by a Laboratory of Social Relations to provide just such training. The new instruments of research included "statistical sampling, interviewing, participant observation, group experiments, coding and machine sorting, community mapping, life-history analysis."[86]

Allport and Boring predicted increased demands for the study of the "human factor" in the atomic age.[87] They saw pressures coming from the federal government, from the local community, and from the university itself.[88] They envisioned a Department of Social Relations along with its laboratory as the vehicle to select and to undertake only the most important projects that would be thrust upon the university.[89] They recounted attempts by American universities over the last decade to deal with the administrative complications posed by the growing synthesis of the three social sciences. Universities took the "manner of least resistance" by creating interdepartmental committees or institutes, such as the Yale Institute of Human Relations.[90] Even Harvard previously had taken only a tentative step of creating an undergraduate concentration in the area of social science, with no move toward interdisciplinary graduate training or research. The committee structure, they concluded, was unsatisfactory because it failed to address the problem. A committee structure, however, was precisely what Boring had advocated when he was resisting the creation of Social Relations. What was required now was recognizing the field by creating a single department for training both undergraduates and graduates. Only Harvard, they said, was prepared to permit "a genuine fusion of the three specialties."[91]

Regarding the effect on Psychology at Harvard, they said, "Psychology-new-style at Harvard will be Psychology-old-style with social and clinical psychology left out."[92] The new Psychology Department would be responsible for all of psychology save those topics dealing with "the individual in the social structure."[93] They acknowledged the potential danger for the discipline in this move by making it harder for social and clinical psychologists in Social Relations to work with the physiological psychologists in the Psychology Department. And, they conceded, the psychology profession disapproved: "At Harvard we have weighed the fusion of the social sciences against the integrity of psychology as a single discipline and have decided in favor of the former, even while the American Psychological Association moves in the opposite direction for the fusion of all psychology."[94]

Allport and Boring also addressed the sensitive situation close to home, noting that the move had divided members of the Psychology Department. Those physiological psychologists remaining in Psychology received nothing in return for the split.[95] In folksy terms, Allport and Boring explained, "The social psychologists could change spouses, but the residual psychologists were merely divorced."[96] They struggled to find a silver lining in the divorce for the psychologists in Psychology old style; they mustered up two advantages. The first was the freedom of the psychologists to associate more closely with the natural sciences: "Psychology can now be classed at Harvard as a natural science, instead of perpetually having to straddle social science and natural science."[97] The second was the benefit of narrowing the focus of the field. "Specialization, moreover, has its strength; there is no doubt that both kinds of psychology will grow faster when each has its own separate pasture."[98] As support of this claim, they cited the growth of Psychology when it split from Philosophy at Harvard in 1934.[99] In short, they argued that the Psychology Department would score a net gain in the transaction because of the ability to become more focused on its specialties: "What is lost in breadth is gained in unity, and Psychology's efforts can become more concentrated in certain directions. For instance, the laboratory can again come to dominate the Department."[100]

Many events heralded the creation of the Department of Social Relations: profound personal and professional dissatisfactions among key faculty members; new movements in the relevant disciplines; the wartime experiences of returning faculty; and a supportive, forceful administrator in Dean Paul Buck.[101] At last, on January 29, 1946, the cumulative pressure imposed by these various forces resulted in the formation of the Department of Social Relations.[102] Now it remained to be seen what the Levellers would do with their new department.

4

The First Five Years

A Golden Age
but Integration Proves Elusive

The enormous, unfocused, almost millenarian exhilaration that attended the social relations department in the 1950s, and what we who were there then were pleased to call its Project—the construction of "A Common Language for the Social Sciences." Bliss was it in that dawn; but the golden age was . . . all-too-brief.

—Clifford Geertz

In fact, though modern art was not much talked about in our conversations, the department in its conceptual disunity resembled one of those self-destructing sculptures by Yves Tanguy.

—Norman Birnbaum

As the Department of Social Relations came into existence, it rode a wave of enthusiasm about interdisciplinary efforts in the social sciences, a wave that its founders had helped set in motion, through both their informal, clandestine pursuits at Harvard as well as their wartime research.[1] And the department's creation, in turn, precipitated a broader national movement toward interdisciplinary methods of research.[2] In post–World War II American academia, interdisciplinarity had become a "virtue" unto itself, and Social Relations was the vanguard.[3] The Levellers, who once pursued their passions on the periphery, now commanded center stage. Their disciplines—social and clinical psychology, sociology, and cultural anthropology—had become not only respectable but exquisitely in demand, earning a new moniker, the "behavioral sciences."[4] Other interdisciplinary social science programs, although not modeled on

Social Relations, sprang up around the country at Yale, Princeton, Berkeley, Minnesota, Wisconsin, Michigan, and North Carolina.[5]

As historian Jamie Cohen-Cole frames it, "interdisciplinary social science was hot in Cold War America," and "American academics, administrators, and foundation officials saw it as paving the road both to better theory and to the production of practical results."[6] David Riesman likened the social sciences post–World War II to "a Cinderella who has come into splendor" and is "unexpectedly courted by the princes of government, industry, and the universities."[7] Many social scientists now viewed the most vital issues for study as ones that "fell between disciplines," such as small-group interaction, mobility, personality, values, national character, and decision making.[8] It was more than simply a dramatic move to newer methods, tools, and topics of investigation. Interdisciplinarity came to be seen as an "unqualified good" that in the Cold War period "meant not only creativity, but also democracy, rigor, and practicality."[9] To some intellectuals, it became a valued "character trait," a sign of an open mind with the mental flexibility and creativity necessary to understand the complexities of human behavior.[10] Rigid disciplinary focus became associated with a narrowness unable to "tolerate" complex or ambiguous situations.[11]

ORGANIZING A COMPLEX NEW DEPARTMENT

The Department of Social Relations began operations in the summer of 1946, and by the fall term its staff was complete. The first permanent members of the department included those most responsible for its creation: Talcott Parsons, Clyde Kluckhohn, Gordon Allport, and Henry Murray (although Murray did not officially return until 1947).[12] Other original members given tenure were Robert White, Pitirim Sorokin, Carle C. Zimmerman, George Homans, and Samuel Stouffer.[13] Nontenured founding members included Leland C. DeVinney (Sociology), Stanley G. Estes (Clinical Psychology), Oscar Handlin (Social History), Eugenia Hanfman (Clinical Psychology), Donald McGranahan (Social Psychology), Jerome Bruner (Social Psychology), Thelma Alper (Clinical Psychology), Sheldon Korchin (Social Psychology), Arthur K. Davis (Sociology), and Robert F. Bales (Sociology).[14]

The department augmented its initial complement the following academic year with the appointments of George E. Gardner (Clinical Psychology), C. F. Mosteller (Statistics), Erich Lindemann (Clinical Psychology), Richard L. Solomon (Social Psychology), Benjamin Paul (Social Anthropology), Mahlon Smith (Social Psychology), David Aberle (Social Anthropology), and Leo Postman (Social Psychology).[15] During its maiden year, Social Relations offered courses in all the disciplines encompassed by its charter: Anthropology and Modern Life, Opinion and Communication, Cultural Differences and International Understanding, Immigrant Culture in Transition, and Dynamic Psychology. Graduate courses took a less unified approach to the field of Social Relations.[16] The part of the program aimed at integration consisted, for the most part, of a series of proseminars considering methods, problems, and concepts of Social Relations as a whole.[17] The department also offered seminars in areas of special interest to the faculty, such as Culture and Personality, Comparative National Psychology, Sociology of Small Groups, and fieldwork in Clinical Psychology.[18] Social Relations acquired a nickname, as nearly everything does at Harvard: Soc Rel, pronounced "sock-rell."[19]

Any new department faces the daunting task of organization and planning, but the Department of Social Relations, avowing a diversity of interests and devoted to synthesis, courted disaster. The department began with a policy of decentralization, attempted in two ways. First, each subfield was given great autonomy in course offerings and requirements for advanced degrees.[20] In addition to respecting internal diversity, there was the practical problem of graduates finding jobs in an academic world still structured around traditional disciplines.[21] The department decided that "the credentials of our trainees should be fully validated in terms of the standards of each of the three disciplines."[22] Second, decentralization was sought by separating responsibility for research, graduate, and undergraduate instruction.[23]

THE LABORATORY OF SOCIAL RELATIONS
AND THE CARNEGIE CORPORATION

The most novel undertaking, drawing on Parsons's earlier visits to research facilities around the country, was the establishment of the Laboratory of Social Relations, parallel to the department. It would not be a laboratory in the traditional sense of a place where scientists conduct technical experiments, but rather an administrative vehicle for funding and supporting research projects by members of the department.[24] But the choice of name was certainly in keeping with Parsons's vision of creating a new science with all the trappings.

The question of how to finance such a venture was resolved when the laboratory found a benefactor in the Carnegie Corporation, which had been impressed by the wartime research of Samuel Stouffer and Alexander Leighton.[25] While director of the Research Branch of the War Department, Stouffer's principal superior had been General Frederick H. Osborn, a Carnegie Corporation trustee.[26] Prior to the end of the war,

Carnegie experienced a reorganization of its own, appointing two top officers familiar with Harvard and academia in general.[27] The new president was Charles Dollard, who had been a member of General Osborn's staff during the war and thus was thoroughly familiar with Stouffer's work. Dollard, with his brother John (a sociologist), was also a close friend of Clyde Kluckhohn.[28]

Kluckhohn, among the Social Relations faculty, had the longest and closest relationship with Dollard and the Carnegie Corporation.[29] He had received a cross-training fellowship from Carnegie before World War II.[30] Kluckhohn also had been a roommate of Charles Dollard at the University of Wisconsin and, through a shared interest in psychoanalysis, became friends with John Dollard.[31] And it was John Dollard who had encouraged Kluckhohn to pursue training in psychoanalysis and to incorporate it in his culture and personality studies of the Navajo.[32]

When Charles Dollard became president of the Carnegie Corporation, John Gardner became vice president. Gardner was a psychologist and, like Dollard, was interested in recent developments within the social sciences.[33] Gardner would become secretary of health, education, and welfare under President Lyndon Johnson and later the founder of Common Cause.[34] It was through connections such as these that the work of Stouffer and others in the Social Relations enterprise had become known and respected.[35] Stouffer would direct the laboratory, and he, along with Talcott Parsons, wanted a highly flexible fund to support younger faculty members just beginning research programs.[36] They met with President Conant and Dean Buck to discuss how the laboratory might be financed.[37] Given Harvard's links to the Carnegie Corporation through Kluckhohn and Stouffer, they decided that an application to the corporation might prove fruitful.[38]

They agreed that Conant's signature would give the greatest weight to the request.[39] The plan succeeded, and the Carnegie Corporation awarded the laboratory a five-year grant of $30,000 per year, which was later extended to a ten-year period. The laboratory, the heart of the research efforts of the new department, was off to a sound financial start. Indeed, the support of the Carnegie Corporation to both the Laboratory and Department of Social Relations was critical in these early years. The corporation made total grants of $335,000 to the department during its first ten years.[40] And the logic behind the corporation's largesse was clear. The sum was large but not excessive, in keeping with the corporation's strategy of providing strategic assistance yet keeping it "small enough to ensure major financing by Harvard."[41] The Carnegie plan was "to commit Harvard so heavily to the Department of Social Relations as to cut off any line of retreat when foundation support comes to an end."[42]

The Carnegie Corporation strongly believed in the merits of interdisciplinary research, surpassing the efforts of the Ford Foundation and other institutions to promote the new tools needed to develop the social sciences in this promising direction. Gardner made supporting interdisciplinary research a priority. In his view, such research was critically important for the future of these young disciplines: "Every thoughtful person who has taken a serious look at the whole range of the social sciences is convinced that great gains will come from what has been called the 'integration of the social sciences.'"[43] The Carnegie Corporation's focus was not lost on the social scientists seeking funding. At Harvard, this "bias in patronage" led to the "belief that the large research project, especially if dressed up as 'interdisciplinary' gets first call on foundation funds."[44] The research at Social Relations attracted funding and, in turn, helped secure a deeper commitment of Harvard to such work.

It was not only research labeled interdisciplinary that attracted funding, and it was not only Carnegie that had the funds. According to Harvard-trained anthropologist David Schneider, the American academy post–World War II was awash in money: "And of course we [Americans] were rich then; richer than anybody else by far. If you could think of anything plausible to do, you could get the money someplace—from the National Science Foundation, the Office of Naval Research, or the National Institute of Mental Health, from Ford or Rockefeller or Rand or the Social Science Research Council—to do it."[45] Samuel Stouffer, the principal mediator between Harvard and the Carnegie Corporation, convinced Harvard administrators that Carnegie favored the funding of research projects rather than the salaries of faculty.[46] President Conant and Dean Buck agreed to emphasize Harvard's long-term commitment to the Social Relations Department and its research, rather than any one faculty member. In this way, Carnegie hoped to ensure that interdisciplinarity became a "normal feature of the social sciences."[47]

The laboratory was independent, responsible not to the department but to the dean of the Faculty of Arts and Sciences. It was governed by a director, associate director, and executive committee, all appointed by the dean of the Faculty of Arts and Sciences.[48] It remained, however, an integral part of the department, according to Parsons: "Its administrative task is twofold: 1) The facilitation of research, a task which may involve the provision of funds, space, and facilities; and 2) cooperation with Department of Social Relations in training graduate students, the social scientists of the future, in research techniques."[49] It maintained a close relationship with the department on all major policy decisions largely because most laboratory appointees were also department members.[50] Thus, Parsons expected that departmental training and curriculum prerogatives would be "respected in the formulation of Laboratory policies."[51] The laboratory had no research program. Rather, members of the department "may enlist the support of the Laboratory in a promising research project of any sort." The only limitation was that the research "embraces the four instructional fields of the department: Social Anthropology, Social Psychology, Sociology and Clinical Psychology."[52]

For a laboratory associated with a groundbreaking department dedicated to a fusion of the disciplines, there was only the briefest nod to that interdisciplinary mission. As Parsons explained, "Support of research is not allocated by field, and a fresh approach to any social science problem from more than one disciplinary point of view is especially encouraged."[53] Such encouragement, however, had a light touch. Parsons also said, "Team research is not encouraged at the expense of individual efforts; rather, the matter of collaboration is left to individuals according to their scientific tastes and preferred modus operandi."[54] In short, there was a great deal of freedom and few practical restraints on the type of research to be conducted at the laboratory.

GRADUATE AND UNDERGRADUATE PROGRAMS

Social Relations also sought decentralization by dividing responsibility between graduate and undergraduate instruction.[55] It established two autonomous committees to administer these programs. The Committee on Higher Degrees was responsible for the graduate program, while the Committee on Undergraduate Instruction was responsible for the undergraduate concentration.[56] This, then, represents the organization of the Department of Social Relations: three relatively autonomous units responsible for research, graduate work, and undergraduate instruction.[57] The overarching goal of the department was to synthesize its three disciplines.[58] Some faculty members, most notably Parsons, viewed the enterprise as a vehicle for developing a new scientific field.[59] In keeping with this attitude, Parsons described the department's priority as follows: "We have hence felt that our first obligation lay in our role as contributors to the scientific development of our field and to its integration."[60] He felt this could be achieved by luring promising scholars, facilitating research, and training graduate students.[61]

This mission statement largely ignored undergraduate instruction. Social Relations recognized that it would be unable to maintain an elite "preprofessional" undergraduate concentration only for those students hoping to become scholars in the field.[62] Thus, while making it possible for such students to advance as far as possible, the department also "assumed the obligation of administering a program of concentration in one of the 'large departments' which had only a minority of preprofessional people concentrating in them."[63] Parsons considered the large, nearly overwhelming undergraduate enrollments to be a "burden."[64] Two years after it came into existence, Social Relations had the second-largest undergraduate enrollment in the college with six hundred students, and its introductory course, with nearly nine hundred students, became the largest elective course.[65]

Social Relations was popular for three principal reasons. First, it was new, and the novelty factor alone attracted some students.[66] Second, the department acquired a reputation for offering easy courses—"guts" as they are known at Harvard—and this appealed to certain students. Parsons acknowledged that the department attracted a "disproportionate number of students in the lower rank groups," and the faculty worried about this tendency.[67] Third, easy classes or not, many students in the postwar period, especially returning World War II veterans, were genuinely interested in understanding society and their role in it. Social Relations was in the right place at the right time. Of course, this motivation was not quantifiable, but as David Riesman observed,

> among thoughtful students in the postwar years, there has developed a preoccupation with private life, with human relations rather than international relations. Thus, while some students enter anthropology or sociology who would once have gone into law, politics, or economics—that is, to better the world or their positions in it—many others enter the more social sciences in order to better their understanding of themselves.[68]

Why was Social Relations so attractive to veterans? Homans and Allport taught the introductory course, the most popular elective course at the college.[69] Homans, a returning veteran himself, attributed the attraction of Social Relations to the desire of veterans to make sense of the chaos they saw in the world: "[Veterans] were more serious minded and mature than most peacetime undergraduates, and their experiences in the war, including the very fact of the war, taught them that something was much amiss in the world and that its problems could be solved only by a new approach, especially one that centered on 'people.' The new department, they felt, might supply what they were seeking."[70] Allport agreed, observing that "veterans were flocking back with a keen interest in the basic social sciences, which they vaguely felt, must hold some solution to the troubled world's problems."[71]

According to Parsons, the department's obligation to "general education"—in other words, undergraduates—had two bases. First, all educated citizens should gain an understanding of themselves and society. Second, it was necessary for the development of "our science" that laymen tolerate and even support it.[72] Parsons felt this support was important because he considered science a "revolutionary" force:

> The continual introduction of new knowledge into our culture is bound to be disturbing in some respects, and new benefits are always to some extent accompanied by new difficulties and risks which some would like to avoid. . . .
> We feel that adding to this understanding of our work on the part of people likely to be influential in later life is itself a contribution to the essential social conditions for the development of our science and hence its future benefits for the society.[73]

But it was the graduate training program that Parsons considered the most important way in the long term for the department to "promote its prime objective of helping to advance its own scientific field."[74] By training its share of the "coming generation of social scientists," Social Relations could seed academia with adherents of the new discipline.[75] And presumably they could in turn influence the next generation. Social Relations adopted a dualistic approach to graduate education. The department had to give sound training in each of the subfields of sociology, social psychology, clinical psychology, and social anthropology and yet strive for integration of these disciplines.[76] Each subfield enjoyed considerable autonomy in setting degree requirements and course offerings, but this freedom was tempered by oversight of the Committee on Higher Degrees.[77] The policy from the outset for higher degrees was to give the "best possible training in both theory and research techniques" and to balance the requirements of recognized professional competence in each of the four fields with "the highest possible level of integration of the fields with each other."[78] In administering the program, Parsons also attempted a balancing act, this time between allowing each group within the department the responsibility for meeting the requirements of its own degree program and providing "an element of unity implemented above all through the work of the Committee on Higher Degrees" in which all four fields were represented.[79]

Parsons was especially proud of an innovation in the research program for graduate students, which he viewed as "unique over such a wide range of subject matter"—the requirement of field training for the PhD degree in all fields.[80] The period of such training would be from six months to one year and would ensure that each graduate of the PhD program would have "first-hand knowledge of the details of research operation."[81] Parsons believed that, "whether he [the graduate] was to engage in field research himself afterwards or not, this could not fail to be of the utmost value to him in understanding the process of science building."[82]

As Social Relations sought to integrate research and study in its four disciplines, it also had to provide the highest possible training and competency in each based on what was recognized nationally as professional competence in stand-alone departments of psychology, sociology, and anthropology. The tension between being the best in each discipline, as measured by traditional departments, and integrating those disciplines would prove to be a major obstacle. On top of all these organizational challenges, Social Relations committed itself to building a new science of social relations recognized by specialists and laymen alike. Pursuing and achieving these goals demanded a great deal of the new department and its policies. Despite the challenges, the department started soundly in all areas: its research program and faculty appointments, graduate training, and undergraduate instruction.[83] Much of this, no doubt, was owed to the high degree of enthusiasm brought to the bold new venture by all concerned.[84] Rapid growth in terms of staff and student enrollment was immediate.[85]

THE EARLY YEARS: MORE MULTIDISCIPLINARY THAN INTERDISCIPLINARY

The department's success in meeting its goals and achieving a measure of leadership in the social sciences at large is not easily quantified. Evaluating the research performed by the Department and Laboratory of Social Relations in an exhaustive manner would be required to reach a definitive judgment on that score. Reviewing the major areas of research, however, provides a fair idea of the range of topics investigated and the methods of research.[86] Talcott Parsons's report, *Department and Laboratory of Social Relations*, and Samuel Stouffer's report, *Laboratory of Social Relations*, listed research projects and findings. The Parsons report is more comprehensive, but Stouffer's summary provides greater detail on each area of research. The wide range of topics investigated by the laboratory is impressive. In his report on the first ten years of its research, Stouffer divided the work of the laboratory into ten general areas (e.g., perception, motivation, learning), describing briefly the work in each area.

In reviewing the report, the paucity of projects involving more than one discipline stands out. Research completed in the Department of Social Relations did not appear radically more interdisciplinary than research undertaken in the predecessor departments or the component disciplines of Social Relations.[87] The bibliography appended to the report indicated that despite the interdisciplinary framework of the department, members continued to pursue largely individual projects or collaborations with a colleague in the same discipline.[88] Indeed, Stouffer never referred to interdisciplinary work in his description of the research contributions of the laboratory. The bibliography is incomplete, as Parsons affirmed, but it is the most comprehensive list of publications of the laboratory to that date. Of the 425 papers cited, 206 are by single authors, and of the 219 articles with coauthors, most are from the same discipline.[89] Thus, it appears at least by this metric—however imperfect—that members continued to work in a manner typical of others in their disciplines elsewhere.[90] It is more accurate, then, to label the laboratory and department as multidisciplinary rather than interdisciplinary. Of course, some social scientists may argue that the most fruitful interdisciplinary and integrative work stems from the convergence of two or more disciplines "under one skull."[91] Indeed, some members of the Social Relations Department borrowed concepts, theories, and assumptions from fields other than their own, incorporating these in their individual work.[92]

As discussed, from its inception, the laboratory received generous funding from the Carnegie Corporation precisely because of its professed interdisciplinary character. Ironically, such largesse proved to be partially responsible for the laboratory's failure to pursue truly interdisciplinary work. The funding from Carnegie came with "so few strings" that it only reinforced the lack of a departmental requirement to pursue projects that would integrate the department's subfields.[93] Stouffer, the director of the laboratory, had a free hand in funding "avowedly speculative projects."[94] Thus, he faced no pressure to focus on projects or a "single methodological training regime for graduate students" that would fulfill the department's goal of creating a new theory of social science.[95] He also backed individual researchers rather than research problems, so there never was an official research program.[96] Consequently, the laboratory never became a "corporate intellectual reality" or a "drill ground for graduate students."[97]

Sociologist David Riesman, who joined the department in 1958, found it a "shock" when he arrived "to discover how little impact on the Department the Laboratory of Social Relations had."[98]

> I believe that a fuller account of a partial failure of the joint Department must lie at the door of Samuel Stouffer's management of the Laboratory, where he brought virtually no students into it, leaving a great majority of graduate students to work on a level often too grandiose, although sometimes much more concrete under Talcott Parsons's conscientious direction.[99]

Riesman found that "the Laboratory did not provide a 'shop' as I had expected it would, and thus it did not balance the theoretical pretensions of the Department."[100] Although its intellectual achievements cannot be questioned, the laboratory "did little to advance or clarify the case for a fundamental behavioral science," and even its most diverse projects did not promote integration.[101] George Homans, another sociologist in the department, summarized: "The laboratory was not divisive, but neither was it a strong force for integration."[102] The department sought to promote unification outside of the laboratory. Homans described one such effort—the cross-disciplinary seminar on methods:

> In the early days of the new department, when, except for the founding fathers, most of us did not know one another well, either personally or intellectually, we made heroic efforts "to integrate." For one thing, we held for a year or more a seminar on methods, in which each of the staff gave at least one lecture on the methods of research he or she considered appropriate to the study of social relations.[103]

As noted in the review of the laboratory's output, the faculty produced few scholarly works of an interdisciplinary character. One notable example is *Personality in Nature, Society, and Culture*, the 1948 book by founders Clyde Kluckhohn and Henry Murray, which viewed personality through the disciplines of psychology and cultural anthropology.[104] Most of the book consisted of articles selected by Kluckhohn and Murray, but they also wrote the first two chapters, setting forth their conception of personality and its determinants: biology, social group membership, social roles, and specific personal circumstances. The *New York Times* favorably reviewed the book, and it was a classic in the field for many years.[105] An epigram summarized the authors' view of the challenge in studying human nature: "Every man is in certain respects: (a) Like all other men; (b) Like some other men; (c) Like no other man."[106]

SEARCHING FOR A THEORETICAL FOUNDATION: BETTER LATE THAN NEVER

Social Relations was already two years old when Chairman Parsons began efforts to develop a theoretical foundation for integrating the department's component disciplines. Integration was not happening naturally, and it was becoming apparent that the department was failing to live up to its "founding principles."[107] Parsons realized that a major effort was needed, and he turned to the Carnegie Corporation for help. The result was the Carnegie Project on Theory. It was the most ambitious project within the department or laboratory, and it most nearly reflected the goal of the Department of Social Relations, i.e., the integration and advancement of the social sciences relevant to the field of social relations.[108] Funded by a grant from the Carnegie Corporation and later supplemented by laboratory funds, the project began in 1949 with the ambitious objective of the theoretical unification of the behavioral sciences. Such a

unifying theory was, according to Isaac, the "holy grail of the postwar
human sciences," not just at Harvard but throughout academia, so the
pressure on Parsons to deliver was enormous, both reputationally and
institutionally.[109]

Only now did Parsons and his colleagues begin to focus on a theoretical
foundation for the undertaking. It gave the appearance that the department was unsure of itself as a discipline and was something of an ad hoc
affair. Even the student newspaper, the *Harvard Crimson*, noted bluntly
that, "three years after its founding, the Social Relations Department, is
stopping to analyze what it's teaching."[110] Parsons said the project would
seek "to codify previous study on the subject" and "to identify areas of
agreement."[111] It was disingenuous, however, for him to suggest that a
theory, or meaningful fragments of one, existed and that it simply needed
to be codified. Parsons and his colleagues needed to create the theory.
Harvard had gotten ahead of itself in establishing the Department of Social Relations "before a consensus had been reached either on the nature
of 'basic social science' or the means by which that prospective science
should be taught."[112] Four men devoted their full energies and time to the
project, but strangely only one—Parsons—was from the department.[113]
Dean Buck arranged for Parsons to be relieved of all administrative and
teaching duties for the fall term.[114] Parsons recruited to the effort Edward
C. Tolman of the University of California, Edward A. Shils of the University of Chicago, and Richard C. Sheldon, a social anthropologist and a
Fellow of the Russian Research Center at Harvard.[115]

The lack of full-time participation by Social Relations faculty other
than Parsons implied that he could not rely on colleagues within the
department because of "expressed preexisting fissures."[116] Shils was a
sociologist and social theorist, as was Social Relations member George
Homans, but Homans openly disliked Parsons, thus precluding any collaboration.[117] Parsons invited Tolman, a behavioral psychologist, to join
the project, despite the presence at Harvard of the most renowned experimental psychologists in the country: Edwin G. Boring, B. F. Skinner, and
S. S. Stevens.[118] Given that Social Relations was created in part to allow the
social and clinical psychologists to escape the hostility of the experimental
psychologists, Parsons could hardly have invited them to participate.

The point of departure for the Carnegie Project was "Assumptions of
Basic Social Science," a document prepared primarily by Murray and
Kluckhohn as an outgrowth of a department seminar, "Problems and
Concepts of Social Relations."[119] Parsons recognized the need to unify
the disparate intellectual impulses in the new department. He hoped to
achieve this synthesis in part through a seminar allowing faculty members to share their methods of studying the social sciences and to attempt
to develop a common theoretical framework.[120] The seminar met weekly.

Senior faculty members would formulate concepts, which would be critically reviewed in subsequent meetings of junior scholars, those below the rank of full professor.[121] The distinction rankled the junior members, who had no input in setting the theoretical agenda.[122] Asked to be mere "underlaborers" for the project, some of the junior faculty revolted, and "one after another, David McClelland, Alex Inkeles, Richard Solomon, Leo Postman, Jerome Bruner, and George Homans stepped forward to challenge Parsons on the conceptual premises of the Project."[123] David Schneider, a graduate student in anthropology, also recognized in 1948–1949 the general dissatisfaction of several faculty members, "who had no use for Parsons's grand design," including "[Samuel Andrew] Stouffer, for instance: if Kluckhohn was an imperialist and wanted culture to explain everything, Stouffer tended to want statistics to explain everything. This is the way it was, and this is the way it was going. Stouffer couldn't account for change in any way."[124]

It is ironic that Parsons, who had led the revolt against the established orders of Sociology, Psychology, and Anthropology at Harvard resulting in Social Relations, was himself now on the receiving end of an insurrection within the new department he chaired. Parsons believed that the functional significance of a pattern of behavior was the key to understanding a social system.[125] His approach was known as structural functionalism, and sometimes more broadly as the systems perspective.[126] It held that individuals learn the roles needed for society to survive, and the most effective way to study, and to explain, human life is to view it in terms of behavior that sustains society.[127] Some of the junior faculty disagreed, arguing that the concept of function played no explanatory role.[128] As Joel Isaac has described, based on his incisive review of the minutes of the seminar, "a report on the meeting of 'Group 2' (the general seminar) held on October 3, 1949 noted a 'feeling of uneasiness' about the term 'functional': Ordinarily by the term 'functional' is meant that actions produce consequences which will maintain structure. An empirical question immediately presents itself: Are all actions functional? Do they maintain the system?"[129]

McClelland and Bruner could think of no behavior that was not "adjustive or adaptive in some sense."[130] McClelland challenged Parsons, noting that any behavior could be viewed as functional depending on the perspective of the viewer: "Take as an example the training of Army officers. If it is good training it is functional to the Army, disfunctional [*sic*] to the officers' families (the officers get killed), and what would be the function to personality?"[131] Homans, one of the leaders of this disaffected group, mocked the seminar:

From time to time the seniors sent down to the juniors memoranda on the current state of their deliberations, on which we were supposed to comment and provide them what was already being called "feedback." As I remember it, the seniors never paid any attention to our reactions, and the junior committee withered away, but not until we had reached with some pleasure a scientific generalization: the number of boxes (categories) in Parsons's theoretical scheme increased weekly as the square of 4. Our meetings stopped when we reached 256. It was spineless of us not to wait and see where the series would, if ever, end.[132]

Not surprisingly, involvement of the junior members in the seminar "petered out" before the project concluded, and Parsons focused his attention on the senior members.[133] Even among the senior members, however, enthusiasm waned. Parsons imbued the project with a scientific approach typically reserved for experiments in a real laboratory with beakers and technical apparatus. He often employed the term "breakthrough" when he referred to the project's progress and presented the theorizing that comprised the project as science itself.[134] In narratives he prepared for the seminar participants, he would recount advances in the debates and the resolution of a problem "with the precision of date-and-time lab results."[135] Indeed, in optimistic reports to the project's underwriter, the Carnegie Corporation, he claimed that, "within the last two weeks a very important theoretical break-through has occurred which will allow us to attain a level of order and clarity of the whole field which I don't think any of us thought possible when we began."[136] Parsons's "obsession with making theory into a scientific-empirical event" led him to tape the two weekly seminars for later analysis as studies in small-group dynamics. Not only did he regard the project as science, but he wanted the process itself studied scientifically as well. To him, it was "science in action."[137]

TOWARD A GENERAL THEORY OF ACTION: FAILS TO PROVIDE INTEGRATION

After countless discussions and revisions over a nearly three-year period, a "general statement," together with individual articles, was published in 1951 under the title *Toward a General Theory of Action*.[138] Parsons and Shils were the editors of the book, with the following scholars contributing individual articles: Edward C. Tolman, Gordon Allport, Clyde Kluckhohn, Henry Murray, Robert R. Sears, Richard C. Sheldon, and Samuel A. Stouffer.[139] The book fell short of being a truly group effort. Ostensibly, Parsons and Shils coauthored the 198-page "centerpiece" in the book, "Values, Motives, and Systems of Action," which, along with its additional twenty-eight pages of charts, constituted approximately one half of the book.[140] Isaac, however, asserted that Parsons alone drafted this section, diluting even further the synthesizing nature of the effort.[141] In what was hoped to be the theoretical foundation of a department devoted to an interdisciplinary approach, there was little actual collaboration.[142]

In a book of 495 pages, the most the group could agree on as genuine coauthors was a twenty-four-page "General Statement" with the less than groundbreaking title, "Some Fundamental Categories of the Theory of Action."[143] Even then, Kluckhohn was "slightly uncomfortable" on one significant point: "the relation of social structure, social system, role, and culture."[144] He wrote a lengthy dissenting footnote, claiming that "the present statement does not give full weight to the extent to which roles are culturally defined, social structure is part of the cultural map, the social system is built upon girders supplied by explicit and implicit culture."[145] With faint praise, he welcomed the statement because "in the present stage of social science it is highly useful to behave experimentally with reference to conceptual schemes."[146] Sheldon also dissented from the general statement, objecting to the conclusion that "culture, though existing as a body of artifacts and as systems of symbols, is not in itself organized as a social system. Therefore, culture as a system is on a different plane from personalities and social systems."[147] Allport made only a minor prepublication comment, "As for the title of the book: I like your suggestion, but suggest the insertion of 'social' thus *Toward a General Theory of Social Action*. Otherwise people may think it a book in physics!"[148]

The opening sentence of the book declared its ambitions: "to contribute to the establishment of a general theory in the social sciences."[149] Nils Gilman found the use of the singular striking: the book was an attempt to establish a "monolithic and exclusive theory" to codify all existing knowledge systems; it was nothing less than a "bid for theoretical hegemony."[150] It was only an opening bid, however, as the authors conceded that more work was needed.[151] They acknowledged the challenge of creating a synthesizing theory, stating, "The empirical complexity is immense, and the unexplored areas are, in the light of present knowledge, Stygian in their darkness."[152] Tempering the project's original lofty goals, they concluded that the "general outlines of the nature of action systems sketched here" would require "more precise and explicit conceptualizations of action and of the ways in which they are interrelated."[153]

Despite the defections of the junior members of the seminar and the tepid support of senior members, Parsons gamely asserted that the synthesis of ideas in the book was a major achievement and would shape the future of the social sciences. It was a valiant exercise in putting a positive spin on the venture: "We feel that the present effort belongs in the context of a major movement, whose significance to the future of social science far transcends the contributions of any one particular group. If we have helped to deepen the channel of the river and remove some obstacles to its flow, we are content."[154] The groundbreaking nature of the book, according to Parsons, was the fusion of the thinking of nine social scientists from various disciplines: four psychologists, three sociologists, and two anthropologists.[155] He contended that not only were several influences and sources discernible, but each author had been "notably influenced by more than one 'school' and more than one discipline."[156] Despite many difficulties for the authors in overcoming their differences and the "blind spots" in each of their respective disciplines, Parsons maintained that they had succeeded, and the book demonstrated that "many streams of thought are in the process of flowing together."[157]

At the heart of the book was a conceptual structure that could be used, according to Parsons and Shils, to analyze any feature of human life.[158] The structure was comprised of a set of five dichotomies called pattern variables:[159]

1. Affectivity–Affective Neutrality
2. Self-Orientation–Collectivity-Orientation
3. Particularism–Universalism
4. Ascription–Achievement
5. Diffuseness–Specificity

This was their "attempt to formulate the way each and every social action, long- or short-term, proposed or concrete, prescribed or carried out, can be analyzed into five choices (conscious or unconscious, implicit or explicit) formulated by these five dichotomies."[160] They claimed that individuals and societies consistently position themselves on one side of these dichotomies, and the variables provide a framework for understanding the values they have adopted.[161] They viewed the dichotomies as an "analytic machine" manifesting the "technical sophistication" of their theory.[162]

In the late 1970s at Harvard, even those who knew and respected Parsons quipped that *Toward a General Theory of Action* may have been a breakthrough, but it was so complicated and theoretical that only he could understand it.[163] There was some truth in this characterization, not only for this book but for what came to be known as Parsonian theory. When Parsons retired in 1973, the *New York Times* wrote, "The substance of Parsonian theory, so complex and abstract that few professional sociologists claim to understand it fully, defies summary."[164] It is, as sociologist Edward C. Deveraux Jr. of Cornell described, "vast and tangled, a veritable jungle of fine distinctions and intertwining classifications."[165]

Harvard sociologist Daniel Bell defended his colleague against these charges, reminding Parsons's critics that "there is no science of the particular; it is necessary to generalize."[166] The beginning of modern science required scientists to study abstract properties, such as mass, velocity, and acceleration, rather than concrete bodies. Only then, he contended, could they create a system that "describes the Newtonian universe."[167] Parsons—trained in biology and economics—sought to do the same in sociology.[168] He "repeatedly warned his readers that he was not dealing with concrete phenomena but with 'analytical abstractions' a set of logical categories into which all social actions would fit."[169] According to Bell, this "helps to explain why Parsonian theory is so complicated that few sociologists, much less laymen, claim to understand it fully."[170]

Others such as Clifford Geertz, a graduate student at the time (later a well-known cultural anthropologist), belittled the Carnegie Project on Theory, claiming the resulting book was "grandly architectonic" and its efforts to create abstractions of human behavior "a great assemblage of boxes and arrows."[171] It was true. The book's effort to create abstractions of human behavior relied on dozens of pages of drawings, diagrams, boxes, and charts. At times it resembled a handbook of mechanical and electrical engineering rather than a theory for a new social science. Pages 286–87 displayed a dizzying array of boxes and arrows purporting to show the model for explaining the behavior of "going to a particular restaurant when hungry."[172] Pages 305–16 of the chapter on learning and psychodynamic mechanisms, for example, relied heavily on nine separate figures of "belief-value matrix[es]" full of "causal arrows," "lassos," "alleys," and "goal boxes."[173] Pages 247–75 contained figures with fewer arrows, but numerous charts and boxes explaining the "Components of Action Frame of Reference" and the "Transcendent-Achievement Ideal," among other concepts.[174]

The Carnegie Project and its work product failed to bring about a synthesis in the study of human behavior.[175] Although it had several printings and appears to have been read widely outside the Harvard community, *Toward a General Theory of Action* did not have a major impact on the social sciences.[176] David Riesman, then a sociologist at the University of Chicago, who later joined the faculty of Social Relations, believed "the effort to construct a 'general theory' was imperialistic and abstract."[177] He considered it a vast overreaching by Parsons and so "grandiose in its claims" and with such "pretentiousness" that it "hid [Social Relations'] real accomplishments in recruitment and training."[178] Cohen-Cole offered a contrary view, contending that the book was one of the "central texts of Cold War social science," with its "position on theoretical integration" playing an important role nationally.[179] The reviews of the book were "overwhelmingly negative."[180] A mixed review in the *Journal of Abnormal and Social Psychology* described the increasing common interests among psychologists, anthropologists, and sociologists, and the "zeitgeist" that personality, society, and culture should not be pursued in "complacent departmental isolation."[181] Any attempt to bring unity from this "conceptual trinity" was bound to generate interest, but an effort from these prominent scholars made it particularly noteworthy:

> When such a distinguished and varied group of authors as those responsible for the present volume undertake to lay out the groundwork of a "general theory of action" into which each of these foci is to be articulated in its proper place, social scientists are justified in viewing the enterprise with a mixture of interest, hope and misgiving. All these reactions seem warranted by this ambitious, difficult, rewarding, and exasperating book.[182]

The review criticized the book's title for suggesting the work was an "integrated treatise" by the authors when the book's core "Values, Motives, and Systems of Action" was authored only by Parsons and Shils.[183] Moreover, some of the individual contributions by Allport, Kluckhohn, Stouffer, Sears, and Murray either had been published previously or failed to bear any direct relation either to the conceptual scheme presented by Parsons and Shils or to the general statement of all nine collaborators.[184] Indeed, the review concluded that it was impossible to assess the book in toto and resorted instead to considering each chapter on its own:

> The book as a whole, thus, must be said to reflect not the unity of the social sciences but the healthy diversity of the Harvard department. Beyond questioning the judgment of bringing it out as a single work and a group product, and noting a certain pretentiousness in identifying it with *the* theory of action, there is little that a reviewer can say about the entire volume. The several contributions require consideration in their own right.[185]

The department used it extensively internally, where it was referred to as the "Yellow Book" for its bright jacket cover and it served as a catalyst for further discussion of the synthesis of the disciplines within Social Relations.[186] Predictably, the book occasioned interdepartmental squabbles: some members saw it as a theoretical manifesto for the entire department and revolted.[187] At one department meeting, Parsons suggested that everyone read the book in the hope that it might guide their teaching and research.[188] In a defining moment for Social Relations, Homans objected. He felt that Parsons was imposing the book as departmental doctrine, and he spoke out at a meeting of the department against what he viewed as "pressure" on faculty members to read, let alone adopt it.[189]

Decades later, Homans recalled declaring at the meeting, "There must be no implication that this document is to be taken as representing the official doctrine of the department, and no member shall be put under any pressure to read it."[190] He said a "dreadful silence followed my attack," but eventually Samuel Stouffer, a senior faculty member, supported him and agreed that the book should not be considered official department doctrine.[191] Homans, pleased with himself for standing up to this perceived pressure, wrote, "Afterwards many of the junior members thanked me for what I had done. My seniors at last realized I was a bit of a rebel."[192] A rebel with a cause, however, because Homans was guarding his own intellectual turf.[193] He recently had published his theory-based approach in *The Human Group*, which was "profoundly at odds with Parsons's action theory."[194]

Throughout their careers, the Parsons-Homans skirmishes became part of the lore of sociology, both inside and outside of Harvard.[195] In any case, the department never adopted the theory put forth in *Toward a General Theory of Action* as orthodoxy.[196] And there was no further attempt to create a unifying theory and common language for Social Relations.[197] Although Parsons's nemesis Homans predictably derided the book, he conceded that "for some years" Parsons's structural functionalism remained "the dominant school of thought among our graduate students in sociology."[198] Nils Gilman aptly characterized *Toward a General Theory of Action* as an attempt at "institutional self-justification."[199] But that effort to find a theoretical basis for Social Relations failed, effectively dooming the department's dream of creating a new and interdisciplinary science.

EBULLIENT EARLY YEARS: AN ACADEMIC ROLLER COASTER

Notwithstanding the failure of *Toward a General Theory of Action* to provide a unifying foundation for Social Relations, there was enormous energy and enthusiasm among the faculty in those early years. Several participants believed there was no social problem incapable of being systematically studied—and solved—by employing the most effective methodologies from their constituent disciplines. David McClelland, a junior faculty member of the Social Relations Department at that time, reflected on the heady atmosphere: "We had a wonderful time . . . dreaming dreams about how to foster basic science in a way that would also contribute to human progress."[200]

Parsons, as noted, hoped to create a new science and believed Social Relations was part of a great movement in scientific thought.[201] He was driven—according to one of his most well-known students, Robert Bellah—by the "ideal of an abstract content-free theoretical science from which one could deduce the laws of social life."[202] Graduate students in Social Relations shared this excitement in varying degrees. Clifford Geertz, a cultural anthropologist, said there was a sense

that Parsons "was going to be the Newton of social science."[203] He
glowingly recalled those early years:

> the enormous, unfocused, almost millenarian exhilaration that attended the
> social relations department in the 1950s, and what we who were there then
> were pleased to call its Project—the construction of "A Common Language
> for the Social Sciences." Bliss was it in that dawn; but the golden age was, as
> is the case with the assertive and the nonconforming, as well as the exciting,
> in academia, all-too-brief.[204]

The exuberance had a price, however, as the department's disorgani-
zation and dizzying diversity exasperated graduate students.[205] Despite
his affection for Social Relations, Geertz found that it was a "maze of
grand possibilities, only loosely related, and some even in serious tension with one another," and "exciting (and it was enormously exciting), a
perilous business."[206] The choices presented by the new, unconventional,
and somewhat amorphous department challenged even the most accomplished graduate student: "With so many ways to turn, so few tracks laid
down, and so little experience of one's own to go by, even small decisions,
to take this seminar, attack that subject, work with this professor, seemed
enormously consequential—a reverseless commitment to something immense, portentous, splendid, and unclear."[207]

Geertz characterized the downside of the graduate program as an academic roller coaster: "At full throttle, it was a wild and crazy ride, if you
cared for that sort of thing and could contrive not to fall off at the sharper
turns."[208] He believed graduate students in anthropology, however, had
one advantage that helped them to stay on track—fieldwork:

> In this maze or maelstrom, or vanity fair, the anthropologist had one thing
> going for him in keeping himself reasonably on course: the realization,
> immediately instilled in him (or—there were a few women—in her) and
> continuously reinforced, that he was going to have to do fieldwork. Unlike
> the others, mere academicians, we had a testing ahead, a place we had to
> go to and a rite we had to go through. The prospect of this moment of truth
> (though in my case it turned out to be two and half years) wonderfully con-
> centrated our minds, gave us a powerful sense of moving toward something,
> or anyway somewhere.[209]

Graduate students Benton and Miriam Johnson described the proseminar required of all incoming graduate students as "a parade of lecturers,
some visiting from other universities. The experience was exciting, sometimes confusing, and for many a little frightening."[210] Arthur Vidich, a
graduate student in anthropology, panned the proseminar. He believed it
had limited benefit, serving primarily as "a kind of collective baptism cer-
emony designed to certify us as members of a common congregation."[211]

It was merely a "display case for senior professors" and gave a "lopsided image of the total Social Relations faculty," with the focus heavily on Parsons, Kluckhohn, and Murray.[212]

Vidich said Murray was known "to ridicule the idea of a systematic sociology" pursued by Parsons, perplexing graduate students with this act of disunity.[213] Vidich criticized the department's offering of classes beyond the proseminar as lacking direction and coherence: "The social relations curriculum debated ideas in all directions. It was full of intellectual confusions and contradictions."[214] For Vidich, there was one bright spot. He considered Henry Murray a welcome counterweight to Parsons's emphasis on a theory of social action: "Murray inhabited the world of Herman Melville and Jungian psychology and provided an antidote to any claims for a rational, objective interpretation of the social world, not to mention the idea of a social system. His view of the social sciences was quixotic and gave courage to those of us who rejected the idea of a closed system."[215]

Vidich believed the proseminar was so daunting in its sheer breadth of material and viewpoints that it failed its interdisciplinary mission. It attempted a "cross-fertilization" of the four disciplines, but it merely created pressure on students to learn just enough about each to pass the examination:

> Exposure to a multiplicity of vocabularies did not lead inevitably to cross-fertilization or to an interdisciplinary perspective. Adding to the centrifugality of disciplinary vocabularies, each of the lecturers recommended the works of authors whom they regarded as significant figures in their fields. . . . It soon became evident to us that no one could grasp the substance or the vocabularies of all the disciplines or read all the books in a semester or even a year. Yet we confronted an examination that included questions involving interdisciplinary knowledge.[216]

To deal with this overwhelming amount of material, the graduate students adopted a strategy employed by law students for generations. They formed study groups of four or five students, and each member was responsible for providing "digests of books and summaries of lecture notes."[217] The group would make copies of the reports and distribute them among members of the group. The students nicknamed the digests "hamburgers."[218] The origin of the term is unknown, but perhaps they were drawing an analogy between fast food providing little sustenance and a cursory method of study. For Vidich, any understanding of the various disciplines gained in study groups was fleeting and barely enough to pass the exam: "By this method, it was possible to acquire secondhand knowledge of dozens of major works prior to the examination. One could appear knowledgeable about books one had never read and courses one had never taken. For me, it led to a certain vagueness regarding which courses I actually took at Harvard and which books I actually read."[219]

Norman Birnbaum arrived as a graduate student in 1947 and studied sociology with Parsons as his thesis advisor. He also believed the proseminar failed to promote the interdisciplinary goals of the department, although it was "interesting" and useful as a "gathering place" to meet other students.[220] Overall, he felt the department had "no sense of common intellectual endeavor" and found the interdisciplinary mission of the department illusory. He emphasized that faculty members were focused on their own disciplinary work, rather than forging a synthesis of the department's constituent elements: "The goal of the Department, the pursuit of a unified social science, which it was quickly apparent to me it simply was not possible, was not being done, and could not be done because these prima donnas, Allport, Kluckhohn, Parsons, Homans, Bruner and some younger people were pursuing their own lines of inquiry which were extremely difficult."[221]

Birnbaum believed "most members of the department thought of themselves as masons, adding bricks to the unfinished . . . edifice of a comprehensive science of society."[222] The problem was that each worked from a different blueprint: "In fact, though modern art was not much talked about in our conversations, the department in its conceptual disunity resembled one of those self-destructing sculptures by Yves Tanguy."[223] Parsons, however, saw himself as much more than a mere laborer; he was an architect with a master plan.[224] Birnbaum remarked that "domed stadiums had not yet come to football, but he [Parsons] had one for society."[225] Despite the general lack of unity, Birnbaum saw two slivers of cohesion among faculty and students in those early days. The first was a belief that they were part of something special and ahead of its time, which unimaginative outsiders simply could not comprehend or appreciate: "The Social Relations faculty, and their most loyal students, conducted themselves as initiates of an esoteric church in possession of truths which a presently unbelieving world would in time have to acknowledge."[226] The second was a "belief in the scientific status of their work."[227]

Despite his criticism, Birnbaum acknowledged the energy and vitality in Social Relations as he placed the venture in a broader context. He believed its faculty members saw that "intellectually the powerhouses of the University, such as those in American Studies, Arthur Schlesinger Jr. and F. O. Mathiessen," among others, were playing by comparison a much larger role within Harvard in shaping the postwar "American empire."[228] If Harvard was rebuilding the world, this new department wanted to be part of it. Consequently, Birnbaum thought "the Social Relations people were running twice as hard to catch up, that is to say, to have something relevant to contribute."[229]

Other graduate students identified tensions and jealousies among the leading figures in Social Relations. David Schneider studied primarily with anthropologist Clyde Kluckhohn, but he also learned a great deal from sociologist Parsons, who was a member of Schneider's thesis committee.[230] According to Schneider, the graduate students sensed there was competition between Parsons and Kluckhohn, adding to the sense of discord in the department: "So, I was very much taken with Parsons. But I wasn't the only one. A large number of the graduate students were, too, and there was a sense that Kluckhohn was competing with Parsons and that if you took sides you were in trouble. Or, at least, I thought so. I was very careful never to really align myself in any simple way with Parsons, but stay 'allied' and loyal to Kluckhohn."[231]

SOCIAL RELATIONS AND MODERNIZATION THEORY IN THE POSTCOLONIAL WORLD

Internal attempts at integration faltered, but the Department of Social Relations nonetheless attracted admirers from outside Harvard. American policy makers, intellectuals, and organizations looking at postwar colonial societies began searching for a "comprehensive strategy for understanding the problems common to those areas of the world that would soon be collected under the rubric of the 'third world.'"[232] The Report of the International Development Advisory Board presented to the U.S. Senate in 1951 expressed the urgent need for such an expansive worldview: "Our strategy must be . . . both global, embracing every part of the world, and total, with political, psychological, economic, and military considerations integrated into one whole."[233] The end of World War II and the ensuing decolonization process and Cold War suddenly made the third world, its diversity of people, and its problems relevant to policy makers and academics.[234] America's intelligentsia believed that only the United States with its vast resources could find the answers. As cultural anthropologist David Schneider observed, "the emergence of the United States as a world power, indeed *the* world power, reviving Europe, containing the Soviet Union, setting the Third World on its developmental course, seemed to suggest that the headquarters of learning and research had moved here as well."[235]

American intellectuals interested in developing postcolonial regions struggled to find a theory to comprehend the third world, suffering a "cognitive crisis" as they floundered.[236] Finally, they thought they had found the answer in the European social theory championed by Talcott Parsons.[237] In their view, the Department of Social Relations and its interdisciplinary and expansive approach to the study of man and society held the key to understanding—and to remaking—much of the non-Western world.[238] According to Nils Gilman, "It was in this context of cognitive and political crisis that intellectuals interested in problems of development of postcolonial regions began to turn to the innovative work being done at the Harvard Department of Social Relations (DSR), particularly the work of DSR's leading light, Talcott Parsons."[239] The needs of U.S. foreign policy makers and the objectives of Parsons and Social Relations converged to help create modernization theory.[240] The theory would influence U.S. social sciences and foreign policy from the late 1950s through the 1960s regarding economic, political, and social change in the postcolonial world.[241] Simply put, the theory sought to understand what was occurring in the postcolonial world and to promote "change that would make these regions more like 'us' and less like the Russians or the Chinese" by becoming modern.[242]

Intellectuals outside Harvard believed the Department of Social Relations would "serve as the launchpad for a radical leap in social science, one that would achieve the old Enlightenment dream of a science of man."[243] To them, the aim for modernization theory—and Social Relations—was nothing less than to create "a universal and general science of society and human behavior."[244] And they gave great weight to Social Relations and the potency of modernization theory for providing "the intellectual gloss for U.S. hegemony during the Cold War."[245] Modernization theory failed to achieve liftoff at the department, but it did exert significant influence on American social sciences for a time. Despite the appeal of his approach to modernization theorists, Parsons largely ignored postcolonial regions and peoples; the only question that mattered to him as a theorist was, "What made the West different?"[246] He was interested in "winning the hearts and minds of deans and fellow academics" and worried little about the populations of the third world.[247] Nonetheless, his work in the early 1950s was embraced by those working on development studies, and it had a significant impact on modernization theory.[248] Modernization theory, however, would lose steam and ultimately run its course by the early 1970s, leaving it largely discredited.[249]

THE RUSSIAN RESEARCH CENTER

The department enjoyed fleeting success with another emerging approach known as "area studies," which had links to modernization theory.[250] Area studies developed from the government's postwar need for information "about little-known but strategically important places and peoples around the world," with Russia as one of the prime examples.[251] The U.S. military and government agencies operated in terms of geographic areas of the world, but universities were organized by disciplines. The interdisciplinary approach of Social Relations seemed the perfect vehicle for bridging this gap in the view of the Carnegie Corporation and its brand of "strategic philanthropy."[252]

Indeed, the Carnegie Corporation chose Harvard for establishing a Russian Research Center (RRC), not because of its expertise in Russian studies, but because of its "strong social relations faculty backed by a supportive administration."[253] The Department of Social Relations and its laboratory were the inspiration both intellectually and organizationally for the RRC.[254] The corporation gave Harvard a grant of $100,000 in 1947, and thereafter "in 1948 additional funds of $740,000 were dispatched in the largest single grant that had yet been made for area study research."[255] The Carnegie Corporation had great confidence in the relevance of Harvard's interdisciplinary approach to area studies. John Gardner expressed the corporation's hope that the RRC would "give impetus to studies that would make use of the best of modern social science methods to understand some of the crucial problems of Russian behavior."[256] The RRC intended to usher in a "new approach to area study."[257] Gardner described the country's need to shift in emphasis from history and languages to a reliance on the social sciences and social psychology in his 1947 article in *Foreign Affairs*, "Are We Doing Our Homework in Foreign Affairs?"[258]

The interdisciplinary cachet of Harvard held such allure that the corporation chose anthropologist Clyde Kluckhohn of the Social Relations Department to be the first director of the RRC, even though he had no previous exposure to the study of Russia.[259] Parsons admitted that Kluckhohn's appointment and lack of any previous connection with the study of Russia or communism "raised many eyebrows in academically conservative academic quarters."[260] Even at Harvard, the selection of a cultural anthropologist, whose early work studied the dreams of Navajo Indians, was met with skepticism. It annoyed Russian sociologist Pitirim Sorokin, who remarked to Kluckhohn as they stood amid a group of graduate students: "Clyde, I read in the *New York Times* that the Carnegie Corporation gave you a half-million dollars to study Russia. Clyde, I do not bear you any malice, but if Carnegie came to me and offered me a half-million to study the Navajo, modesty would make me say no."[261]

Notwithstanding Kluckhohn's lack of knowledge of the subject matter, Carnegie considered him a logical choice as director given his mastery of the research techniques to be employed by the RRC.[262] He had helped to pioneer the techniques used by social scientists in the Foreign Morale Analysis Division of the Office of War Information to analyze Japanese attitudes during World War II. His groundbreaking work in studying Japanese culture and opinion through the analysis of "press reports, information from prisoners of war and general descriptions of Japanese culture" was precisely the type of investigation into Russia that Gardner and others promoting the RRC had in mind.[263] Indeed, the "study of culture at a distance"—as anthropologist Margaret Mead described the analysis of societies inaccessible to direct observation—was essential to the study of behavior in a society as closed as the Soviet Union.[264]

Throughout the McCarthy era and the attacks on Harvard and other universities for alleged communist sympathies, the RRC went unscathed, even though it must have been an inviting target.[265] Senator Joseph McCarthy had scorned Nathan Pusey, Harvard's president, and labeled the university "a privileged sanctuary for Fifth Amendment Communists."[266] Parsons claimed the RRC avoided McCarthy's assaults because Kluckhohn had handled "with great delicacy the politically sensitive problems of a university organization engaged in the study of Communist society."[267] David Price, however, finds this explanation disingenuous because Parsons—and Harvard—knew that Kluckhohn and the RRC were secretly working with the CIA, the FBI, the Pentagon, and the State Department.[268] Kluckhohn had a top-secret security clearance, and the center's "baseline funding" came from the CIA (presumably when the initial Carnegie Corporation funds ran out).[269] Indeed, even before the RRC officially launched, its senior staff met with the director of the CIA, who wanted to establish an ongoing relationship.[270] Within its first two years, the RRC was overwhelmed with requests from the CIA and other government agencies.[271]

Kluckhohn shared research reports prepared by students and staff with the CIA, air force intelligence, and the State Department.[272] Essentially, the U.S. government secretly used the RRC as a research service. The State Department would tell Kluckhohn it was "short of a certain aspect of Soviet activity," and he would then suggest it to a graduate student as a thesis topic, failing to mention the interest of the State Department or that the research would find its way there.[273] Other times, Kluckhohn would suggest to the entire staff a government-authorized topic for a paper or seminar, without disclosing the origin of the request.[274] Once he asked the assistant director of the RRC, Alfred Meyer, to research a topic, telling him confidentially that the request came in a phone call from the local field office of the CIA: "Our uncle in Washington would like to know what you people think about such a problem."[275]

The FBI conducted investigations of Kluckhohn and the Russian Research Center. One report stated that "one of the jobs of Kluckhohn is to obtain pertinent information requested by government departments, and, within limits, shape the research program of the Center to the needs of the United States."[276] Sigmund Diamond questioned whether Kluckhohn was under pressure to cooperate with the FBI because it had information that could subject him to "humiliation" if it became public.[277] The FBI had investigated Kluckhohn in 1943 in connection with an unspecified "episode" on a Navajo reservation in New Mexico.[278] The U.S. attorney in New Mexico requested that the investigation be undertaken "with a view toward prosecution."[279] The Department of Justice sent the file to FBI director J. Edgar Hoover, but no further action is known to have been taken.[280] There is no evidence that either Harvard or Kluckhohn knew about the investigation.[281] As Diamond speculated, if Kluckhohn was aware of the investigation, he would have had "powerful incentive for being cooperative."[282]

Critics contended that so-called extramural government funding of the RRC and other area studies programs constituted "Cold War scholarship," leading to an "American academy saturated with government funds that distorted all aspects of thought within it."[283] David Engerman considered such condemnation overly broad, however, because it fails to consider the results of the research undertaken and whether or not they were slanted to conform to the views of its government patrons.[284] He cited research by the RRC as a prime example of legitimate scholarship that prevailed in the early 1950s notwithstanding its government funding.[285] In his view, the RCC's most ambitious project—the Refugee Interview Project—was scholarly work that "rested comfortably within disciplinary norms" and even challenged claims of its government sponsors about the Soviet threat.[286] The project involved interviews of Russian refugees living in the American-occupied zone of Germany following World War II.[287] Kluckhohn directed the Refugee Interview Project, but most of the work was done by Alex Inkeles, a sociologist coming from the Office of Strategic Services (the precursor to the CIA), and Raymond Bauer, a sociologist with a PhD from the Department of Social Relations.[288] The interviews became the basis for the Harvard Project on the Soviet Social System, which was commissioned (at a cost of nearly $1 million) by the U.S. Air Force's Human Relations Research Institute (HRRI) to develop a working model of the Soviet Union's social system.[289] The model would, among other things, help the air force determine the cities to be targeted for bombing and the propaganda to be disseminated in connection with the attacks.[290]

The RRC's work on this project revealed the tensions in what Engerman refers to as the "academicization" of military life and the "militarization" of academic life in the 1950s.[291] The RRC saw its task of building a conceptual model of the Soviet social system as a scholarly endeavor in keeping with the "grand integration of knowledge to which Social Relations scholars aspired."[292] The RRC was not simply camouflage for classified work, but it was not without its problems.[293] The Harvard scholars contemplated that the military applications—a "relatively minor job" in their view—would be considered only after the academic exercise was completed.[294] The air force saw it differently, complaining that the mission was first and foremost one of military intelligence.[295] The RRC responded to the criticism by reminding its staff that the project was paid for by the air force and by telling them to demonstrate a "semblance of concern" for the needs of the air force.[296]

This marriage of scholarship and military intelligence was rocky. The RRC did not want the Refugee Interview Project simply to be an intelligence-gathering exercise, fretting internally that the air force thought it had "bought a piece of Harvard University" and wanted to get its money's worth.[297] The RRC tried to provide information that was helpful to military intelligence without compromising its scholarly autonomy.[298] It also sidestepped Harvard's ban on classified research projects through a dubious maneuver: the RRC contracted separately with the air force to "funnel into the classified framework some relevant parts" of its research findings.[299] Apparently, this fig leaf was enough for Harvard to claim that the project was "general social science."[300]

Ultimately, the RRC met both its scholarly objectives and the intelligence aims of the air force.[301] The final report, "Strategic and Psychological Strengths and Vulnerabilities of the Soviet Social System," evaluated the strengths and weaknesses of key institutions of the Soviet social system, providing a model to predict the effects on each of various shocks, including all-out war.[302] The study's conclusion, however, was not what the air force wanted to hear.[303] The study rejected the prevailing conviction of the air force that the Soviet Union was an aggressive, unstable country on the verge of collapse, lacking the support of its citizenry.[304] The RRC concluded that if American forces were to attack the Soviet Union, they would not be greeted as liberators.[305] Engerman contended that the RRC's Refugee Interview Project was one of two large government-funded projects of the era (the other was the Smolensk Archive Study for the RAND Corporation by Harvard political scientist Merle Fainsod) that served "to tamp down the threat mongering of their sponsors" and reflected the "hopes—however innocent—that scholars could advance knowledge and serve the national interest simultaneously."[306] Such noble aspirations soon faded, however, as scandals broke in the 1960s about the CIA funding the Congress for Cultural Freedom and the Pentagon supporting Project Camelot.[307]

Of course, the RRC did work for the government beyond the Refugee Interview Project, but an analysis of those projects has yet to be undertaken. Although Kluckhohn surreptitiously steered graduate students and RRC staff to conducting research requested by the government, those researchers were unaware of the government's involvement and could hardly be accused of tilting their results in the government's favor. The government involvement raises questions about the RRC's work but does not automatically invalidate it, as Price explained: "I would not argue that the work of Kluckhohn . . . or others whose research aligned with the interests of CIA or the Pentagon was necessarily of an inferior quality, or that it should not be taken seriously simply because of these relationships, only that it should be read and interpreted with these relationships firmly in mind."[308]

Congressional critics of the air force's support of the RRC and its foray into the behavioral sciences caused the demise of the air force's Human Relations Research Institute, which had sponsored the Refugee Interview Project of the RCC.[309] One senator complained that the RRC was "simply throwing money away," grousing that if military leaders "have not sense enough to know how to counteract Soviet propaganda without hiring a bunch of college professors . . . this defense establishment is in one darn bad shape in my opinion."[310] Another complained that the air force had paid so dearly for a study of Soviet society, rather than of Soviet "targets."[311] The negative attention from Congress gave opponents of the project within the air force the ammunition they needed to push for the termination of its Human Relations Research Institute, and it was dismantled in 1954.[312]

The RCC's fortunes declined with the termination of the Refugee Interview Project. Kluckhohn resigned as director in 1954, signaling the end of the RRC's mission to apply behavioral sciences to the Soviet Union.[313] He reminded his successor that one of the stated reasons for the RRC and its support by the Carnegie Corporation was "the development of scholars and scholarship in the 'Social Relations' area."[314] But that ship had sailed. By 1954, the RRC had lost nearly all connection to Social Relations, either "as an intellectual approach or academic department," becoming little more than a place for scholars of different disciplines to work independently.[315] A visiting committee remarked that it operated as a loose "federation of disciplines," rather than an interdisciplinary organization.[316] The same criticism, of course, applied to the Social Relations Department that had inspired the RRC's creation and organizational model. Given the flaws in the model, it was inevitable that the RRC would suffer the same fate—functioning as a multidisciplinary umbrella organization rather than a truly synthesizing undertaking. Even Inkeles admitted that, although the work of the RRC was of the highest quality in each of its disciplines, it was "not interdisciplinary, experimental, or methodologically innovative."[317] The newer disciplines in the Social Relations constellation had lost ground to the traditional disciplines of government, economics, and most notably Russian history as the primary methods of study.[318] By the time Kluckhohn left, the RRC had no psychologist or anthropologist on its staff.[319]

INTERDISCIPLINARY RESEARCH LOSES ITS LUSTER

Harvard had a singular status within Carnegie Corporation philanthropy in the late 1940s, with large and record-setting grants going to the Department and Laboratory of Social Relations as well as to the Russian Research Center.[320] The interdisciplinary approach the corporation sought to promote, however, proved to be "little more than a short-lived impulse to collaborate in the redesign of social research."[321] The corporation's investments in Harvard and other programs around the country promoting cross-disciplinary research failed to produce the desired results.[322] The RRC's failure as a force for interdisciplinarity is but one example. As Ellen Condliffe Lagemann has observed, interdisciplinary efforts did "not survive the generational conflicts, the postwar geopolitics, the personal loyalties, and the philanthropic encouragement that had given rise to them in the first place."[323]

For some scholars, the post–World War II interdisciplinary movement was simply a fashion that ran its course. Political scientist Robert A. Dahl questioned whether the behavioral approach to social research championed by the corporation was "anything more than [a] mood" that had percolated into prominence after the war.[324] For Engerman, "a wartime experiment had become a fad."[325] Even the Carnegie Corporation that had funded some of the most ambitious efforts in this area conceded the movement's lack of staying power, with President Charles Dollard pronouncing: "A great deal of time is wasted on the premature attempts to produce very large 'syntheses' or 'integrations' of social science fields."[326] Social Relations faculty member Jerome Bruner mused that "the magic university word in those days was 'interdisciplinary.'"[327] Indeed, there was a sense among some on Harvard's faculty that grant writers quickly grasped what foundations wanted to hear and sought to "dress up" large research projects as interdisciplinary to improve their chances of funding.[328] The Ford Foundation even tried to entice economists into the interdisciplinary movement of the behavioral sciences, but they wanted no part of it.[329] They dismissed it, in the words of Milton Friedman, as a mere "fad"—again that descriptor—that would only impede economics from becoming a "mature" science.[330]

Social Relations faced critics at Harvard as students and faculty questioned whether the department was merely a novelty act. Norman Birnbaum and Michael Olmsted, Teaching Fellows in Social Relations, defended the department against attacks of being a nebulous discipline, heavy on theory and light on facts.[331] In a letter to the editors of the *Harvard Crimson*, they conceded that as a new discipline it focused on developing a systematic social theory rather than establishing the facts of human behavior: "Our 'nebulousness' is, of course, a function of the newness of our science: but nebulousness exists on the frontiers of even the most advanced and rigorous of sciences—which we are not. Those of a 'factual' inclination, therefore, have every right to suspect that they may be unhappy in any science."[332] They suggested that, "even at our present relatively primitive level of theoretical development, our work is of some value to those interested in understanding important areas of behavior."[333]

The local attacks intensified as Harvard faculty from other departments challenged the basis for the Department of Social Relations, claiming it was an illegitimate discipline lacking serious standards. One might have expected a certain noblesse oblige from the venerable Department of History, but two of its faculty took the unusual step of publicly criticizing Social Relations. The details of what prompted this spectacle are unknown, but in 1950, undergraduate Adams House hosted a forum on "Social Relations and Its Criticism."[334] One hundred fifty students listened while history professors Arthur M. Schlesinger Jr. and Oscar Handlin assailed Social Relations. Schlesinger claimed the discipline "resorts to statistics and laboratory experiments to back up wild statements," and Handlin mocked sociology as "the study of material left over from government and economics."[335] Handlin's attack was odd given that he had taught social history as an original member of the sociology wing of the Social Relations faculty in 1946, until leaving his position as an assistant professor in 1950.[336] Social Relations did not make him a permanent member as there had been no vacancy, but the Department of History appointed him.[337] Defending the department were psychologist Jerome Bruner and sociologist Alex Inkeles. Inkeles responded to the charge that faculty in Social Relations rated their results too highly with, "There are pretentious men in all fields. I generally agree that there are some good and some bad practitioners . . . but this is true of all work."[338] It is difficult to imagine today any Harvard department justifying its existence in a public forum; the skirmish highlighted just how poorly some in the Harvard community regarded Social Relations. The perception of it as an amorphous discipline dogged the department throughout its existence.

Sociologist David Riesman—then at the University of Chicago but later joining the Social Relations faculty—had another view on this type of attack. He suggested that the criticism by the older social sciences against Social Relations was a "disciplinary home-guardism" motivated by the popularity of the new department and its ability to attract students that might otherwise have concentrated in History, Government, or Economics.[339] He recounted a development at the University Chicago, where a faculty member of Economics attacked a new social sciences program, in which Riesman taught, because it—and especially the course on culture and personality—was "somehow seducing" students into the program and out of Economics, "presumably by talk of such enticing matters as sex and social class."[340]

> Similar attacks greeted the rise of the Department of Social Relations at Harvard, which, formed in 1946, was within two years third in student enrollment. In recognizing the concerns of the post-war students, the Harvard administration was merely giving one further illustration of the democratization of that university, its refusal to hold a snobbish fort for the humanities and the older social sciences . . . and by the same token its attention to trends in the nation at large.[341]

Social Relations failed to integrate its component disciplines. Despite the early enthusiasm of the department's founders, and some senior faculty members and graduate students, as well as important institutions and intellectuals outside of Harvard, which also had invested a great deal of hope (and in the case of the Carnegie Corporation—money) in the department and its promise of creating a new science, the enterprise could not fulfill its central goal of synthesizing its constituent disciplines. There was little interdisciplinary collaboration in research. The Carnegie Project, the single effort to establish a unifying theory for Social Relations, missed the mark. By the early 1950s, it was clear the department was multidisciplinary rather than interdisciplinary in character. Centrifugal forces would continue to pull Social Relations further away from its original mission for the rest of the decade.

5

✦

The 1950s

A Decade of Disunity

The ideas of the originators (Parsons, Murray, Kluckhohn, Allport) have had their day.

—Gordon Allport

Psychology must eventually get back under one roof—a physical roof preferably, but a symbolic roof at least.

—Jerome Bruner

The 1950s was a disappointing decade for Social Relations. The department had not met its original goals. The year 1953 was particularly discouraging; one of the young faculty stars, Jerome Bruner, established his own research project outside the department following years of failing to persuade senior faculty members to address major flaws in Social Relations.[1] Bruner remained a faculty member but no longer participated actively in its interdisciplinary mission. As early as 1948, there were signs that junior faculty members rejected the vision of the Levellers. As noted earlier, many younger members of Social Relations protested the unified theory put forth by Parsons and Shils in *Toward a General Theory of Action*. Bruner was one of them. He continued to voice misgivings about pursuing a grand theory of behavior and the harm it was doing to the department, particularly the study of psychology.

Bruner had received his PhD in psychology at Harvard in 1941 and joined the faculty of the Psychology Department in 1945. Despite his training with the biotropes in Psychology, Bruner was attracted to the Social Relations experiment, and he soon left Psychology for Social

95

Relations. For him, Social Relations had an "extraordinary collection" of faculty, both senior and junior.[2] Happy with his choice, he nevertheless maintained intellectual bonds with the Psychology Department: "[Social Relations] became my new home. I embraced it. But I could never shed the 'old Department' as a 'reference group.' I taught in both Departments. . . . Social Relations eventually became focused upon larger, macrosociological issues. Psychology, perhaps in reaction, narrowed its focus to the details of operant conditioning and psychophysics."[3]

His initial zeal notwithstanding, he became concerned about a counterproductive division between the psychologists in Social Relations and those in Psychology. He also felt that his brand of psychology, what he called the "heart of psychology—the study of the powers of the mind and their enablement—fell neglected between the two."[4] Yet he maintained an optimism about the Social Relations experiment in its early years. He felt that the split in Psychology at Harvard would "disappear" over time "in the growth of one super-ordinate entity: a school, or an institute or what not."[5] In explaining his rejection of an attractive offer to organize a social psychology unit within the Psychology Department at the University of Chicago, he said many of his interests, or "hunches" as he called them, "have precious little to do with what might be called social psychology."[6] He felt "there were few places in the world as congenial to intellectual wanderers as is Harvard," stating that, "for the moment, I am quite satisfied that there is room in the Department of Social Relations for a generalist like myself."[7]

A RISING STAR LOSES FAITH

Bruner soon became less than satisfied. In 1950, he wrote to Gordon Allport expressing his deep concern over psychology within Social Relations, particularly at the graduate level, telling him, "I feel the urgent need to shake things up at the moment."[8] Lamenting the division of psychology at Harvard into two departments, he said it may have been "inevitable but it has in a certain sense begun to be a plain pain in the neck."[9] He added, "We have collected in Cambridge a tremendous array of talent. . . . We must use it to get psychology back on its feet." And to him, that effort included working with the Department of Psychology.[10] He worried about the direction of psychology at Harvard broadly—not just within Social Relations, but also in the Department of Psychology. He thought neither group of psychologists was doing justice to the discipline.

On May 10, 1951, he drafted a long letter to E. G. Boring, the chairman of the Psychology Department, and, although the draft remained in his files designated "letter never sent," it showed his increasing anxiety about

Figure 5.1.   Jerome S. Bruner, 1971. *Credit*: Timothy Carlson, Harvard, 1971. *Source*: Schlesinger Library, Harvard Radcliffe Institute.

the discipline.[11] Based on his long friendship with Boring, he felt he could approach him with blunt criticism of both departments, saying it was "a matter which is none of my business—yet which *is* my business in another sense [emphasis in original]."[12] He insisted that his comments transcended departmental ties or formalities, stating simply, "My loyalty is to psychology at Harvard and I am interested in seeing balance in the field."[13]

His draft was triggered by the impending loss in the Psychology Department of several faculty members, who Bruner feared would "not be replaced with people who can as readily bridge the gap between Memorial Hall [the Psychology Department] and Emerson Hall [the psychologists in Social Relations]."[14] He saw each group of psychologists heading in the wrong direction. Psychology was too narrow in outlook, while Social Relations lacked a clear focus: "There appears to be pressure on the one side to get down-the-line rat-box men, and pressure on the other to get psychologists who look and act as much as possible like physicists or mathematicians."[15] Bruner was "particularly bewildered" by the psychologists in Social Relations.[16] His pejorative reference to "rat-box men" revealed his disdain for the behavioral psychologists in the Psychology Department, a theme throughout his career.[17] He believed that behaviorism ignored key aspects of human mental experience by viewing the mind as a passive learner, merely a stimulus-response mechanism.[18] Rather, he viewed the mind as an active learner, bringing "a full complement of motives, instincts and intentions to shape comprehension, as well as perception."[19] Eventually his works would be credited with helping "to break the hold of behaviorism" on psychology and with leading the "cognitive revolution" in the field.[20]

Sociologist David Riesman agreed partially with Bruner's assessment: "By providing a shelter in Social Relations for psychologists who had been beleaguered in their original home, that home became more monolithic, while the Department of Social Relations was seen by some faculty as amorphous and lacking in proper standards."[21] But Riesman did not believe that if the persecuted psychologists had remained in the Psychology Department they would "have done much to alleviate the more monolithic aspects" of it.[22] In his unsent letter to Boring, Bruner said that each department was attempting to solve its own "internal problems" in the choice of new appointments, rather than focusing on what was good for psychology as a whole.[23] Social Relations had "no coherent plan" in appointments other than trying to "cover a fairly wide spectrum of points of view—a rather odd and indiscriminate policy."[24] But, "what is quite apparent is that our actions are not dictated by the aim of furthering the general development of psychology at Harvard any more than yours are."[25]

He declared, "I deplore the fission" in psychology at Harvard and its consequences.[26] He proposed reuniting all of Harvard's psychologists, arguing "that psychology must eventually get back under one roof—a physical roof preferably, but a symbolic roof at least."[27] Only five years after the bitter divorce between behavioral and social/clinical psychologists, he contended that all components of psychology should be reunified. He reasoned that it was detrimental to teach the discipline of psychology in such a compartmentalized fashion, recommending that "we cease as soon as possible our habit of thinking of three or four *kinds* of psychologists. . . . In short, there is only *one* kind of psychologist," and that "as soon as possible we try to give but one kind of degree in psychology—a Ph.D. in Psychology [emphasis in original]."[28] He ended with a stark warning about psychology's future at Harvard if it continued as a divided discipline: "Let me sum up saying that I am not satisfied to have no control over what psychology across the street is doing and that I think you people have no business being satisfied having no control over psychology outside Memorial Hall. And I doubt that you are satisfied.

Unless we can get psychologists somehow working together here, I see only poor outcomes."[29]

Perhaps Bruner decided the letter was too incendiary to send, or it was merely an exercise in venting his frustration. Boring for his part seemed relatively sanguine about psychology's current predicament at Harvard, although he fiercely opposed the division at the time. Writing to thank Bruner for sharing a copy of the exam in the Social Relations proseminar in social psychology, Boring said, "It is a very good exam and shows that your crowd is getting basic things given them in the way in which they should be given."[30] He reflected on the split in psychology with a rather mild rebuke: "The duplication of work is an odd business."[31] Overall, he found it not such a bad state of affairs: "As to Harvard Social Relations it is a tribute to all of us on both sides that things work so smoothly and with so little tension as they do now. . . . We go ahead and duplicate and nobody worries and the student groups are small enough to get adequately instructed, small enough to have common attitudes and common vocabularies so that communication is not hindered."[32]

Within Social Relations, Bruner apparently (no letter was found) complained to Allport, who sympathized, responding, "Indeed your indictment of our poor department was so devastating and so thorough that I wondered whether anything I might say could refrain you from taking the next train for Palo Alto."[33] Allport assuaged Bruner's fear of being forced to integrate into a grand departmental scheme:

> Please ask yourself if this charge is really fair. It is true that TP [Talcott Parsons] coos and coos when he prematurely writes an integrative book . . . but have you felt forced to integrate? Have you? Does our Department really undermine Harvard's thrice-blessed individualism? I quote your words "If they should, in pairs, or trios, cast their lot with each, that is just fine." Does the Department demand more than that?[34]

Allport admitted the challenge facing Social Relations was "incredibly great," but he asked Bruner to aid the department's "further evolution" and to "consider seeing it through."[35] He ended saying, "All I beg is this: give yourself and us a chance to thresh it out, until the pure grain of your values and intelligence are exposed. The decision will then follow naturally, and it will be good."[36]

Allport's pep talk failed to persuade Bruner. While on sabbatical at the Institute for Advanced Study at Princeton in 1951–1952, Bruner "brooded over the split" in psychology at Harvard. He wrote again to Allport on December 23, 1951, singling out Parsons as a principal concern:

> It seems to me that there is an additional sense of urgency in the situation, and again I must be very blunt. I have had disturbing news from

Cambridge—from Harry Murray and from George Homans and from other friends—about Talcott Parsons. I gather he's in a very auto intoxicative phase and he is acting somewhat megalomaniac about a "social relations point of view" which represents the point of view that comes out of his joint enterprise on theory. . . . I have seen this coming on and it scares the daylights out of me.[37]

Bruner told Allport he was not worried that "Talcott [Parsons] is running away with our show," but rather that "he is pretty blind to some of the needs" of psychology.[38] He added, "Frankly, I would hate to have to sit down with Talcott and talk with him about how psychology should be envisaged over the next decade."[39] Bruner's concern with Parsons was his pursuit of an overarching theory of social behavior that held little relevance for psychology, undoubtedly a reference to the Carnegie Project led by Parsons and the resulting book, *Toward a General Theory of Action*, published earlier that year. "His eye is on some Grand Design of the Social Sciences and while I am in sympathy with his objectives, I still have strong feelings that Grand Design or no, there are some internal rules that make for good psychology and that have relatively little to do in the short run with Grand Designs."[40]

Upon returning from his sabbatical, Bruner, resigned to being unable to effect change within Social Relations, stepped back from the group enterprise. He remained in the department but received permission from the dean to establish a Cognition Project in a Victorian house at 9 Bow Street in Harvard Square.[41] There, physically and intellectually removed from colleagues in Emerson Hall, Bruner pursued his "work on the study of thinking and its development."[42] The move presaged a more pronounced retreat in the years to come: the Cognition Project would become the more formidable Center for Cognitive Studies in 1960.

Of course, Bruner was only one faculty member in Social Relations. But he was highly regarded, both for his interdisciplinary bona fides and his prowess in procuring funding. In the first years of Social Relations, Bruner received more funding from the Laboratory of Social Relations than any other researcher.[43] Not only did he think critically about the department's problems; he wrote about them, leaving a rich record of correspondence on the challenges facing Social Relations in the 1950s. Other faculty members in Social Relations and Psychology began to join Bruner in his dismay over the splitting of psychology between two departments. Indeed, in 1957, Robert White, chairman of Social Relations, and Edwin Newman of the Psychology Department considered a "rapprochement" between the two departments.[44] The discussions were not widely publicized, however, and no action was taken.[45] The idea that Social Relations had damaged the discipline of psychology at Harvard was very much in the air.

SOCIAL RELATIONS:
SCATTERED INTELLECTUALLY AND GEOGRAPHICALLY

Bruner's vexation and subsequent withdrawal underscored two ominous realities taking hold within the Department of Social Relations. First was the failure of the founders to convert younger faculty members to the vision of integrating the department's disciplines.[46] Bruner distanced himself from Social Relations, but at least he remained in the department. By 1954, seven other prominent junior members had resigned to pursue posts elsewhere.[47] The department's insecurity increased as eight faculty members took temporary absences of one semester or more.[48] Chairman Parsons viewed this as a serious problem; to him it seemed as if "the rats were deserting the sinking ship."[49] Second, nothing physically united the diverse elements of Social Relations. No single building housed the department; its various subdisciplines and projects were scattered around Harvard. Bruner had his project on Bow Street. Parsons and Allport, along with most of the sociologists and psychologists, were in Emerson Hall, which served as the "hub" for Social Relations.[50] Henry Murray had his own enclave at the Psychological Clinic at 64 Plympton Street, a comfortable old house, which its inhabitants playfully described as "wisteria on the outside, hysteria on the inside."[51] Clyde Kluckhohn was situated in the Russian Research Center.

Thus, only two of the founders of Social Relations even worked in the same building. This dispersion of the faculty may have "lent a sense of freedom and lightness to academic life" within the department, but it did little to enhance its efforts at integration.[52] The interdisciplinary aspirations—already fading at this point—of Social Relations had stalled. Research in the department involved many talented people, but they largely were working on individual projects, each within his own discipline. Interdisciplinary collaboration continued to be rare. As an institution, it was a multidisciplinary muddle. Allport later pondered whether the timing of the venture or even the vehicle itself had been conducive for integration:

> Intellectual leadership toward the formation of a "common language" in our field came from Talcott Parsons, joined for a time by Edward Shils and Edward Tolman. Whether the effort was premature or whether Harvard's tradition was one of individualism and dissent, it did not turn out to be possible to establish a common basic language for the department. But dyads, triads and small clusters of colleagues did manage to work together on projects of common interest and a general atmosphere of convergence prevailed.[53]

To be sure, some faculty dyads produced notable interdisciplinary works.[54] In 1953 there was the second edition of the successful *Personality in Nature, Society, and Culture* by Kluckhohn and Murray and the publication of *Working Papers in the Theory of Action* by Parsons and Robert F. Bales.[55] In 1955, Parsons and Bales collaborated on another interdisciplinary book, *Family, Socialization and Interaction Process.*[56]

But a few collaborative works and a "general atmosphere of convergence" neither justified nor sustained a department founded on the promise of integrating its disciplines into a new science.[57] The early turn of Social Relations toward a multidisciplinary model is evident in the pattern of senior appointments.[58] The department's intention, initially, was to select candidates not so much according to the specific needs of a subfield, but in terms of the appointees' likely contribution to the development of social relations as a whole.[59] In practice, however, this policy was largely ignored.[60] By the 1950s, the department selected permanent members based principally on their achievements in their respective fields, with little or no regard for their potential for contributing to "social relations" broadly conceived.[61]

There was only "marginal pressure to present candidates who could contribute to the department as a whole, including its neglected undergraduate program, as well as to the advancement of scholarship and training in each of the wings [as the subdisciplines came to be known] taken separately," according to David Riesman, a member of the ad hoc committee that proposed candidates.[62] Riesman noted the additional load for sociologists, who had "to read the publications of candidates in social and personality psychology and in social anthropology."[63] He admitted this "was a burden, of course, but it was also an opportunity to increase my understanding of fields."[64] George Homans also recognized the added workload, but he felt it was manageable in the beginning.[65] There were few members of the department then, and the tenured professors knew the work of candidates for a permanent appointment, so they could reasonably compare their abilities.[66] As the department grew, however, faculty members had difficulties evaluating candidates in fields other than their own.[67]

Promoting integration proved problematic in the graduate programs as well. Neither faculty nor students found the interdisciplinary seminars to be uniformly successful.[68] The department resorted to informal methods of encouraging integration at the graduate level, hoping that students would experience some degree of synthesis through contact with faculty bringing in ideas and materials from fields other than their own.[69] Some faculty members believed that whatever integration was achieved at the graduate level manifested itself not in formal course work but in student dissertations.[70] Objective measurement of such synthesis, however, was difficult.

The undergraduate program faced similar challenges. Like the graduate program, the college concentration failed to find a course that could provide grounding in the field for all students.[71] Consequently, even some faculty members conceded that the department resembled an intellectual "three-ring circus," with distinct acts from anthropology, psychology, and sociology.[72] Although its initial postwar popularity tapered after the peak in 1948, the department continued to be one of the largest in the college. It also continued to attract a disproportionate number of students from the lower-rank groups, although this trend was partially offset in the late 1950s by the increase in premedical students who chose to concentrate in Social Relations.[73] According to David Riesman, the image of an easy concentration (major) was a continuing concern for the department. He believed the faculty wanted "to show that it was not a 'gut' field for jocks—as if jocks were necessarily inferior beings."[74] Social Relations never fully came to terms with mounting a large, popular, and diverse concentration that at the same time attracted students looking for easy classes.[75] The failure to integrate its diverse elements was common throughout the department: in its research, in its faculty appointments, and in its graduate and undergraduate instruction.[76]

PARSONS STEPS DOWN

In 1955, nearing the ten-year anniversary of the founding of Social Relations, Parsons prepared to relinquish the chairmanship. It would not be a triumphant passing of the torch. Instead, it was a milestone most notable for acknowledging departmental failures. Writing to Dean McGeorge Bundy on the selection of a successor to Parsons, founder Gordon Allport conceded that "the ideas of the originators (Parsons, Murray, Kluckhohn, Allport) have had their day."[77] Parsons voiced strong opinions on the selection of his successor. Naturally, he wanted someone committed to the ideals of Social Relations. He told Dean Bundy his two top choices were Sam Stouffer and Clyde Kluckhohn. But he also supported Gordon Allport, Frederick Mosteller (a statistician), Robert White (a lecturer in psychology), Richard Solomon (a psychologist and acting director of the laboratory), and Evon Vogt (a social anthropologist).[78] He ranked Stouffer and Kluckhohn higher, based on their reliability for the "highest level of statesman-like work on the larger policy issues."[79] Parsons questioned whether Allport had the personality for the job, but otherwise thought he had "the general respect and greatest seniority of any" of the candidates.[80]

Parsons also told Bundy there were candidates who absolutely were not suited for the job.[81] He ruled out his nemesis George Homans because of his headstrong personality:

As I think I put it to you orally, we feel that Homans is a rather special kind of individualist who one might say is a bull who, far from avoiding china shops, takes something of a pleasure in seeking them out. He is a very valuable member of the Department from a variety of points of view, but he is anything but catholic and eclectic in his interests or his judgments so he does not seem the suitable type for this particular assignment.[82]

He disqualified Bruner for his lack of commitment to the department:

[Bruner is] also a kind of individualist, but his individuality consists more in an extremely intensive drive in pursuit of particular interests of his own. . . . He has not shown the order of concern for the interests of the Department . . . which seems to be prerequisite for becoming a central symbol of its corporate unity. . . . He has sometimes been openly skeptical of the advisability of having such a Department at all.[83]

Parsons emphasized that his personal judgment of Homans and Bruner was also the "definite consensus of the six full professors at the present time."[84] Parsons vetoed fellow department founder Henry Murray because of his lack of interest in administrative duties and his preference to be a "freelancer," coming in and out of the department and university at will.[85]

Ultimately, Dean Bundy appointed Robert White.[86] Although Parsons supported White as a second-tier prospect, White did not seem capable of, or even interested in, pursuing Parsons's vision. White was a psychologist who had not published widely and lacked the reputation of Parsons, Allport, Kluckhohn, and Murray.[87] His work was not interdisciplinary, and he did not contribute to *Toward a General Theory of Action*.[88] He was not anyone's first choice. Allport did not support White's ascension, although he fit the bill of someone younger to "inherit the mantle."[89] But White was popular within the department, a good administrator, and no one actively opposed him; that seemed enough for Bundy.[90]

The ten-year anniversary of Social Relations gave the outgoing chairman the opportunity to reflect on the department's history, submitting a 127-page report to Dean Bundy, *Department and Laboratory of Social Relations, Harvard University: The First Decade, 1946–1956*.[91] In the section "Background and Origins," Parsons revisited the theme of the 1941 white paper he had coauthored, "Toward a Common Language for the Area of Social Science," one of the key events in the department's prehistory. He said the social sciences of anthropology, sociology, and psychology may have been "slower to mature" than history, political science, and economics, but they "were more fundamental to the development of a *general* scientific study of human behavior than the other three [emphasis in original]."[92] The principal reason for this was their "higher level of theoretical generality on which they have tried to analyze social behavior."[93] Addressing sociology, he explained that it considers the "whole society" and focuses on problems of the "theoretical analysis of social systems on the most *general* level [emphasis in original]."[94] Thus, sociology studies "phenomena, even in our own society, which economists, historians, and political scientists have taken for granted—phenomena like family and kinship, social stratification, ethnic groups and their traditions and conflicts, ecological distribution and succession in the local community, etc."[95] Anthropology "tended to be concerned with the structure and functioning of *total* societies, rather than segments of them like the economic and political."[96] It examines "relatively simple societies" where it is easier to obtain an overview by direct observation than in a complex modern society, although Parsons noted that anthropology has since the late 1930s given more attention to modern societies.[97] The discipline also considers the phenomena of culture in relation to the analysis of social behavior.[98] And psychology was fundamental to all social sciences because it "deals with the motivation of the individual and the mechanisms in his personality through which his performance of social roles and his implementation of the patterns of his culture operate."[99] Although each discipline has its own area of investigation, Parsons maintained that they were "converging with each other in the areas of their intersection."[100] He highlighted the relation of psychology to the other disciplines in the "discovery of the internalization of socio-cultural norms or values as part of the personality structure of the individual, a discovery made independently both from the psychological side by Freud, and the sociological-anthropological side by Durkheim and G. H. Mead."[101]

Perhaps it was only natural for Parsons to reexamine the issue of how the younger social sciences fared against their older siblings at Harvard. After all, the Levellers had predicted their new discipline would overtake the big three at Harvard in importance. But Parsons's apologia had a whiff of defensiveness to it; the department's collective insecurity was frequently all too obvious to graduate students and faculty members. With a chip on its shoulder, Social Relations still had something to prove vis-à-vis the older disciplines of history, government, and economics. Parsons glossed over another sore spot in the department's history, the failed attempt to create a theoretical foundation. He deemed the Carnegie Theory Project a "sufficiently central subject" to warrant mention in the report, but he devoted only a single paragraph on efforts "to take stock of the common theoretical ground between the disciplines which enter into the Department's field."[102] Gone was the bravado that had accompanied the department's founding, the bold predictions of creating a new social science, and the great new movement on which Parsons had staked his professional reputation. He referred to *Toward a General Theory of Action*—

what some at the time thought could be the splitting of the "social atom," making Parsons the Newton of the social sciences—as a mere enterprise that served "to stimulate and focus our thinking in an area of fundamental concern to all of us."[103] He relegated it to the status of a stock-taking exercise: "It is a question whether it might not be profitable to undertake something of the sort at intervals of every ten or fifteen years."[104]

Parsons acknowledged the inability of the department to integrate the field in its courses for graduate students, but he blamed the students for the failure of the two courses that sought to span "the whole field of social relations."[105] The courses—"Problems and Concepts" and "Methods of Research"—were abandoned because of "the feeling of the staff that the background of the students was so inadequate at many points and uneven that it was better not to attempt so ambitious an integration at the beginning of graduate study."[106] Admitting failure in formal attempts at integration, the department mainly "relied on informal methods to promote the process of integration."[107] Parsons neglected to mention, however, one unusual informal method. According to David McClelland, Parsons sought "to provide a common socialization experience" for faculty by bringing in lay analyst Erik Erikson (who would later join the department) to analyze them.[108] It is not known how many faculty members participated, but McClelland recalled, "it didn't work out."[109] It underscored, however, that Parsons realized something was needed to unite the faculty "for the department to continue."[110] Given the failure of the formal methods, Parsons had no choice but to praise the spontaneous approach of integration.

> There is of course a great deal of actual integration in the program of instruction which does not bear the formal label. In lecture courses, seminars and research projects with which the students have contact there is continual use of ideas and materials from fields other than the formal affiliations of the instructor or instructors. The same has been true of a substantial number of students' dissertations. . . . All of this is of course facilitated in a number of ways, by reading work from all the fields, by attending graduate colloquium and staff research meetings sponsored by the Laboratory, by actual collaboration, and, perhaps most effectively of all, by informal discussions of "shop" problems at the staff and particularly at the graduate student level.[111]

The grand theoretician who insisted on making Social Relations scientific, complete with a "laboratory," and who monitored the progress of the Carnegie Project on Theory with the precision—and "Eureka" language— of the physical sciences, now recognized the utility of the informal approach: "On the whole, my own personal opinion is that reliance principally on these informal mechanisms is, by and large, the most effective way to promote the process of integration."[112]

STILL A SHOP CLUB?

Parsons's interdisciplinary odyssey had come full circle. In certain respects, he and his fellow Levellers were back where they started in the 1930s—working informally to exchange ideas and looking for opportunities to cross-fertilize. Of course, they no longer had to meet clandestinely, discussing how the radically new psychoanalysis might be applied to their research, or suffering the derision of their tormentors in the traditional departments. They now had their own department with all the trappings: generous funding from the Carnegie Corporation, a novel laboratory, and a world-renowned faculty. None of that, however, succeeded in creating a new social science supported by a general theory of integration. What the Levellers started in the 1930s as a "sort of shop club" in Parsons's words had grown far beyond that institutionally. At a theoretical level, however, it remained something of a shop club.

In *The First Decade*, Parsons took comfort in a 1954 faculty committee report, *The Behavioral Sciences at Harvard*, stating, "The net outcome seems to have been a strong endorsement of the Social Relations 'experiment' and general commitment to its continuation."[113] Calling the department an experiment is consistent with his downplaying *Toward a General Theory of Action*. Parsons overstated the strong endorsement of the report, however, and he ignored its negative commentary altogether. The closest thing to an endorsement was a mild statement that there seemed to be support among the department's own "staff members" for the "ideas represented in Social Relations."[114] Elsewhere, the report questioned the department's commitment to its interdisciplinary integration, particularly by its founders and more senior faculty. It acknowledged that "the need to leap over old disciplinary lines in fostering a new discipline is strongly represented" by the older supporters of Social Relations, but they left it to the younger members of the department to execute that vision.[115]

The report also published anonymous comments from interviews. One interviewee described the department's flaws with striking accuracy and bluntness, asserting that there was "more than a grain of truth" in the criticism that senior members of Social Relations were paying lip service to interdisciplinary research:

> The Department has hashed over the question of interdisciplinary work innumerable times in the last several years, attempting to achieve by some ingenious formula a result which is impossible because of far more basic conditions than the senior members are willing to face up to. These senior members are in general not interested in interdisciplinary research and tend to withdraw into their disciplines more and more. Their justification is that the task of "integration" should fall to the younger staff members. However, their formula can never work because the senior staff has almost exclusive

contact with graduate students in the first year, thereby furnishing role models for the students and also proselyting the best of them to become their research assistants.[116]

The interviewee charged that the emperor had no clothes and there was no point in pretending Social Relations represented a synthesis of its disciplines unless its senior faculty changed course dramatically:

> I would recommend most emphatically that unless the University administration is willing to commit three or four new permanencies to the Department of Social Relations and the senior members are willing to commit these to persons of genuinely interdisciplinary orientation, that your committee recommend that all pretense of integration of the several disciplines in the Department of Social Relations be stopped.[117]

The anonymous critique was correct. Following the failure of the Carnegie Project on Theory, the department made no further attempts at integration on a theoretical level. Even during the golden age of Social Relations, graduate students often felt overwhelmed by the disunity. Apart from two or three collaborations between senior faculty members on cross-disciplinary works, they went their own single disciplinary ways. One of the founders, Gordon Allport, for example, conceded that from the beginning of Social Relations, "my own teaching continued much as it always had."[118]

AN ILLUSTRIOUS TRIO JOINS THE DEPARTMENT

In at least one area, however, the trend away from the interdisciplinary mode abated.[119] In 1959, Dean McGeorge Bundy and President Nathan Pusey had the opportunity to make three senior appointments to Harvard's faculty. They made three bold and unconventional choices, bringing to Harvard men of demonstrated interdisciplinary habit and conviction who were free to select their departmental affiliation.[120] All three chose Social Relations. They were David Riesman, Erik Erikson, and Laurence Wylie.[121] Through no initiative of its own, Social Relations thus acquired three individuals cast in the mold of the department's original aspiration.[122] And unlike most faculty members, each was well known to the public through their popular books.

The most famous of the trio was sociologist David Riesman, whose book *The Lonely Crowd* became the best-selling book by a professional sociologist in American history with 1.4 million copies sold.[123] The book even landed him on the cover of *Time* magazine on September 27, 1954.[124] Harvard sociologist Orlando Patterson praised him as "The Last Sociolo-

gist" in the *New York Times* upon Riesman's death in 2002, explaining that
his colleague had written not only a hugely successful sociology book, but
"arguably one that has had the widest influence on the nation at large."[125]
In its 2002 year-end edition "The Lives They Lived," the *New York Times*
lauded Riesman as the "Big Thinkster" and the "most influential sociologist of the era."[126] Riesman reached Americans beyond the academy at
a time when "sociologists for a while rivaled even psychiatrists in their
ability to explain everything about everything."[127]

Figure 5.2.   David Riesman, 1973. *Credit*: Lilian Kemp *Source*: Schlesinger Library,
Harvard Radcliffe Institute.

Surprisingly, Riesman did not have a doctorate in the social sciences.
He received a law degree at Harvard and had been a law clerk to Supreme
Court justice Louis Brandeis. Nonetheless, he was a kindred spirit to the
founders of Social Relations and their interdisciplinary goals. He had
been strongly influenced by neo-Freudianism, having studied with leading psychoanalyst Harry Stack Sullivan and having undergone analysis
with Erich Fromm. These experiences led him away from the law and to
the pursuit of character studies in a social context.[128] His course for Harvard undergraduates, "American Character and Social Structure," was
immensely popular.[129]

Riesman came to Harvard from the University of Chicago, where he had been a professor of social science. He said he chose Social Relations over the Government Department, "to the great disappointment of my former mentor, Carl Friedrich, a Harvard government professor, because of Social Relations' multidisciplinary character and its unusually gifted faculty and students."[130] Ever the lawyer, he chose his words carefully, however, significantly describing Social Relations as *multidisciplinary*, not *interdisciplinary*. Riesman had no reservations about joining the department despite its failure to integrate its disciplines. Indeed, writing in 1956 before being offered the position, he described the limitations of a departmental venture such as Social Relations, without naming it outright:

> Other packages bring together anthropology, sociology and psychology. If we look at the latter, we can see there are enough terminological and stylistic distinctions among the three disciplines to keep unifiers busy for several generations; and what we find in practice is frequently a course jointly taught by members of three departments, all competing for majors or graduate students, while at the same time making efforts, more or less valiant or successful, to adopt a joint conceptual frame—at worst a sort of pidgin English, with, for instance, psychologists learning to say "culture" or "social structure" from time to time; at best ascetic adoption of terms derived from some overarching scheme like that of Talcott Parsons. What Freud termed "narcissism with respect to minor differences" can preoccupy such a faculty indefinitely.[131]

Of course he was describing Social Relations and its graduate proseminar; it was the only program in the academy attempting to integrate those three disciplines. And although he credited the efforts as "more or less valiant or successful," it was faint praise. He dismissed the notion that real integration was occurring. The disciplines were merely appropriating terminology from one another.

Erik Erikson had no doctorate degree, and indeed had not even gone to college, but as a lay analyst he achieved recognition with specialists and laymen alike with the publication in 1950 of the best-selling *Childhood and Society*, introducing the now well-known concept of identity crisis.[132] The book had a significant impact on the field of child development and influenced younger analysts to appreciate cultural anthropology and social psychology.[133] He also published a highly acclaimed psychobiography of Martin Luther, *Young Man Luther*, in 1958.[134] And he would win a Pulitzer Prize and National Book Award for another psychobiography, *Gandhi's Truth*, published in 1969.[135] According to Howard Gardner, a renowned developmental psychologist and professor of cognition and education at the Harvard Graduate School of Education, Erikson was "intellectually charismatic."[136] Gardner was an undergraduate at Harvard who con-

centrated (majored) in Social Relations, and Erikson was an important
mentor, serving as his junior and senior year tutor.[137] Erikson became
a colorful addition to the Harvard community: "Blond, blue-eyed, and
Viking-tall, Erikson was 'the most arresting figure on campus,' Gardner
said, remembering his straight-backed stride. In those days, swimmers at
Harvard's Indoor Athletic Building did their laps without wearing bath-
ing suits. 'Even naked,' a friend told Gardner, 'Erikson looks 10 percent
more distinguished than anyone else.'"[138]

The third member of the trio was Laurence Wylie, who came to Harvard from Haverford College, where he had been chairman of the Romance Languages Department. He joined Social Relations as the Clarence
Dillon Professor of French Civilization, which had the unusual perk of an
annual case of wine from the Chateau Haut-Brion, owned by the Dillon
family.[139] In 1957, he published a groundbreaking study of life in a small
town in France, *Village in the Vaucluse*, which received wide acclaim and
soon became a classic.[140] The book was considered popular social anthropology and not standard French literature, however, and this annoyed
the Romance Languages Department at Harvard, where Wylie had a
joint appointment with Social Relations.[141] The department's snobbery
led Dean Bundy to quip that it "seems that languages and literatures are
not necessarily the central method of inquiry into French civilization."[142]
Wylie's course on French culture and society was popular with students,
and it was one of the first at Harvard to use movies.[143] Students dubbed
it "Frogs and Flicks."[144]

The three appointments increased the star power of the Social Relations faculty and proved popular with students, both undergraduate and
graduate. Although their individual styles drew on various disciplines,
each largely went his own way and did not contribute to the integration
of the department's disciplines. For example, they did not rely on statistics in the way that psychologist Sam Stouffer of the Laboratory of Social
Relations and others did. Nor did they align themselves with the abstract
scientific-sounding approach of sociologist Talcott Parsons, which Riesman, for his part, found "grandiose."[145]

Riesman and Erikson sometimes received criticism for their less rigorous and "seemingly artistic approach to scholarship."[146] Howard Gardner, an admirer of both men and their brand of scholarship, employed
the terminology of art in favorably describing their work as drawing
"more informed individual and societal portraits than traditional science:
not putting forth claims that could be 'tested' in the sense of Karl Pop-
per, but rather sense-make syntheses that sought to capture the world in
its complexities."[147] Their individual specialties and approaches, while
interdisciplinary in certain aspects, did not involve collaboration with
the other disciplines in Social Relations. They neither participated in the

department's interdisciplinary dyads and triads cited by Allport nor published collaborative cross-disciplinary works.

Riesman collaborated successfully with other sociologists (Nathan Glazer and Seymour Martin Lipset among them), but not with psychologists or anthropologists, whose work he nevertheless often incorporated into his own. His peers considered him an "interpretive sociologist who drew upon more specialized work and on other disciplines, especially anthropology and psychology, in his effort to distinguish forest from trees."[148] Indeed, Riesman—and Erikson—are prime examples of what Howard Gardner called "synthesizing" minds capable of investigating big issues drawing on the tools of several disciplines.[149] Riesman's individual interdisciplinarity was impressive, but it did not further the mission of the department.

The difficulty of the interdisciplinary enterprise became increasingly apparent by the end of the 1950s.[150] Faculty members grew frustrated and unhappy.[151] Bruner had distanced himself from the department. Senior members withdrew into their own specialties. Even one of the founding fathers, Clyde Kluckhohn, became disillusioned.[152] Colleagues suspected that he wished to return to the Anthropology Department, where he already held a joint appointment.[153] It didn't help that he moved his office from Social Relations' Emerson Hall to the Peabody Museum, home of the Anthropology Department.[154] The early ebullience of Social Relations evaporated, leaving the department with a shaky self-image. David Riesman expressed surprise at the department's lack of self-esteem when he joined it in 1959: "To come from the Sociology Department at the University of Chicago, with its immense self-confidence and pride, in no way feeling inferior either to the natural scientists or the (frequently inhumane) snobs in the Humanities, to the Department of Social Relations with its defensiveness vis-à-vis the traditional Harvard was something of a shock."[155]

Despite failing to meet the ambitious original goals, the first ten years of Social Relations can be fairly labeled as positive and productive.[156] All wings of the department had some of the most important scholars in the country.[157] Reports on the first group of PhDs trained by the department were encouraging.[158] Already they had authored several noteworthy books.[159] Many graduates had received full professorships, several had become department chairmen, and one had even risen to the position of dean.[160] The enthusiasm generated by a new venture, a remarkable faculty, and the spirited leadership of Talcott Parsons as chairman were credited for this success.[161] The approaching decade, however, would present difficulties even the most dedicated leadership and illustrious faculty could not overcome.[162] The lack of synthesis in the research, graduate, and undergraduate programs in the 1950s would grow more apparent.[163]

The trend toward faculty appointments premised on traditional disciplinary interests would continue.[164] The department's innovative efforts had not led to the establishment of a field of social relations within, let alone beyond, the confines of Harvard University.[165] With no common language or unifying theory, it was adrift.[166] The rest of academia did not start interdisciplinary departments modeled on Social Relations, save for a small doctoral program at Rice University, which was later disbanded because the faculty considered the program as "less than competitive."[167] Faculty members of all component disciplines voiced profound personal and professional frustrations. The department remained an anomaly in an academic world structured around the traditional disciplines.[168] In all its guises, Social Relations reflected a multidisciplinary character rather than the radically different interdisciplinary image to which it had originally aspired.[169] The 1960s would bring new challenges to chip away at the department's fading unity and its reputation, at Harvard and beyond.

6

✝

The 1960s
Drugs and Departmental Drift

The old values are at stake—academic freedom, freedom of consciousness, the freedom of the nervous system. Who controls your cortex?
Who decides on the range and limits of your awareness? If you want to
research your own nervous system, expand your consciousness, who is
to decide that you can't and why?

—Timothy Leary

The trouble is that I think your consciousness is expanded and the result
I don't like. It isn't the old Tim that I knew and loved and supported.
If you ever decide you don't like the alienated ecstasy so much, let me
know. I keep holding hope against hope that you'll get tired of it and
get back to being the useful psychologist you once were.

—David McClelland

Underlying the mounting difficulties of the Social Relations Department in the 1960s was a debilitating trend—a pronounced return
to the original academic disciplines.[1] The interdisciplinary hiring of the
early 1950s had devolved in the 1960s to blatant logrolling, with each
wing demanding its own share of hires.[2] Young faculty members came to
Harvard lacking any strong interdisciplinary leanings.[3] Social Relations
held little significance for them except as an organizational umbrella
under which to pursue their own specialized work.[4] Established faculty
members also began shifting their interests.[5] Jerome Bruner, an early
skeptic of the department's interdisciplinary ambitions, established an

independent research enterprise where he could pursue his studies in cognitive psychology.[6]

Bruner, regarded as a master "grant swinger" by his colleagues, received a quarter of a million dollars from the Carnegie Corporation in 1960 to establish the Center for Cognitive Studies (he already had distanced himself from the department in 1953 with his Cognition Project on Bow Street).[7] He procured additional funds for the center from the National Institutes of Health and the National Science Foundation.[8] Bruner partnered with George Miller of the Psychology Department to establish the center outside of the Department of Social Relations, imbuing it with an interdisciplinary approach.[9] Indeed, they founded the center precisely to compensate for what they perceived to be the narrowness of the Departments of Social Relations and Psychology.[10] They envisioned the center as a "unifying force, a neutral place where students from both Social Relations and Psychology could meet and educate each other."[11]

Bruner and Miller wanted to study the mind—how normal people think—a topic they felt their respective departments neglected.[12] The Psychology Department was ruled by B. F. Skinner and behaviorism and S. S. Stevens and psychophysics; there was no interest in the study of mental processes.[13] The Social Relations Department had faculty that studied only the abnormal mind or the interactions among groups of people.[14] Bruner and Miller claimed their approach had to be more interdisciplinary in practice than the Social Relations Department because "the study of cognitive processes . . . [was] clearly not an enterprise that [could] be entrusted to any single discipline."[15] The center's researchers, visitors, and directors included people from such diverse fields as psychology, linguistics, philosophy, biology, mathematics, anthropology, pediatrics, history, psychiatry, and psychoanalysis.[16]

Rather than breaking out in such bold fashion, other faculty members simply returned to their original fields.[17] The most dramatic example was Clyde Kluckhohn's move to the Peabody Museum, the home of the traditional "sticks and bones" anthropology he had fled in 1946.[18] Such departures followed the inclinations and frustrations of members of the department, but movements in the social sciences at large also played a role.[19] One such trend was the move away from the school of culture and personality that had once united cultural anthropology and clinical psychology.[20] Faculty and graduate students alike increasingly avoided this area of research whose very rise in the 1940s had helped establish the Social Relations Department.[21] Anthropology was retreating from the so-called soft areas of study. As David Riesman pointed out in 1958,

> I believe we can detect something like a nativist or third-generation reaction in anthropology, as well as in a number of the other newer disciplines which

have suffered frustration in attempts at integration. There has been a movement away from the culture and personality school, a renewed preoccupation with special methodologies, an almost pathetic eagerness to show that anthropologists of either sex are as tough-minded, hard-headed scientists as any critic from another discipline could ask.[22]

Sociology also was moving in a direction uncongenial to the aims of the department.[23] The field was turning away from the micro interests that had allied it so closely with psychology and the ideology of Social Relations.[24] Enthusiasm for employing psychoanalytic thought in sociology and other disciplines waned.[25] Increasingly, sociologists were becoming concerned with macro issues that linked their discipline to economics and government.[26] The sociologists within Social Relations, particularly new arrivals, were not immune to this trend, which gained momentum throughout the decade.[27] Such developments foreshadowed difficulties because psychoanalytic theory had initially been an important element melding the various strands of Social Relations.[28]

Already weakened by these trends, the department suffered a set of blows in 1960 that made matters worse.[29] Two of the founding fathers died unexpectedly.[30] Clyde Kluckhohn suffered a heart attack, and Samuel Stouffer succumbed to leukemia.[31] Although Kluckhohn, disappointed with the department, had already distanced himself from it, his death nonetheless was a symbolic loss.[32] More ominous was the passing of Samuel Stouffer.[33] As head of the Laboratory of Social Relations since its inception, Stouffer had been a vital leader.[34] Robert F. Bales assumed leadership of the laboratory, but times had so changed that it became a less and less integral component of the department.[35] Most responsible for this development was a new trend in government funding of research.[36] Beginning in the mid-1950s, funds increasingly went to individual researchers, such as Bruner, thus undermining the function of centralized facilities like the Laboratory.[37] Compounding the losses of Kluckhohn and Stouffer was the retirement in 1962 of Henry Murray, one of the Levellers, who had helped establish the department and had guided the early development of clinical psychology.[38]

A BAD TRIP FOR SOCIAL RELATIONS

The department soon faced internal contention that mushroomed into national, even international prominence.[39] In 1960, two members affiliated with the department's Center for Research in Personality, Timothy Leary and Richard Alpert, began research on psilocybin and other consciousness-expanding drugs.[40] Leary was a lecturer on clinical psychology, and

Alpert was an assistant professor of clinical psychology and education.[41] At the time, psychedelic drug research was just beginning in America and had not yet set off any alarm bells.

Leary had been brought to Harvard in 1959 by the director of the Center for Research in Personality, David McClelland, who also would become the chairman of the Department of Social Relations in 1962.[42] McClelland was a highly regarded figure in twentieth-century American psychology, known primarily for his efforts to bring empirical inquiry to the study of human personality and motivation.[43] He published his most widely cited book, *The Achieving Society*, in 1961.[44] Despite some personal setbacks, Leary had been a rising star in mainstream psychology when he first came to Harvard.[45] McClelland admired Leary's book, *The Interpersonal Diagnosis*, and he hoped that Leary would help "to get our Ph.D. clinical program going at Harvard."[46] Indeed, Leary would get things going at Harvard, but not in the way McClelland had imagined.

Figure 6.1.   David McClelland, 1982. *Credit*: **Lilian Kemp** *Source*: **Schlesinger Library, Harvard Radcliffe Institute.**

Timothy Leary is remembered today as the high priest of hallucinogens, clad in a Nehru-collar shirt and draped in love beads. But when he arrived at Harvard in 1959, he was, in his own words, dressed as the very "caricature of a professor."[47] He ridiculed his button-down shirt and tweed jacket with leather elbow patches as the bland "varsity uniform" of the day.[48] The only outward hint of his rebellious streak was his choice of footwear—white tennis shoes, which he wore everywhere.[49] In the conformist culture of Harvard in the late 1950s, his choice of footwear should have alerted his colleagues that he might not stay in step, let alone toe the academic line.

He began his academic duties by teaching the advanced graduate seminar on the theory and practice of psychotherapy.[50] Rather than assigning students to clinics and hospitals, which had been the standard approach, Leary encouraged them to deal with real-life problems in ghetto community centers, skid rows, orphanages, and jails.[51] Traditionally minded faculty, including McClelland, expressed concern with his methods and the vagueness of his approach.[52] Some younger faculty members, however, were intrigued, and Leary gained a small following.[53] One of the beguiled was thirty-year-old Richard Alpert, an assistant professor of Clinical Psychology and Education. Alpert later gained fame as Ram Dass, a spiritual leader with a devoted following and a 1971 best-selling book, *Be Here Now.* Initially the two bonded over being bachelors and the only faculty members to hold night office hours in the Center for Personality Research.[54] They soon discovered they also shared a disdain for the establishment.[55] According to Leary, the "two rebellious pals, Tom Sawyer and Huck Finn, were role models" for their friendship in those early days.[56]

Returning to Cambridge in the fall of 1960 after a visit to Mexico and his first experience ingesting psilocybin mushrooms, Leary said he had been transformed by "the deepest religious experience of my life."[57] Convinced that psychedelic drugs would radically change the practice of psychology, he and Alpert undertook three projects based on psilocybin. The first, the Harvard Psilocybin Project, was strikingly simple in design. Graduate students and faculty members from Harvard and other universities and seminaries in the Boston area would take a controlled amount of psilocybin and then write a report about the experience.[58] In the second, he and Alpert undertook a rehabilitation program for inmates of Concord Prison, hoping to demonstrate that ingestion of psilocybin could reduce recidivism rates.[59] In the third project, known as the Good Friday Experiment, they gave psilocybin to divinity students from Andover Newton Theological Seminary to determine whether it could induce a religious experience.[60]

In late 1960, Leary took his first steps toward becoming a figure in the counterculture, making friends with Aldous Huxley, famous for recounting his psychedelic trip on mescaline in the 1954 book *Doors of Perception.*[61]

Leary had written him to describe his experience ingesting psilocybin mushrooms in Mexico.[62] Huxley was just down the road in Cambridge at MIT, and soon the two met for lunch at the Harvard Faculty Club.[63] It went well. Leary asked Huxley if he would like soup. Huxley asked what kind, and Leary scanning the menu replied, "Mushroom soup."[64] Laughing at that omen, they proceeded to discuss the most effective way to study consciousness-expanding drugs.[65] Huxley was one of the first high-profile authors, philosophers, poets, musicians, and counterculture personalities to populate the Leary orbit. Allen Ginsberg, the famous Beat poet, became another, living for a time in the attic of Leary's home (William Burroughs reportedly lived there for a time as well). Leary claimed that he had "turned on" Burroughs, Jack Kerouac, Arthur Koestler, Neal Cassady, and Robert Lowell, among others, to psilocybin. Ginsberg also encouraged Leary to initiate Willem de Kooning, Franz Kline, and Dizzy Gillespie, but there is no evidence he acted on Ginsberg's advice.[66]

Not all the trips led to converts. Koestler said of his experience, "There's no wisdom there. I solved the secret of the universe last night, but this morning I forgot what it was."[67] Kerouac also failed to become an enthusiast, writing to Leary of his last trip, "Got high but had funny hangover of brainwashed emptiness— . . . Me take no more."[68] Lowell professed to having a profound experience, telling Leary, "Now I know what Blake and St. John of the Cross were talking about."[69] But Leary did not believe him, contending that the dose was "too low to produce transcendental effects."[70] Leary remarked, "My take with Kerouac and Lowell is that we are batting zero for two in the Life-Change Revelation League."[71] Leary and Ginsberg thought if Lowell had a positive experience it would encourage other intellectuals to jump on the psychedelic bandwagon.[72] They argued whether giving Lowell a stronger dose might be in order. Leary thought they should have given Lowell the option for a "heavy dose experience and go all the way."[73] Ginsberg, mindful of Lowell's repeated hospitalizations for manic depression, vetoed the idea, saying he did not want to go down in history as "the guy who put America's leading poet around the bend."[74]

These were not random encounters. Leary had mounted a concerted campaign to connect with those he called "great men."[75] Sometimes he was introduced by a trusted intermediary, such as Ginsberg, who had provided admission to the "Beatnik network."[76] But the biggest draw in making these connections was Leary's "seemingly unlimited supply of psychedelic drugs."[77] The drug company Sandoz had synthesized psilocybin, the hallucinogen in the mushrooms, and provided Leary with a large bottle of the pills based on nothing more than Leary's request on Harvard stationery for a supply to use in his research.[78] The pills arrived with a cheery, if unscientific, note: "Here's a starter kit to get going and please send us a report of the results."[79] Whether tripping with William Burroughs in Morocco or inviting Isak Dinesen, author of *Out of Africa*, to take psilocybin in Denmark (then seventy-five, she declined, stating that "she was filled with enough fantasies without any external stimulation"), Leary in less than three years morphed from button-down lecturer in Social Relations to a jet-setting Johnny Appleseed of psilocybin.[80] Eventually he would become a full-blown counterculture icon, exhorting a generation to "turn on, tune in, drop out" and attracting the ire of President Richard Nixon, who labeled Leary "the most dangerous man in America."[81]

As Leary and Alpert's research progressed in the Harvard Psilocybin Project, it became less experimental, acquiring a party-like atmosphere; Leary even renamed it the Harvard Psychedelic Project.[82] They insisted that the psilocybin be administered in a natural nonclinical environment—often the living room of a private house or apartment.[83] In the fall of 1961, they began holding drug sessions with students enrolled in their course.[84] Stories of mystical orgies circulated throughout the student community, alarming faculty and administrators alike.[85] Alpert reportedly was "using drugs with undergraduate men in exchange for sexual favors."[86] Harvard ordered Leary and Alpert to cease using undergraduates as subjects in further drug research. Leary found the exclusion unfortunate given the tremendous interest from undergraduates and their ability to obtain the drug on their own: "Following our contract with the University, we excluded undergraduates, who were the most interested group of all. Drugs were becoming ultra-trendy. Every weekend the Harvard resident houses were transformed into spaceships floating miles above the Yard."[87] He was troubled that undergraduates were being deprived of a profound and positive experience, all because of "occasional mishaps that caught the attention of the authorities."[88] The "mishaps" were two undergraduates who went to mental institutions after taking psilocybin and mescaline.[89] Leary thought the student experience with psilocybin was a positive one:

> The drug enthusiasm of Harvard undergraduates continued to haunt us. In this, the third year of our research, the Yard was seething with drug consciousness. If we prudishly refused to turn them on, no big deal. They scored supplies from Boston or New York. Several enterprising chemistry students constructed home labs to make the stuff themselves. For the most part the drug epidemic sweeping Cambridge seemed benign. Hundreds of Harvard students expanded their minds, had visions, read mystical literature, and wrote intelligent essays about their experiences. It seemed to us they were benefitting.[90]

Part of the problem stemmed from what he saw as the "chronic tendency of students to tell everyone *everything*."[91] He said the administration got nervous upon receiving complaints from parents: "Dozens of bright youths phoned home to announce they'd found God and discovered the secret of the universe."[92]

Social Relations faculty associated with the Center for Research in Personality were shocked by the apparent lack of controls and the haphazard experimental approach.[93] McClelland received a growing number of complaints. He organized a private meeting for members of the center, including graduate students, on March 14, 1962, to address the matter and to clear up misconceptions about the drug research.[94] Battle lines were drawn: Leary and Alpert versus Herb Kelman and Brendan Maher, two other professors in the department.[95] McClelland assured graduate students the drug research was not part of the clinical program and they were not obligated to participate.[96] Kelman, a lecturer in social psychology, emphasized the ambiguity facing graduate students in the department, many of whom were unsure whether the drug sessions were curricular or extracurricular.[97] He criticized the laxity of the research standards, arguing, "The program has an anti-intellectual atmosphere. Its emphasis is on pure experience, not on verbalized findings."[98] One student said Alpert had told him that if he was not interested in research on drugs there was no point in continuing his studies in clinical psychology.[99] Kelman maintained that a cult was forming among the students most heavily involved in the drug sessions.[100]

Maher focused his line of attack by citing scientific studies about the dangers of psilocybin and the need for it to be administered by a physician. He grilled Leary, "Have you bothered to read the literature in your own field?"[101] Leary thought Kelman was a "formidable rival" with "undeniable clout in Washington" for his success in obtaining grants and fellowships, but that some of his animosity was due to jealousy because fewer graduate students gravitated toward him and his "tame questionnaire projects."[102] He dismissed Maher, who was British, as a "dour rat-lab experimentalist known for his rigid insistence on teaching students exactly the same way he had been taught in medieval English universities."[103]

Leary and Alpert denied they had coerced any student into participating in the research, claiming their procedures were approved by the Food and Drug Administration, the University Health Services, and Sandoz Labs (the supplier of the psilocybin).[104] They said psilocybin was a powerful drug that deserved study of how it could be harnessed to advance man's growth. "What could be more important for the future work in the psychological and sociological studies? How is this not in line with our task here at Harvard?"[105] They considered that their work was in the tradition of William James and that any attacks on it violated academic freedom. Leary charged that McClelland's private meeting was a setup, contending he had been "ambushed by the Harvard Squares," a play on Harvard's geographic location at Harvard Square and the conventional views of his detractors.[106] Despite the rancor, however, he felt "the meeting ended on a note of civilized coexistence" when a committee was formed to study the matter.[107] That resolution was harmless enough, allowing for the continuation of Leary's research, but it was far from the end of things.

The meeting, as it turned out, was not private. A reporter for the *Harvard Crimson* had wormed his way into the session, and the paper printed a story detailing the departmental quarrel.[108] Boston newspapers soon seized on the news, and the controversy received widespread attention. For the first time, the simmering strife in Social Relations was no longer confined to Harvard Yard; it had hit the wire services and was now painfully public.[109] On March 20, 1962, the Massachusetts State Food and Drug Division began an investigation, resulting in a decision allowing the studies to continue if a physician was present during administration of the drug.[110] Public controversy abated temporarily, but difficulties persisted within the department and the Harvard community. The executive board of the Laboratory of Social Relations appointed an ad hoc committee to advise on further drug studies. Professor Robert Freed Bales, the director of the laboratory, proposed that the supply of psilocybin be held in custody of the University Health Services, to be dispensed only through the laboratory.[111] Leary agreed to this stipulation, but Alpert did not. Nothing was settled before the summer of 1962.[112]

The following fall, Leary and Alpert returned from Mexico where they had been conducting further drug "research." They promptly formed an organization as another platform for continuing their research, christening it the International Federation for Internal Freedom (IFIF). Meanwhile, back in Cambridge, the Harvard administration grew increasingly concerned about drug use on campus. John Monro, dean of Harvard College, and Dana Farnsworth, University Health Services director, took to the *Crimson* to warn undergraduates of the hazards of taking "mind-distorting drugs" and to dismiss the intellectual justification for using them.[113] The alert made the front page of the *New York Times*.[114] A flurry of letters and articles followed, most notable of which was the counterargument made by Leary and Alpert. They claimed that the Harvard administration's statements were "reckless and inaccurate" from a scientific viewpoint and urged the Harvard community to "keep an open mind"—an apt plea from those promoting consciousness-expanding drugs—and to focus on scientific data rather than the advice and "grown up responsibility of faculty members."[115]

Denying the accusations that they allowed undergraduates to participate in the experiments, Leary and Alpert cast their rebuttal in terms not only of academic freedom but of freedom of one's own body and consciousness:

> What is at question is the freedom or control of consciousness, the limiting or expanding of man's awareness. . . . The old values are at stake—academic freedom, freedom of consciousness, the freedom of the nervous system. Who controls your cortex? Who decides on the range and limits of your awareness? If you want to research your own nervous system, expand your consciousness, who is to decide that you can't and why?[116]

They portrayed themselves as brave pioneers sharing their research and its implications with their "fellow Americans" and demonstrating "the unusual potential of the nervous system" to those volunteering as research subjects.[117] Indeed, they said Harvard should take pride in being the first university to wrestle with the drug controversy. It was only "fitting and natural that the Harvard intellectual community be the first to grapple with this new philosophic and practical issue and that the University of William James be given the first chance to accept or reject the educational potentialities of consciousness-expanding drugs."[118]

Leary and Alpert announced in the fall of 1962 that they would divorce their drug research from Harvard and conduct it under the auspices of IFIF, but the research remained a source of controversy.[119] In April 1963, Leary stopped showing up to teach his classes, and the university removed his name from the payroll, apparently without firing him outright.[120] Later the Harvard Corporation passed a resolution memorializing the action, stating that Leary "has failed to keep his classroom appointments and has absented himself from Cambridge during term time without permission."[121] One of the last contacts the department had with Leary was an exchange between him and Professor Robert Freed Bales.[122] Turning to leave after a discussion of the controversy, Leary queried, "Freed, do you think I'm psychotic?"[123] Bales pondered the question for a moment and replied, "Tim, I just don't know."[124]

Following Leary's departure, McClelland wrote to him, telling him that IFIF was "dangerous as are all people who promote widespread use of the drugs" and that he would have no choice but to tell the public that Leary was misleading them.[125] He expressed his certainty that the use of psychedelic drugs "really alters consciousness so as to alienate people from the world," and "my best evidence is what has happened to you, Dick [Alpert], and others who have repeatedly taken these drugs."[126] McClelland, Leary's friend and the man who had brought him to Harvard, made a final poignant plea:

The trouble is that I think your consciousness is expanded and the result I don't like. It isn't the old Tim that I knew and loved and supported. If you ever decide you don't like the alienated ecstasy so much, let me know. I keep holding hope against hope that you'll get tired of it and get back to being the useful psychologist you once were.[127]

Harvard publicly dismissed Alpert later that month after university officials learned he had given drugs to an undergraduate, thus violating his earlier agreement not to do so.[128] It was the first time in the twentieth century that Harvard had fired a professor, thus singling out the Department of Social Relations and its faculty for this dubious distinction.[129] Alpert defended his actions, saying he had given the drugs as a friend and not in his role as a professor.[130] Alpert admitted his guilt, and he said of the incident, "Someday it will be quite humorous that a professor was fired for supplying a student with 'the most profound educational experience of my life.' That's what he told the Dean it was."[131] The student was Ronnie Winston, son of famed jeweler Harry Winston.[132] How his confession came about was a melodrama all its own. According to one version of events, another undergraduate, Andrew Weil, a friend of Winston, supposedly encouraged him to incriminate Alpert.[133] Weil allegedly was "moonlighting as a spy for the Harvard Administration, helping President Pusey get the goods on Richard Alpert."[134] Weil later gained fame as a best-selling author and founder of a holistic medicine empire, even appearing on the cover of *Time* magazine. In a 2016 documentary film, he would say only that he "played a key role in getting information which eventually led to Alpert's being fired."[135]

Weil was a legitimate journalist for the *Harvard Crimson* with an obligation to follow a story, but he purportedly harbored a personal grudge against Leary and Alpert.[136] He and his friend Ronnie Winston previously had approached Leary, volunteering to be research subjects in the Harvard Psilocybin Project.[137] Leary refused because they were undergraduates, but he did give Weil a clue as to where they could obtain mescaline.[138] Neither Leary nor Alpert trusted Weil because he was a reporter.[139] Alpert also met Winston and became friendly, even infatuated with him, inviting Winston but not Weil into the small and exclusive psychedelic club at Harvard.[140] Weil's anger over this snub reportedly fueled his zeal in attacking Leary and Alpert.[141]

Weil knew Winston was taking drugs with Alpert. He also knew that no other students were cooperating with Pusey's investigation.[142] According to one account, Weil told Winston's father that his son got drugs from Alpert and likely would be mentioned in an upcoming article on Alpert.[143] But if Winston would voluntarily talk with the administration, then perhaps his name could be kept out of it.[144] Winston talked; Alpert was fired.

Alpert disputed Harvard's stated reason for his dismissal. He contended he was fired not only because he had given drugs to an undergraduate but because he was gay: "My claim to fame was that I was thrown out of Harvard. They always say it was because of the drugs but it wasn't only the drugs, it was also my homosexuality."[145] Leary also claimed Alpert's sexual orientation was the cause of his firing: "Dick was ousted for something more romantic. He got caught up in the middle of a love triangle involving an editor on the *Harvard Crimson* staff."[146]

A BLACK EYE FOR THE DEPARTMENT

Following the firing of Alpert, the *Harvard Crimson* published an editorial coauthored by Weil, savaging Alpert and Leary as "propagandists for the drug experience" who violated "the one condition Harvard placed upon their work; that they not use undergraduates for subjects for science experiments."[147] The editorial denounced the duo as charlatans:

> Far from exercising the caution that characterizes the public statements of most scientists, Leary and Alpert, in their papers and speeches, have been given to making the kind of pronouncement about their work that one associates with quacks. The shoddiness of their work as scientists is the result less of incompetence than of a conscious rejection of scientific ways of looking at things. Leary and Alpert fancy themselves prophets of a psychic revolution designed to free Western man from the limitations of consciousness as we know it. They are contemptuous of all organized systems of action—of what they call the "roles" and "games" of society.[148]

The *New York Times* reported on Alpert's dismissal, mentioning Leary but focusing on Alpert.[149] The story exploded beyond Harvard.[150] Unflattering articles in a variety of newspapers and magazines followed, some with sensational titles such as "The Strange Case of the Harvard Drug Scandal" in *Look* magazine and "The Hallucinogenic Drug Cult" in *The Reporter*.[151] Other newspapers and magazines covering the story included the *Boston Globe*, the *Boston Herald*, *Esquire*, the *Ladies' Home Journal*, the *Saturday Evening Post*, *Time*, and *Newsweek*.[152] The *Look* article was long, detailed, and provocative. The author—no stranger to Harvard or the players in the scandal—was none other than undergraduate Andrew Weil, who now was prosecuting his seeming one-man campaign against Leary and Alpert far beyond Harvard and its student newspaper. And he did so without disclosing his connections to Alpert, Leary, and Winston or his role in gathering the information that led to the ouster of Alpert.[153] The most titillating remark in the article was that "an undergraduate group was conducting covert research with mescaline. There were stories of students and others using hallucinogens for seductions, both hetero-sexual and homosexual."[154]

Psychedelic drugs were not well known among the general public in 1963. These articles changed all that and associated Harvard and Social Relations with the growing drug culture. The psilocybin research of Leary and Alpert in the Department of Social Relations had become em-broiled in a national scandal with broader repercussions for the country. Leary, liberated from university restrictions and the "Harvard Squares" who had vexed his vision for promoting psychedelic drugs as the cure to man's ills, could now freely spread his signature message to turn on, tune in, drop out. He was now fully committed to "a lifelong quest of going beyond the limits of ordinary consciousness" and would play his part in fueling the rise of the 1960s counterculture.[155] The psychedelic drug scandal in the Social Relations Department did not create the coun-terculture, but it certainly launched Leary into becoming one of its most noted protagonists.[156]

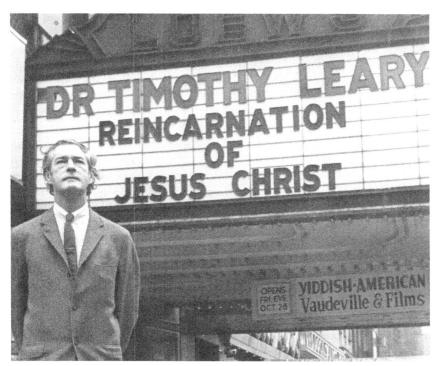

Figure 6.2. Timothy Leary, Village Theatre in New York City, circa 1966. Everett Collection Historical / Alamy Stock Photo.

The Leary-Alpert episode gave the department, particularly the clinical psychology wing, a black eye both within Harvard and throughout the broader intellectual community.[157] Internally, the scandal divided students and caused a tremendous headache for Leary's early champion McClelland, now the chairman of the Department. McClelland, nearly from the beginning of Leary's research, had voiced misgivings, privately and publicly, arguing in a faculty meeting that the "history of the [Psilocybin Project] has been marred by repeated casual ingestions of the drug."[158] Years later, he admitted, "I began to realize there were only a few subjects and many researchers, which meant that the researchers were taking more of the drug than anybody else."[159] The last straw for McClelland was when Leary convinced McClelland's mother-in-law, well into her seventies and recovering from a recent stroke, to take psilocybin.[160]

Social Relations professor Brendan Maher harshly criticized Leary and Alpert's drug research and how it affected graduate students who chose not to participate. Echoing the complaints aired by Kelman at the supposedly private departmental meeting, Maher asserted, "There was an in-group and an out-group. There were mornings when one might go into the building and find that one-third of the graduate students in a course one was teaching were wearing sunglasses in March. Because they had been up all night. It was an in-group of the illuminati versus the rest."[161] Graduate students complained to Maher that Leary was sending the message that if they were too uptight to take the drugs, then perhaps they did not belong in the field of clinical psychology.[162] Maher explained his concern: "When you're a graduate student looking for a degree in clinical psychology, that's a pretty powerful message to get."[163] Years later, Leary referred to Maher as "our old rival" and countered that it was Maher and other conservative faculty members who signaled to graduate students that their careers would be jeopardized if they associated themselves with Leary and Alpert's research.[164] Leary claimed that their veiled threats frightened students, who depended on reference letters and "old-boy networks" to advance their careers. He claimed Maher had told students, "This drug-taking is a campus fad like goldfish-swallowing. Can you really expect to be recommended for a good job if your research here involves schoolboy pranks?"[165]

Internationally, too, the reputation of Harvard and Social Relations suffered. In 1961 Leary and Alpert spoke at a prestigious six-day conference in Copenhagen, the Fourteenth International Congress of Applied Psychology.[166] Speakers at the opening session included Aldous Huxley and Social Relations' own Henry Murray. It was that evening's session that got weird, however, as Leary and Alpert, who some observers thought were high at the time, praised the wonders of psychedelic drugs.[167] Leary addressed the methods of changing human behavior and claimed that the most effective way of doing so was "by the use of psilocybin or LSD to cut through the game structure of Western life. You win today's game with humility. You lose tomorrow's game with dignity."[168] One Social Relations faculty member in the audience, Leary's nemesis Herbert Kelman, dismissed the lecture as unscientific and nothing more than a sales pitch for psilocybin: "Basically a paean to the drug experience. I could find nothing of substance. I am not prone to making diagnoses but I remember one Danish psychologist saying it sounded like the talk of someone who had been on drugs for a long time."[169]

The audience scorned Alpert. He praised the power of a drug-induced visionary experience to produce love, charity, and peace.[170] Several psychiatrists in the audience received great applause when they rose to denounce—"in seven languages"—nonmedical psychologists for addressing drugs at all.[171] After the conference, Danish psychologists descended on Leary, claiming he had "set Danish psychology back twenty years."[172] Unfazed, Leary countered with his characteristic boldness that in twenty years, the conference would rank alongside the lectures of Isaac Newton and Charles Darwin before the Royal Society.[173] According to George Litwin, a graduate student in Social Relations who had worked with Leary, the Danish conference seriously damaged Harvard's image:

> This event was decisive as far as Harvard and its reputation in the field was concerned. It was a radical testifying for psychedelics as opposed to a carefully literate presentation of what these new materials might offer us as potential in our field. . . . They totally crossed the line as far as those in the field were concerned. . . . By the time they got back [to Harvard], the furor was raised. Thousands of people all over the world had heard them testify to some new drug, which they were obviously on, and it was a disgrace to Harvard.[174]

The Leary-Alpert affair discredited the department. It was divisive, particularly among the clinical psychologists, an administrative nightmare for administrators, and it generated opprobrium internationally. The effects of the scandal are impossible to quantify, but it is certain that so incendiary an incident did not help a department already struggling with other difficulties.[175]

HARVARD DEBATES THE FUTURE OF SOCIAL RELATIONS

Growing concern over the future of the behavioral sciences at Harvard, and Social Relations in particular, prompted Dean Franklin Ford in 1963 to appoint an ad hoc committee to study the matter, with David McClelland, chairman of Social Relations, to lead the committee.[176] McClelland submitted a final report to Ford in May 1963. Weary from wrestling with Leary and Alpert for two years, he sounded a note of frustration as he confronted a new and existential challenge to the department—formal calls for its dissolution coming from within its own ranks.

McClelland used the report as an opportunity to take stock of Social Relations seventeen years after its founding. He acknowledged a number of disadvantages of the present configuration.[177] Some of the members, the anthropologists in particular, wanted to reconstitute a department along disciplinary lines. Graduate students sought a degree in a discipline and were confused by the situation at Harvard. Staff members also expected a disciplinary title. Most importantly, he conceded that "few courses are really interdisciplinary and there is much confusion in labelling courses so that some dealing with analogous subject matters are labelled Psychology and some Social Relations."[178] This was a stunning admission for the leader of a department founded on an interdisciplinary vision. Second, he admitted that, "even in Social Relations, integration has not gone as far as might be intellectually profitable."[179] He found the lack of integration most pronounced in social psychology, where "the social psychologists, who happen to have Ph.D.s in Sociology, have had little direct influence over the program leading to the Ph.D. in Social Psychology."[180] Finally, there was "the sheer size and complexity of the Social Relations Department."[181] Members of the department were reluctant to take on "administrative chores, such as keeping track of the budget, appointments, courses, and records of candidates for undergraduate and graduate degrees."[182] He noted that many science departments had "more or less tenured administrators" to handle such business affairs, and even if no changes were to be made in the department's structure, it needed a "business manager."

On the positive side, he believed Social Relations was at least a "going concern" at the undergraduate level and a clear success "in turning out Ph.D.s who are well grounded in their disciplines but with a broader viewpoint than they would be likely to get in an exclusively disciplinary program."[183] In his view, the strongest case for keeping the department in its present format was the employability of its graduates: "Social Relations Ph.D.s are clearly in demand, as a special breed. This is the intellectual objection to returning to the narrower organization of the disciplines."[184] At the same time, he conceded that change seemed inevitable: "I don't see how we can keep the present system going when only 3 of us have a strong investment in it."[185]

After two months of consulting with department members to gather a consensus, he thought he had a satisfactory agreement.[186] Each "wing" of Social Relations would return home to its original department, i.e., social anthropology would rejoin the Department of Anthropology, social and clinical psychology would return to the Department of Psychology, and sociology would revert to being a Department of Sociology. The individual departments would label interdisciplinary courses as Social Relations. McClelland envisioned two additional administrative layers, presumably to ensure that the interdisciplinary character of Social Relations would survive if the department dissolved into traditional departments. The first layer would be called committees of instruction or "programs" for each component of the new departments, so the wings of Social Relations would retain "many of the powers usually given to Departments."[187] The programs would appoint staff, administer the budget in consultation with the dean, and have the power to award all higher degrees.[188] Graduate students would apply to a department in the behavioral sciences but would be admitted by a program.[189] The second layer would be an overall "coordinating committee" of the programs composed of the chairmen of each program along with a permanent executive secretary.[190]

In the final meetings of the committee, McClelland expressed surprise that his convoluted restructuring of Social Relations was rejected. To be fair, he had set an impossible goal, trying to keep an interdisciplinary venture alive in a configuration that would include at its heart a return to three traditional disciplinary departments. He was striving, in his words, for a "kind of compromise formula which would keep the best of both worlds."[191] His colleagues countered with a more basic solution. Professors Vogt, Douglas Oliver, and Bruner advocated "simply decomposing Social Relations into its constituent elements" as they existed prior to 1946 with no additional level of programs or committees on instruction.[192] McClelland and others found such a dissolution too radical a step to be taken immediately, but the ensuing discussion ruled out any consideration of the more complicated structure that he favored. He concluded there was no consensus "in favor of my plan or any plan for that matter . . . just a feeling that a return to disciplinary departments would be simpler and better."[193] Faculty and administration were now actively examining the problems of Social Relations and its future. It was a watershed moment in the department's history—the first time Harvard officially broached the failings of Social Relations and its possible dissolution. Certainly, Bruner and others had sounded misgivings for years, and informal discussions had cropped up about reuniting the disciplines, but now it was formally on the agenda with the administration.

Months after McClelland submitted the report, the angst in the department went public when the *Harvard Crimson* published an article, "Social Relations at Harvard after Seventeen Years: Problems, Successes and a Highly Uncertain Future."[194] Written by Andrew Weil, the same undergraduate who had played a role in the Leary-Alpert episode, the article focused on the administrative problems highlighted by McClelland. Weil described the cumbersome and time-consuming administrative side of a department with four subdepartments or wings and numerous members with joint appointments in other departments. Social Relations had many problems, the most immediate being administrative: "The department is as large as some small colleges and demands an elaborate governing organization. But of its huge staff (114), few devote their full energies to the department."[195] In Weil's view, and presumably the view of his unnamed sources within the department, Social Relations had become so large that it was simply unmanageable, concluding that the job of chairman "had become too much for one man."[196]

WILLIAM JAMES HALL: NEW HOUSE, UNHAPPY HOME

Weil also previewed "the greatest change ever to hit the Department"—the plans for a new building that would house all personnel of both Departments of Social Relations and Psychology.[197] He captured the apprehension of department members regarding the upcoming move: "No one has the slightest notion of what will happen on Divinity Avenue," but the new building "has already brought into focus all of the accomplishments and problems of Social Relations and has led everyone in the Department to reflect on the future of Harvard's behavioral studies."[198]

Social Relations was geographically diverse. Each of the four wings had set up operations in seven comfortable enclaves scattered around the campus.[199] Sometimes, as in the case of the Psychological Clinic, it was an old house.[200] Another outpost was Jerome Bruner's Center for Cognitive Studies.[201] Emerson Hall housed many of the sociologists and social psychologists.

The scattered fiefdoms united under a single roof in 1965 upon completion of William James Hall, and the Social Relations Department shared the fifteen-story building with the Psychology Department.[202] Well-established figures in the Psychology Department also had to relinquish their longtime and highly customized environs to take up residence alongside members of Social Relations.[203] The base of operations for the experimental psychologists in the Department of Psychology was the basement of Memorial Hall. S. S. Stevens had his Psycho-Acoustic Laboratory at one end, and B. F. Skinner had his famous Harvard Pigeon Lab at the other. The Harvard administration had been determined to house the two warring tribes of psychology in a single complex.[204] The move was a fait accompli.

The creation of the Center for the Behavioral Sciences to administer the new complex suggested that the administration was hospitable to the idea of uniting the departments under a divisional umbrella. Indeed, there

Figure 6.3. Emerson Hall, Harvard University. HUV 51 (2-5b), olvwork369554. Harvard University Archives.

was much talk along these lines.[205] The center, however, never became more than an administrative entity providing logistical support for the inhabitants of William James Hall.[206] With the center assuming sufficient responsibility for research management, the Laboratory of Social Relations, once a key component of the department, went out of existence.[207] Even the name—the Center for the *Behavioral Sciences*—rankled Gordon Allport, the longtime critic of behaviorism. It seemed to transport him back to 1939 and his speech railing against operationism. The term suggested a surrender to the narrow dictates of behaviorism and its emphasis on the experimental over the humanistic in psychology.[208] Indeed, in remarks at the installation of the portrait of William James and in front of his behaviorist colleagues, he criticized the name of the center, saying it was misplaced in a building named for the great psychologist.[209] The new enterprise was continuing its namesake's "search for harmony among the psychological, social, physiological, and moral sciences—and we hope in the same catholic spirit."[210] But he cautioned that James did not have to contend with the many disciplines, theories, and developments that "seethe like intellectual ferments within these walls," thus ensuring that "harmony, of course, is still a distant dream."[211]

He believed the discipline remained a fractured one, and the "dispersion, disparities, contradictions in the so-called behavioral sciences are more evident today than ever before."[212] Allport skewered the phrase as an invention of "grant dispensing foundations" and a seductive concept that James would object to becoming "a dogma of method or theory."[213] He ventured that James would find the moniker "amusing" given that none of the activities within the Center for Behavioral Sciences dealt exclusively with behavior.[214] Nearly thirty years later, the old wounds had not healed for Allport:

> I am not fond of the label "behavioral sciences" now in vogue. From a certain point of view, it is harmless enough, but to me it somehow implies that if we were all to embrace the creeds of positivism and behaviorism, all our problems would be solved. I cannot agree. Our methods would be restricted, our theories one-sided, and our students would be intimidated by a tyrannical and temporary scientism.[215]

Allport's take on James and the behavioral sciences lives on in the lore of the Psychology Department, where the wind-tunnel effect around William James Hall is said to be the spirit of James (famously open-minded on spiritualism) trying to enter in order to protest behaviorism.[216]

None of the new tenants liked the building. Members of the Social Relations Department had to relinquish their cozy houses and hideaways for the cold, sterile hallways of William James Hall.[217] Allport, for example, "found it a wrench to leave Emerson Hall, which as a student and teacher I had inhabited continuously for fifty years."[218] Professors in the Psychology Department were similarly disgruntled. B. F. Skinner was said to have been "dragged kicking and screaming out of Memorial Hall" after he had spent decades modifying the Pigeon Lab to his precise requirements.[219] When he moved to the new building, he commandeered the entire seventh floor to replicate his secluded empire. The elevator doors opened to a display of two bumper stickers proclaiming his sovereignty: "Think Behavior" and "God is a VI"—VI is an abbreviation for "variable interval schedule of reinforcement" and a joke only a behaviorist would readily appreciate.[220]

Icebox. Shinto Gothic.[221] Embarrassing phallus.[222] Thus was William James Hall ridiculed when it was completed in 1964. Space on campus was desperately needed to accommodate the increasing number of students, so Harvard decided to "build up."[223] At fifteen stories, it was Harvard's first high-rise building and integral to the university's nascent commitment to modern architecture on campus. For the building's design, Harvard turned to architect Minoru Yamasaki, who had designed

Harvard's Engineering Science Lab in 1962.[224] Yamasaki was a master of the architectural style known as the New Formalism, which featured symmetrical facades, columnar arched supports, and smooth unadorned white walls.[225] He later gained renown as the architect of the 1970 design of the World Trade Center.[226] Harvard hardly set unique expectations for the new building, telling Yamasaki upon his hiring that it did not conceive of William James Hall as "a monumental work or of unusual artistic importance."[227] The administration's conventional ambitions for the exterior of William James Hall contrasted with its lofty aspirations for what might be achieved on the interior. Harvard hoped the building—named for the father of American psychology—might reconcile its two groups of estranged psychologists.

Figure 6.4.   William James Hall, Harvard University. https://
commons.wikimedia.org/wiki/File:William_James_Hall,_Har
vard_University.jpg

The interior layout proved problematic because it discouraged casual interchange either on individual floors or from floor to floor.[228] Critics thought it had too many floors, with slow elevators and "dreary corridors" that overall "tended rather to divide than unite us."[229] George Miller, Jerome Bruner's partner in the Center for Cognitive Studies, believed the move "destroyed" the collegiality that had been a hallmark of the center.[230] Most of the faculty sorely missed the meetings over lunch so typical of many of the outposts of Social Relations, as William James Hall opened with no luncheon facilities whatsoever.[231] Ironically, Social Relations, the one Harvard department devoted to the study of human relations, was housed in a facility with a design wholly neglecting those relations in the real world.

Students and faculty nicknamed it Billy Jim, not out of affection but simply because Harvardians nickname everything. It was a far cry from stately Emerson Hall that had stood in Harvard Yard since 1905, housing the Departments of Philosophy, Social Ethics, and Psychology. Displayed above the central elevator in the lobby of the new building was a quote from namesake William James: "The community stagnates without the impulse of the individual. The impulse dies away without the sympathy of the community."[232] The quote comes not from James's work in psychology but rather philosophy: *The Will to Believe: And Other Essays in Popular Philosophy*, and an essay therein entitled "Great Men and Their Environment."[233] Was it intended to be aspirational, a message of hope that the new building might reconcile the great men (still mostly men at this point) of psychology? Or was it meant as a daily reminder that in a community of scholars considering the same subject, there should be room for a multiplicity of individual viewpoints and contributions? Gordon Allport thought it was a worthy antinomy to adorn the lobby because it captured "the incontestable truth that there are on the one hand, biological and psychological laws governing the conduct of the individual, while at the same time, there are incontestable social, societal, and cultural laws of equal restraint."[234] Whatever the case, the old battle lines remained between experimental psychologists studying the individual and his physiological impulses and sociotropic psychologists studying man as he functions in society.

The new environment stirred little sympathy between the two groups, and the residents constituted a captious community. Apart from unhappiness about the building's design, everyone squabbled over the allocation of space.[235] Representatives of the Psychology Laboratory, the PsychoAcoustic Laboratory, and the Department of Social Relations bickered incessantly.[236] Distrustful of the new neighbors from Social Relations, Edwin Newman, chairman of the Psychology Department, demanded that after-hours access to Psychology's floors be restricted to faculty with a separate access key.[237] Despite the intentions of President Pusey, Dean Ford, and faculty members of both departments who had fought to obtain the new building, the process of uniting the behavioral sciences in one place backfired. It only served to further separate Psychology from Social Relations, and the groups within Social Relations from each other.[238] The chilly relations among its inhabitants ensured that William James Hall was as much an icebox inside as out.

CLINICAL PSYCHOLOGY SHOWN THE DOOR

Social Relations faced further fragmentation through the loss of its clinical psychology degree program.[239] Clinical psychology at Harvard had always been under a cloud.[240] The early scorn from colleagues and administration encountered by clinical pioneer Henry Murray had been circumvented by the creation of Social Relations, where clinical psychology found a secure and congenial setting for a time, notwithstanding the bad publicity from the Leary-Alpert debacle.[241] But such a professional training program had always fit uncomfortably under a Faculty of Arts and Sciences.[242] The training of clinicians required a skillful clinician to direct the program. At the same time, however, the director had to be an outstanding scholar in order to gain appointment to the faculty.[243] It was hard to find someone who could wear both hats. A candidate with outstanding qualifications as a clinician often lacked a scholarly background, and vice versa.[244] Many on the ad hoc hiring committees passing on such appointments felt that selecting an individual who appeared weak on the scholarly side, no matter his strength in other areas, would "debase the coinage" of the faculty.[245] It became nearly impossible to find someone who met both criteria.[246]

As a result, the clinical program at Harvard found itself in the mid-1960s without a full-time, permanent member of the department.[247] It received strong criticism from the American Psychological Association and the National Institute of Mental Health, the latter saying it would withhold grant funds if a remedy was not forthcoming.[248] Finally, in 1967, the department found the seemingly perfect candidate, and Social Relations named Norman Garmezy, a clinical psychologist from the University of Minnesota, to head the program.[249] He had a distinguished record as both clinician and scholar. In a bizarre twist, however, Garmezy resigned before he even left Minnesota.[250] He claimed he had been misled by Chairman David McClelland about the extent of his administrative duties.[251] The two men exchanged bitter letters in the *Harvard Crimson*. Garmezy said he did not come to Harvard because "the department was not committed to the development of a program that would bear Harvard's stamp of excellence."[252] He criticized Social Relations as seeking to maintain a "noble purity" in its research and failing to appreciate the importance of clinical work.[253] He also lamented the "immaturity" of university departments nationwide—including Harvard—for neglecting clinical studies: "How can you understand a field as complex as psychology without observing patients?"[254]

The high-profile resignation of Garmezy dealt yet another blow to the reputation of Social Relations. Most important, however, it signaled the end of a frustrating struggle to maintain a clinical psychology program within Harvard's inhospitable environs. Finally, in March 1967, the department voted to drop its degree program in clinical psychology.[255] Responsibility for maintenance of a clinical training program was assumed by an interfaculty committee from the Graduate School of Education, the Divinity School, the Medical School, and the Faculty of Arts and Sciences.[256] But the new program in clinical psychological and public practice encountered several setbacks of its own and was discontinued within a few years, thus ending the remaining vestige of what was once a cornerstone of Social Relations.[257]

The department lost yet another charter member with the death of founder Gordon Allport in the summer of 1967. The passing of Allport, a strong advocate of the department and one of the most influential leaders in social psychology nationally, coupled with the loss of clinical psychology, left little hope that Social Relations could maintain allegiance to its original ideals.[258] Allport's last word on the state of psychology was published posthumously in 1968. He was pessimistic, deploring the discipline's focus on the mechanistic at the expense of the humanistic.[259] Defending his style of psychology until the end, he named those fellow psychologists who also avoided behaviorism's limitations:

> The irrelevance of much of present-day psychology to human behavior comes from its emphasis on mechanical aspects of reactivity to the neglect of man's wider experiences, his aspirations, and his incessant endeavor to master and to mold his environment. Of course, not all psychologists have this blind spot. Carl Rogers, Abraham Maslow, Gardner Murphy, Harry Murray, and many others have clearer vision.[260]

Kluckhohn had died in 1960, and Murray had retired in 1962.[261] With the death of Allport, the ranks of the Levellers had thinned to a single man—Talcott Parsons, their intellectual ringleader.

SOCIOLOGY: AN OLD RIVALRY RESURFACES

The 1960s were tough on the psychology component of Social Relations, but sociology also had problems as the long-standing Homans-Parsons feud flared into public view. The enmity erupted first as an internal departmental matter in 1952 when Homans rejected Parsons's suggestion that the Social Relations faculty might benefit from reading *Toward a General Theory of Action*. In 1964, Homans continued his attack on the theoretical approach of Parsons. This time, however, he had a bully pulpit. Homans had ascended to the presidency of the American Sociological Association and used his presidential address to lambaste Parsons's structural functionalism and its practitioners, Parsons and one of his star pupils, Neil Smelser, who now was an eminent professor of sociology at Berkeley.[262]

Homans's move was reminiscent of Allport's 1939 address as president of the American Psychological Association, when he mocked the experimental psychology and animal studies so central to the work of his colleagues in the Psychology Department. Allport diplomatically refrained from naming his faculty colleagues: Lashley, Boring, and Stevens. Homans, however, showed no such restraint in his takedown of the functional school. He named names: Parsons and Smelser. His blunt opening set the stage for settling an old score:

> I am going to talk about an issue we have worried over many times. I have worried over it myself. But I make no excuses for taking it up again. Although it is an old issue, it is still not a settled one, and I think it is the most general intellectual issue in sociology. If I have only one chance to speak *ex cathedra*, I cannot afford to say something innocuous. On the contrary, now if ever is the time to be nocuous.[263]

Homans contended that functionalism focused unduly on assessing behavior based on an individual's membership in a particular group or his fulfillment of a particular function in society. He also criticized the theory for emphasizing abstract categories in the social system and how equilibrium is achieved in the system, rather than examining the behavior of man using what Homans called "psychological explanations."[264] He believed the needs of man—not society—explain behavior.[265] He argued, according to sociologist William Sims Bainbridge, that the functionalists were "ignoring the real topic of social behavior, which is individual human beings interacting with each other."[266] With his customary sarcasm, Homans summarily dismissed the approach of Parsons and Smelser:

I am being a little unfair to functionalists like Parsons and Smelser if I imply they did not realize there were people around. The so-called theory of action made a very good start indeed by taking as its paradigm for social behavior two persons, the action of each of whom, sanctioned, that is, rewarded or punished, the action of the other. But as soon as the start was made, the authors disregarded it. As the theory of action was applied to society, it appeared to have no actors and mighty little action.[267]

Their alleged failure to consider individual actors was the basis for the title of Homans's speech, "Bringing Men Back In"—that sociology should study man rather than abstract roles and functions. In his critique of Smelser's work, *Social Change in the Industrial Revolution: An Application of Theory to the British Cotton Industry, 1770–1840*, Homans said, "Let us get men back in, and put some blood in them."[268] Reviving his crusade against Parsons's attempted theoretical unification of Social Relations, he took a swipe at the highly abstract *Toward a General Theory of Action*, saying, "This is the type of box you get into when you think of theory as a set of boxes. For this reason, no one should hold their style of writing against the functionalists. The best of writers must write clumsily when he has set up his intellectual problem in a clumsy way."[269]

Homans's speech, later published as an article, caused a "firestorm" in the field, eliciting a torrent of articles in response, with sociologists suggesting "bringing back in" a number of other things to the discipline.[270] Closer to home, the speech must have seemed to his fellow sociologists that Homans reveled in deriding the structural functionalist school that had been a principal focus within Social Relations for many years.[271] His attack could only have increased tensions among the sociologists.

REORGANIZATION PLANS FLOATED

The urgent need for some realignment was evident in a reorganization scheme drafted in the summer of 1967 by Roger Brown, the chairman of Social Relations, and Richard Herrnstein, the chairman of Psychology.[272] They proposed a combined Department of Behavioral Sciences, a bold step but not without precedent.[273] A concrete move in this direction had occurred as early as 1962 when several Social Relations courses were cross-listed with the offerings of the Psychology Department.[274] Members of the Social Relations Department such as Brendan Maher, Jerome Bruner, and Roger Brown had joint appointments in Psychology as well.[275] Brown and Herrnstein detailed their proposal in a ten-page plan, which included the rationale for the combined department, its structure, undergraduate concentration requirements, graduate program requirements, and a listing of courses in psychology.[276] Basically, it provided for a Department of Behavioral Sciences with degree programs in Psychology, Sociology, and Social Anthropology.[277]

Two factors motivated the plan. First, there was growing concern among psychologists within the Psychology Department that their department was too narrow.[278] Second, many of the psychologists within Social Relations wished to be affiliated with a more comprehensive psychology program.[279] Brown and Herrnstein approached members of both departments with the idea in the fall of 1967.[280] The faculty strongly disapproved of the plan and rejected it. Although the plan failed, it planted the idea of reorganization in the minds of many faculty members.[281] The spirit of the plan was resurrected the following spring when Social Relations proposed to offer joint appointments to psychologists of the Psychology Department.[282] Social Relations backed off, however, in the face of many objections.[283]

Dissatisfaction with Social Relations ran high among sociologists and social anthropologists. David Maybury-Lewis summarized the feelings of the latter group: "We (nearly all the social anthropologists) felt that Social Relations had become a bureaucratic monster, which hampered rather stimulated interdisciplinary work."[284] It was true. Others had made the point formally at least as far back as the 1963 ad hoc committee report on the future of the behavioral sciences at Harvard. Members of Social Relations devoted far more time to administrative tasks than did members of other departments in the university.[285] Each wing held its own meetings, and all then gathered again for full departmental meetings.[286] The social anthropologists had a triple burden because many of them held joint appointments in the Anthropology Department and were thus required to attend those meetings as well.[287] The meetings of the permanent members of Social Relations were an added burden for senior faculty from all wings.[288] The sprawling nature of the department caused another serious problem that underscored its lack of integration. As the department expanded, faculty members could no longer assess candidates for a permanent appointment outside their own fields when it came to making a recommendation.[289] They simply accepted the recommendation of faculty members in the relevant field.[290] As Homans explained,

> by 1970, though, when it was a question, for instance, of making an appointment in the field of personality psychology, the sociologists and others would simply have to take the word of the psychologists as to which of the candidates was really able. They themselves would not even have heard of their names and were quite unable to judge their published works. This condition is thoroughly unhealthy. The department had simply grown too large.[291]

Restiveness mounted, and predictably Harvard formed a committee to review the situation. Members included the chairmen of Social Relations, Psychology, and Anthropology as well as the "wing chairmen" from within Social Relations and the director of the Center for Behavioral Sciences. This group proposed to reorganize as three departments— Anthropology, Psychology, and Sociology—and to establish a strong committee to regulate and to promote interdisciplinary interests.[292] The plan differed only slightly from the earlier Brown-Herrnstein proposal by giving more autonomy to each department. The Social Relations Department firmly rejected it on April 16, 1968. Obsession with reorganization did not end with this meeting, but other events intervened in 1968–1969 to divert everyone's attention. Social Relations, weakened by scandal and departmental drift, would not escape the end of the decade before reeling from one more body blow.

7

+

The Final Unraveling

*Soc Rel 149 Disrupts
and Sociology Departs*

Everyone is demanding his own piece of turf. Eventually, each professor will have his own department.

—David McClelland

[Social Relations] had ceased being a department in the sense of interacting socially or intellectually.

—Seymour Martin Lipset

Social Relations 148 and 149, undergraduate classes in Social Relations, burst like bombshells over an already restless academic scene.[1] Harvard in the late 1960s was no stranger to student uprisings against the Vietnam War. The wave of protests that first hit Columbia and Berkeley campuses soon rocked Harvard Yard, often supported by the organizing skills of the radical group Students for a Democratic Society. Indeed, Harvard had the largest SDS branch in the country with two hundred members.[2] The years 1967–1969 were turbulent ones at Harvard. In 1967, the SDS held a Dow Chemical recruiter hostage for several hours in Harvard's Mallinckrodt Chemical Building, demanding his written promise that DOW (the maker of napalm used in the Vietnam War) cease interviewing students.[3] Students also demanded the abolition of Harvard's Reserve Officers Training Corps (ROTC) program.[4]

Against this highly charged background, a group of radical graduate students in the summer of 1968 planned a new course, "Social Change in America."[5] They found a sympathetic faculty member in Thomas Cottle, assistant professor in Social Relations, who, in his words, agreed to serve as their "cover."[6] In the "easy style in which these things were once done at Harvard," Cottle took the idea to George Goethals, the vice chairman of the department, who sent a request to Dean Franklin Ford to add the course for the fall semester.[7] An unknown assistant to Dean Ford approved the request automatically, and thus the SDS achieved a "major success" in getting permission for its course, according to Harvard professors Seymour Martin Lipset and David Riesman.[8] It now had an official platform to reach—and to radicalize—large numbers of students.[9] According to one teaching fellow, "Harvard SDS organized Social Relations 148–9. . . . Graduate students, older undergraduates and a few off-campus radicals teach the course in sections."[10]

Social Relations 148, or Soc Rel 148 as it was commonly called, would, according to its prospectus, "examine three of America's central social problems: imperialism, race, and labor."[11] At the first class, organizers added a fourth topic—an overview of radical theory.[12] It was the first course in Harvard's history to have undergraduate instructors.[13] It was popular, attracting 350 students.[14] Early in the semester, rumors circulated that the course sought to convert students to a radical political ideology, that grades would be assigned randomly, and that undergraduates would lead many of the sections.[15] The *Harvard Crimson* reported that course organizer and teaching fellow Michael H. Schwartz told students the instructors were considering a "nonsense" grading system that would determine grades in a random manner unrelated to the quality of course work.[16] Adding to the buzz about Soc Rel 148 was the announcement that Eldridge Cleaver, the Black Panther "minister of information" and presidential candidate of the Peace and Freedom Party, would lecture in the course, even as he was on trial for murder in California.[17]

Social Relations faculty worried that the original plan for the course had not disclosed the plans for random grading.[18] The plan also alarmed administrators. Seeing a flyer for the course, President Nathan Pusey thought it was a spoof.[19] He asked Dean Franklin Ford if the faculty had authorized the course. If so, he had some straightforward questions: "Is it to be a course of scholarly objectivity and high standard? Is it being given by a member of our faculty and will he have control of the content and grading?"[20] Ford relayed the questions to the chairman of Social Relations, Roger Brown, who said the department had concerns but saw value in a course with a stated political position.[21] One student recalled it was not just a "gut" (an easy class, in Harvard parlance) but a "roaring gut," surpassing even the legendary guts of Natural Science 10, Introduction to Geology (commonly "Rocks for Jocks") and History 136, European Oceanic Discovery (commonly known as "Boats").[22] Cottle, the faculty member who fronted for the course, set the standards, believing that "fruitful discussion around a table" had the same value in terms of grading as a term paper.[23] Soc Rel 148 was a popular and provocative course, but it was a mere ripple of controversy compared to the turmoil that erupted over the sequel course that spring, Soc Rel 149.[24]

Jack Stauder, a young instructor in social anthropology, proposed to teach Soc Rel 149, "Radical Perspectives on Social Change." Ostensibly it would cover the same topics as its predecessor, but in greater depth, with sections on topics such as "Leninism," "Sex-Role Oppression in the United States," "Imperialism and the University," and "The American Maelstrom."[25] Enrollment swelled to 758 with forty-five sections.[26] Of these sections, only fourteen were taught by Harvard Corporation appointees, only three of whom were Social Relations graduate students.[27] Nineteen Harvard undergraduates and several Harvard and MIT graduate students constituted the remainder of the teaching staff.[28]

Senior Social Relations faculty had "second thoughts" about Soc Rel 149, questioning Stauder's ability to attest to the competence of the section leaders drawn from other schools.[29] They discussed plans to drop the course, but the *Harvard Crimson* got wind of it and students protested the planned move. Faculty and students debated the merits of the course, but it was like "two streams of consciousness that flowed smoothly past each other."[30] No compromise was reached. One student on the teaching staff threatened, "If you don't let us teach our course, we won't let you teach yours."[31]

Soc Rel 149 coincided with the zenith of the student upheaval that spring. In April 1969, the SDS led a forceful takeover of University Hall, which housed the dean of the Faculty of Arts and Sciences.[32] Upon the request of Harvard's president, Nathan Pusey, four hundred state troopers and local police in full riot gear removed the protestors from University Hall, injuring 45 and arresting 197.[33] In retaliation for the ouster, students engaged in a protest strike that paralyzed the university.[34] Faculty members kept a lookout for three nights over Widener Library amid rumors that the SDS planned to burn it down.[35]

The semester's zeitgeist included students questioning the very premise of the university and seeking a full reorientation of Harvard education.[36] A group of students known as the "Conspiracy against Harvard Education" pushed this agenda with leadership from *Harvard Crimson* president James Fallows (now a celebrated writer at the *Atlantic*) and others.[37] They claimed students felt "discontent, alienation, and unfulfillment" because they "are serving the University's needs, without the University responding to serve theirs."[38] In the trippy language of the day, the *Crimson* exhorted students to attend an informational meeting of "the Conspiracy": "Are you unhappy with the education that Harvard is selling you? Do you want to talk about some far out ideas for changing it?

Come to an open meeting of The Conspiracy against Harvard Education at 7:30 p.m. tonight in Lowell Lecture Hall."[39]

Soc Rel 149's use of uncertified and seemingly unqualified section leaders was only part of the controversy. The most volatile element was the avowed goal of the course to convert students to radical politics. SDS members, who had planned and staffed the course, now had the means to proselytize to hundreds of students.[40] Soc Rel 148–149 provided "an excellent base for organizing within the University," according to one of the planners.[41] The organizers designed the course as a "bridge" between mere detached interest in a politically radical worldview and "a commitment to action in the Movement."[42] That call to arms, as manifested in Soc Rel 148–149, likely contributed to the SDS takeover of University Hall. Steven Kelman, the leader of the Harvard Young People's Socialist League—a rival radical group—believed Soc Rel 148–149 played a crucial role in preparing for the takeover by "indoctrinating a large number of wavering liberal-radical types and especially presenting them with a sense of the strength and invincibility of the New Left steamroller."[43]

Figure 7.1.   Student protestors inside University Hall during the takeover at Harvard, April 9–10, 1969. HUA 969.71 (1), olvwork724078. Harvard University Archives.

Leading by example was Stauder, the only faculty member convicted of trespassing in the University Hall seizure, and thirteen of the section leaders in Soc Rel 149, who were also arrested.[44]

The course's political advocacy bitterly divided the faculty of Social Relations and the wider Harvard community.[45] Supporters within the department claimed the course was an innovative venture, which could scarcely be denied, and they raised the banner of academic freedom, invoking the specter of illegitimate regulation.[46] Critics decried the introduction of political advocacy into an academic community.[47] There was a sentiment at Harvard that Social Relations, still suffering a hangover from the Leary imbroglio, had become a department with loose standards, "one in which not everything, but a lot went."[48] Soc Rel 149 was a flash point for the entire Harvard faculty, adding tension to the already frayed relations between the conservative and liberal "caucuses" that had evolved in response to the general student unrest.[49]

By normal academic standards, Soc Rel 149 was a farce.[50] Instructors uniformly gave honor grades, reading lists (intellectually respectable in some of the sections) were generally narrow and short, and one course recruited students to organize for Cambridge rent control.[51] Reports circulated that liberal and conservative students were harassed in sections for not readily accepting a radical perspective.[52] Some black students claimed they were placed involuntarily in an all-black section.[53] It became a nationwide story. The *Washington Post* ran a two-part article on the controversy, with headlines "Radicalism Course Splits Harvard: Trust Is Gone" and "Student-Led Course Shatters Tradition at Harvard." The article described the "remarkable radical invention" of Soc Rel 148–149 as a course that "twitches every nerve end of conventional academics."[54] Challenged about the competency of the seminar leaders, Stauder responded angrily, "That's a lot of bull——."[55] He complained, "They love to cut things into little categories—specialization—it's crazy, they love to put us down."[56] Questioned about his qualifications to teach a seminar on imperialism, he replied dismissively, "Imperialism is very simple. It screws people. It takes (to teach) a large perspective, which the average academic hasn't got."[57]

The quirky grading approach of Soc Rel 148 carried over to its sequel Soc Rel 149 in the spring semester. Indeed, David Finkelhor, one of the undergraduate architects of the course, opposed giving grades at all: "We would really like not to have grades. Grades are used to socialize people to the industrial system we have."[58] But the department required that grades be given. To foil this oversight, Finkelhor planned to give an A to any student who turned in a paper, a B to any student with regular attendance, and a B– to the rest.[59] One section leader promised a B to everyone, but students could get an A if they requested it; predictably all the students asked for one.[60] James Glassman, an undergraduate and editor of the *Harvard Crimson*, said he probably would give every student who showed up to his seminar the same grade, either an A or a B.[61] He was also willing to accept photographic essays or pen-and-ink drawings in lieu of a paper.[62]

The debate boiled throughout the spring term as course leaders and students fought plans to regulate or to eliminate the course for the following year.[63] Again, the cry of academic freedom and political oppression sounded.[64] The academic year 1968–1969 ended without any resolution, the embers tamped down but still flickering. The SDS had become a spent force but got a last gasp when Harvard gave its representative five minutes to address the June 1969 commencement.[65] The speaker failed, however, to reignite the passions of the previous months. Seniors hissed and booed when he exceeded his time limit.[66] Ultimately he was led off the stage among cries of "throw him out!"[67] The department agreed to offer Social Relations 148 again in the fall of 1969, but it forbade undergraduate and graduate students from teaching if they had been disciplined by the university following the Dow incident and the University Hall occupation.[68] Stauder objected, claiming this would exclude his most committed staff, and he canceled the course.[69] The Soc Rel 148–149 tempest ended just like that. No doubt the restriction played a role, but Roger Brown, then chairman of Social Relations, believed the fervor of the previous year had simply evaporated over the summer.[70]

The crisis passed, but the event sorely weakened the department.[71] As in the case of the Leary-Alpert episode, Social Relations found itself ruptured and ridiculed.[72] But the wounds inflicted by Soc Rel 148–149 were more damaging than the black eye of the psilocybin saga.[73] The latter had pitted faculty members against one another on professional grounds: those arguing the drug experimentation was valuable and protected by academic freedom versus those contending it was a sloppy and dangerous affair, undeserving of being considered serious research. Soc Rel 148–149, however, divided the department politically.[74] The split mirrored the ideological divide of the broader Harvard faculty: a liberal caucus supporting the militant students and a conservative group siding with President Pusey and viewing the radicals as a threat to liberal democracy.[75] The tumult created by the course took a grave toll.[76] Several faculty members were afflicted with ulcers; one suffered a heart attack.[77] One faculty critic of the course received death threats from a radical student.[78]

Some faculty in the department believed Social Relations would have disintegrated eventually, but the Soc Rel 148–149 shambles dealt the final blow.[79] For one senior member in Social Relations, sociologist George Homans, the course was the "precipitating cause" of the department's downfall.[80] He excoriated the department's leaders, "otherwise good men," for allowing it to be taught at all.[81] The uproar deepened the political and personal schisms that overlay the already tense professional disagreements.[82] Mired in mistrust and "permanent ill feelings," members of the department abandoned hope of reaching consensus on any issue.[83] For Homans, "it came to the point at which I could not bear to listen in department meetings to the bleatings and wafflings of the foolish, hypocritical, and self-righteous 'liberals.'"[84] The blunt, longtime nemesis of Talcott Parsons believed Social Relations would have fragmented "sooner or later," but for him Soc Rel 149 made life in the department intolerable: "I wanted out, and one of the purest pleasures I have enjoyed from no longer being a member of the Department of Social Relations is my freedom from ever having to pay the slightest serious attention to such people again. If they will stick to their business, they are often good fellows, but as academic statesmen, they make me puke."[85] Homans was eager to leave, and so were other sociologists.[86] Despite his acid-tongued attacks, however, he denied being the instigator of pushing sociologists to abandon the department. Rather, he credited sociologist Harrison White for promoting the theory that sociology would be better off in its own department.[87] According to White, sociology would have the ability to "wangle more new appointments" as an independent department rather than as a mere wing of Social Relations.[88]

AN UNCOMFORTABLE EXAMINATION BY OUTSIDERS

Preceding the drama of Social Relations 148–149, another event agitated the department. In 1968, Dean Franklin Ford appointed an ad hoc committee to assess the current state of the behavioral sciences, particularly Social Relations. The members were James Davis (a sociologist from Dartmouth), Neal Miller (a psychologist from the Rockefeller Foundation), Fred Eggan (a social anthropologist from the University of Chicago), and Robert K. Merton (a sociologist from Columbia University).[89] After a single brief visit, the committee essentially put the matter back in the lap of the affected departments.[90] The committee agreed that "some kind of restructuring seems called for but that it will be better if this can be achieved slowly by a series of small changes rather by a single, large drastic overhauling."[91] It proposed strengthening psychology, anthropology, and sociology, but at the same time establishing "a number of quota faculty posts to be held in a common pool . . . to meet general needs, and especially to keep alive the possibility of making distinguished interdisciplinary appointments."[92] The committee recommended keeping the status quo, saying, "Meanwhile 'Social Relations' (including sociology and those from the other disciplines who might choose to belong) should continue as a separate viable entity."[93]

It was felt that the most appropriate first step would be for you [Dean Ford] to refer the matter back to the Executive Committee in William James Hall (and presumably through its members to the various departments involved) with the request that they now: (1) Reconsider the matter (in light of any instructions you may wish to give them from the discussion you heard in the *ad hoc* committee); and (2) then suggest what seems to them the most promising new kind of organization for their several disciplines.[94]

One member of the committee, James Davis, a professor of sociology from Dartmouth, wrote separately to the dean. He found it "bad policy to have two Ph.D. programs feeding into the same employment market," i.e., two types of anthropologists and two types of psychologists coming out of Harvard.[95] It "confuses applicants and potential employers and dissipates the strength of the two teaching units."[96] He said this criticism implies reunifying anthropology and "less clearly" reunifying psychology.[97] With respect to psychology, he acknowledged that "no university anywhere has managed to work out a comfortable niche for social psychology, though the statistical mode is to have it in psychology."[98]

Davis also noted "the demography of the situation" in which several of the men opposed to a reunification of the departments would be retiring soon, suggesting a phased solution was worth contemplating.[99] He thought "re-departmentalization" was the obvious trend, but he was disappointed to see the end of Social Relations and its attempt to surmount parochialism in conventional departmental structures.[100] Davis offered his analysis that "the flaw in Social Relations was not that it combined social sciences but that it built the content of those unions into its structure."[101] He believed that the trend in social science was interdisciplinary, but "not in terms of one grand integrated edifice."[102] Rather, he viewed it as "constantly changing collaborations between specialties" and that the "natural unit of collaboration" is not the department, but groups of two or three men within departments.[103]

Sociologists saw the committee's comments as critical of their wing, heightening the uneasiness already felt within that group.[104] They thought sociology at Harvard was unnecessarily constrained in two respects. First, the national trend in the discipline was toward alliance with economics and government, not psychology and cultural anthropology.[105] Second, confined within a department dominated by psychologists, they felt that their freedom to develop such macro links to economics and government was severely inhibited.[106] One senior member of Social Relations, Robert Freed Bales, a social psychologist, described these developments:

A good deal of the sociology taught at Harvard since the formation of the Department of Social Relations has been social psychology. . . . However, times are changing as all the disciplines within the department undergo natural growth. A new center of gravity for sociology may be forming around the large-scale focus linking with government, economics, international studies, modernization of underdeveloped societies, and the like.[107]

Davis, in his letter to Dean Ford, also cited the need for sociology at Harvard to recognize these changes and to recruit the relevant faculty. He praised the faculty of luminaries but criticized the department for neglecting the teaching of research methods:

> Indeed, I can think of only two or three men in the world whose reputation exceeds that of Parsons, Homans, Bales, Lipset, and White, and you seem to be on the track of at least one of them. Rather, we felt that the department has a high ratio of desert to meat and potatoes. In particular, it needs a man in demography and ecology, the intellectual foundation for the burgeoning applied areas of "urbanism" and "social change." It is my further opinion that the department has not excelled in teaching its graduate students research methods, as opposed to theory. This may be why the research productivity of Harvard Ph.D.'s in Sociology has sometimes been disappointing.[108]

Talcott Parsons made his feelings known prior to the meeting of the ad hoc committee, seemingly trying to blunt any attempt to justify the breakup of the department into its constituent elements.[109] He told Roger Brown, chairman of Social Relations, "I think the most important thing I want to say is that I am skeptical of the formula of a straight and direct reversion to the pattern of three totally independent departments in the Social Relations area."[110] He acknowledged "the pull" that the Anthropology Department had on the social anthropologists in Social Relations, but he maintained that current intellectual trends would make relationships between anthropologists and sociologists "more important in the future."[111] He also recognized the desire among some of his fellow sociologists, most notably Alex Inkeles, to cultivate relationships with government, history, and economics.[112] To Parsons this was not, however, a reason for Sociology to secede from Social Relations: "There is still a strong burden of proof on him who would break sociology out of Social Relations in the name of it's [sic] freedom to cultivate this sort of connection."[113] The biggest problem in Social Relations, according to Parsons, was social psychology.[114] Parsons worried that "sociology would be greatly impoverished" by the loss of contact with social psychology, and he doubted that social psychologists would "feel comfortable in a pure, old-style Department of Psychology where a certain category of experimentalists carried relatively the heaviest weight."[115]

SOCIOLOGISTS HEAD FOR THE EXITS

In 1969, a group of frustrated sociologists called for an independent Department of Sociology. Led by Professor Ezra Vogel, they met informally and, according to the *Harvard Crimson*, decided to "make plans for the creation of an autonomous sociology department."[116] The first step was appointing a committee "to work out feasible plans for the new department with other concerned groups—undergraduates, graduates, and faculty members in other wings of the Social Relations Department."[117] Vogel cited three reasons behind the move. First, sociology as a discipline had been relatively weak under Social Relations in comparison with sociology departments at large universities, such as Columbia and Berkeley.[118] Second, sociology was moving from psychology and cultural anthropology toward more macro problems: "The frontiers in sociology now seem to be in the consideration of social problems and public policy," and sociologists wanted more contacts with economists, political scientists, and historians.[119] Third, the Social Relations Department had become large and difficult to administer.[120] An overarching concern of the sociologists—although one not specified in the *Crimson* article—was their small size in contrast to comparable universities.[121] As the only disciplinary group subsumed wholly under the banner of Social Relations, they wanted more faculty appointments and greater access to the dean.[122]

One of the highest-profile faculty members in the Vogel group was Alex Inkeles, who was increasingly impatient about the plight of his discipline at Harvard.[123] The third-most-senior sociologist in the department, he believed sociology was constrained in making the needed macro links to government and economics. Inkeles criticized Social Relations and the harm it was doing to sociology, and as early as 1968 he had argued internally that sociology should break with Social Relations and become independent.[124] In the middle of the growing debate and discord, Inkeles accepted the offer of a professorship at Stanford University. Although he had advocated for an independent Department of Sociology at Harvard, he left for a position that was not in sociology but rather was a university professorship in the School of Education.[125] The departure of one of Harvard's most prominent sociologists created a panic among those who remained.[126]

Occurring against the background of concern over their small size and ever-weakening ties with the other disciplines in Social Relations, the abrupt departure of Inkeles was the last straw for the sociologists.[127] Within days, they hatched secession plans.[128] The psychologists and anthropologists within the department feared the ramifications of such a move, and the department became consumed with even more meetings, discussions, and hand-wringing.[129] Sociologist Harrison White, chairman of Social Relations, noted the harmful effects of the constant debate in his annual report for the year: "There seemed to be fewer beginnings of major new efforts, and perhaps a slackening of interest in basic scientific work. Another year or so of turmoil might be more costly than would be immediately apparent."[130]

In April 1970, under White's leadership, the sociologists proposed leaving Social Relations to become an independent Department of Sociology.[131] Echoing the observations of Bales and the concerns of Inkeles and the Vogel group, White said that sociology at Harvard needed to move beyond its ties to social psychology and to focus on its links to other disciplines with a broader focus.[132] Other universities were moving in this direction, and he implied that Harvard was missing this trend. Ironically, this argument was the same one Parsons had used in the 1940s to justify the creation of Social Relations—Harvard would be left behind in a wider movement. White believed Harvard should establish a "simple" new department untethered to psychology, one free to develop relations with other more relevant disciplines:

> Sociology remains entwined with psychology, especially social psychology, but the balance shifts toward intellectual interests shared with history, government, economics, and area studies. Even the new work concerned with small groups and individual attitudes is related much more explicitly to nuances of the broader institutional setting—whether with an eye to policy relevance (Matza, Berkeley) or to building new axiomatics for theory (Davis, Dartmouth; Garfinkel, UCLA). An appropriate framework for the new trends is a simple new department, in broad agreement on these new directions but with flexibility for individual members to build special ties to a wide variety of fields.[133]

He also believed a stand-alone Sociology Department would have an easier time attracting the funding necessary to build these new networks and alliances with other disciplines: "More resources will be needed and can be much more easily sought—funds can be raised more effectively—by such a department, not drained of time, energy, and attention by cumbersome existing arrangements with largely psychological specialties."[134]

Psychology professor David McClelland proposed an alternative.[135] Rather than disaggregate Social Relations into three departments (Sociology, Anthropology, and Psychology), he advocated adding a fourth—a Department of Social Psychology.[136] This new department would include personality, social, and developmental psychology. The social psychologists opposed reuniting with the experimental psychologists they had fled in 1946. After three days of caucusing and one special meeting of the Social Relations faculty, no consensus was reached on the direction forward, but there was one dramatic moment amid all the wrangling.[137]

Talcott Parsons rose above the din to address the full faculty of the department that he had helped to create with the promise of a new and revolutionary science.[138] With Allport and Kluckhohn deceased, and Murray long retired, Parsons was the last of the Levellers, standing alone before the disheartened members of a department in disarray. He reminded them of the great traditions of Social Relations, but he had concluded that its dissolution was unavoidable.[139] Then he turned and "slowly left the meeting room (some said, with tears in his eyes)."[140]

Reluctant to lose what many perceived as the core of the department, the non-sociologists nevertheless acceded to the wish of their colleagues to become independent.[141] The split became official on July 1, 1970.[142] It was a grievous event for Parsons. Not only was his dream child dismembered, but his old adversary George Homans assumed the chairmanship of the new Department of Sociology. Social psychologists took the news hard, worried about the future of their own discipline. Social psychologist Thomas Pettigrew said, "What's left is a kind of 'Remnant Relations.' It makes very little intellectual sense and is extremely bad for the development of social psychology."[143] He suggested keeping social psychology in the department with clinical and developmental psychology, while spinning off social anthropology to the Anthropology Department, but that proposal met with little enthusiasm beyond the social psychologists.[144] His backup plan was to create a separate Department of Social Psychology.[145] Fellow psychologist David McClelland disagreed with Pettigrew. He argued, "We could make sense out of the department [Social Relations] if we wanted, but if Pettigrew pushes hard enough for independence, he can win."[146] Exasperated, McClelland said, "Everyone is demanding his own piece of turf. Eventually, each professor will have his own department."[147]

Sociology leaving Social Relations was big news at Harvard, but it also garnered national attention. The *New York Times* covered the transition, describing it as "the end of an experiment that had united sociologists with scholars from other disciplines whose work was closely related."[148] It quoted Homans, the new chairman, who cited two developments for the move. First, Social Relations "had grown so large (50 professors and 601 undergraduate majors) that it had become unwieldy" and faculty interests "so diverse that intellectual and social interaction had become difficult."[149] Second, sociology had shifted in emphasis toward areas of urban and racial problems and away from the "micro scale" analysis of individual behavior, thus drawing sociologists closer to political scientists and economists than the anthropologists and psychologists in Social Relations.[150] The article also quoted David Riesman, who agreed that sociologists were becoming more closely aligned with economists: "We wanted to give people a chance to work on economic development without having to take a course in personality theory."[151] Previously, Riesman had resisted the change, maintaining that the Social Relations Department was a good model for interdisciplinary work.[152] Fellow Harvard sociologist Seymour Martin Lipset thought Social Relations was simply no longer viable, "It had ceased being a department in the sense of interacting socially or intellectually."[153] Two days later, the *New York Times* had more to say about sociology leaving Social Relations, as a book reviewer cheekily linked the timing of its departure with the recent publication of *The Coming Crisis of Western Sociology* by Alvin W. Gouldner: "The crisis of Western sociology enters its second day. Next month, almost as though the professors had been reading Alvin W. Gouldner's book, Harvard will re-establish an independent Department of Sociology, ending 24 years of interdisciplinary group-grope (sociologists, psychologists, anthropologists) under the 'social relations' umbrella."[154]

The sudden loss of sociology crippled the department.[155] As the only "complete" discipline within Social Relations, many in the faculty considered it central to the department.[156] Now all the constituent elements of the department were eroding. Social Relations had dropped clinical psychology, and its ties with social anthropology were weakening. Most of its anthropologists held joint appointments with the Anthropology Department, and many were increasingly pulled in that direction.[157] Similarly, some psychologists had been increasing their ties with the Psychology Department. The formal exit of two of the original four subfields (sociology and clinical psychology) was compounded by the loss of several founding members. Amid such disintegration, a commitment to interdisciplinary collaboration was wishful thinking. Indeed, Roger Brown, chairman of Social Relations from 1967 to 1970, declared that the notion of integration had "become a joke" because there was no core curriculum or even a single course required of all graduates.[158]

DEAN JOHN DUNLOP DEMANDS ORDER

Clearly, Social Relations needed revision, and it did not lack for suggestions.[159] A flurry of meetings and discussions yielded nearly a dozen plans but no constructive action. Schemes of every sort circulated through the corridors of William James Hall.[160] One envisaged a Department of Social Psychology and Sociology with faculty members of Social Relations free to affiliate with either this new creation or the Departments of Anthropology, Psychology, or Sociology.[161] Another proposed a broadly construed Department of Social Psychology. Some plans harked back to the Brown-Herrnstein proposal of 1967—a broad department with several subunits.[162] Yet another suggestion advocated separate Departments of Social Anthropology, Social Psychology, and Psychology.[163] Some plans emphasized interdisciplinary collaboration (such as an executive committee to regulate this activity), while others laid out well-defined departmental boundaries.[164]

What was left of Social Relations (social anthropology and developmental, social, and personality psychology) was overwhelmed by a torrent of proposals, amendments to proposals, counterproposals, meetings, memoranda, and arguments about reorganization.[165] Confusion reigned—departmental minutes were not recorded for the year, and most business was conducted through the various wings.[166] Some at Harvard now referred facetiously to the Department of Social Relations as the Department of "Residual" Relations.[167] In the fall of 1971, President Pusey appointed yet another ad hoc committee, this time to advise specifically on what should be done about the Psychology Department at Harvard. The committee suggested that Psychology's focus had narrowed and that the only remedy was a merger with the psychologists of the Social Relations Department. Dean John Dunlop—an economist specializing in labor economics—supported a straightforward solution along these lines. For such a fusion, however, leadership was needed from an individual acceptable to both groups. Each group was extremely apprehensive about what they might lose in such a union. The consensus candidate for the chairman of a reconstituted Department of Psychology was Gardner Lindzey, vice president of the University of Texas and a nontenured member of Social Relations from 1948 to 1953.[168] Lindzey had received his PhD in the Psychology Department, and both factions respected his work.[169]

Finally, amid the cacophony, Dean Dunlop summoned the permanent members of Social Relations and Psychology to a meeting.[170] The question of a merger was the agenda. The members could not agree, largely because members of the social psychology wing of Social Relations objected. Convinced that the only sensible move was a merger, Dunlop pressured the group toward agreement. In a decisive display of decanal power, he broke the resistance by reminding the group that "the dean makes up the budget for your departments."[171] The role of a Harvard dean in the life cycle of Social Relations was pivotal; Dunlop's move in ending the department was the bookend to Buck's move in creating it. As David Riesman noted at the time, "it is interesting that top administration was important in both the creation and the ending of the Department: in Paul Buck's central role about which Talcott [Parsons] has often commented, and in John Dunlop's at the present."[172] The added twist is that Dunlop also had played a role in the creation of Social Relations, having coauthored as a young Economics professor—along with department founders Parsons and Kluckhohn and others—the most important document in the department's prehistory, "Toward a Common Language for the Area of Social Science."[173]

At the May 16, 1972, meeting of the Faculty of Arts and Sciences, the chairman of the Psychology Department, Edwin Newman, presented a motion formalizing the merger and establishing the Department of Psychology and Social Relations.[174] George Goethals, chairman of Social Relations, seconded the motion. It passed with language expressing the hope that the new department would remain true to the interdisciplinary ideals of the defunct Department of Social Relations:

> That the Department of Social Relations and the Department of Psychology be combined administratively into a single department, broad and inter-disciplinary in character, effective July 1, 1972. It is intended that the new department retain the programs and breadth of interests represented by the two former departments and that for the present it retain the names of each as the Department of Psychology and Social Relations.[175]

The rest of the motion defined the scope of the new department. It would have three graduate degree programs: (1) experimental psychology, (2) personality and developmental studies, and (3) social psychology. These three graduate programs would also constitute the areas of specialization in the Department of Psychology and Social Relations.[176] The undergraduate programs and degrees of the two existing departments would be transferred intact to the new department, and undergraduate concentrators in either department could continue in their present program for their degrees as now defined.[177] Faculty members would agree on a "department-wide undergraduate program" involving faculty members from all three areas of specialization and offering "options for both a broad interdisciplinary concentration and more focused specialization."[178]

In certain respects, the death of Social Relations paralleled its birth, and not only in the key role played by senior administration. Just as movements within the disciplines fueled the creation of the department, new academic affiliations and alliances made the Social Relations setup incompatible with the interests of younger faculty members with no loyalty to its original interdisciplinary goal. The topics that had united the founders and early faculty of Social Relations, such as small-group interaction, personality, and values, were now out of favor. They were replaced by macro-oriented themes of inquiry into social and urban problems, more closely linked to government and economics than psychology and social anthropology. Sociologists felt this change most acutely. After years of proposals, lobbying, and wrangling, administration and many faculty members finally admitted that Social Relations was no longer viable. The forceful intervention by Dean Dunlop in 1972 to end Social Relations recalled Dean Buck's decisive action in 1946 to create it.

8

Conclusion and Summary

As we say, it was a good try, and a life of twenty-four years is a long one for a noble experiment.

—George Homans

I am . . . convinced that the Social Relations Department was a creative enterprise.

—David Riesman

Shifts in academic styles, personal and professional dissatisfactions, and the advent of younger faculty interested in new affiliations played crucial roles in the dissolution of the department just as they had in its formation. The integration, at any level, of several disciplines (however closely related) is no mean task; establishing a new science based on such synthesis is harder still.[1] In addition, Social Relations hoped to develop a graduate program based on an integrated curriculum. The department's fundamental flaw was failing to integrate its component disciplines. The single most ambitious attempt to this end, the Carnegie Project on Theory and its work product, *Toward a General Theory of Action*, failed, although for a brief time the book served a useful catalyzing function within the department. The absence of a theoretical integration precluded the fulfillment of the larger goal of the department—developing a scientific field of social relations. The hubris of the founders in seeking to create the Social Relations Department before there was a tested theory to support a discipline of Social Relations is striking. Harvard's decision to implement such a plan is equally remarkable. In the early 1940s, the Levellers

159

believed they could see a new behavioral science emerging on the horizon. In the end, however, it was a mirage.

To be fair, optimism was not entirely unwarranted given the wartime research in social science, which was decidedly interdisciplinary in character. In the academy, a movement also was afoot, with Yale establishing its interdisciplinary Institute of Human Relations. And the Levellers themselves had produced work supportive of the new approach: Parsons's 1937 *The Structure of Social Action*; the 1939 trial undergraduate program in the area of social science; and the group's 1941 manifesto, "Toward a Common Language for the Area of Social Science."

The professors and their sympathetic dean pushed forward, driven in equal parts by ego and exigency. The Levellers were confident they could create a new science. Dean Paul Buck wanted to mend the rifts within the Psychology and Sociology Departments. Murray, Allport, and Parsons were desperate to escape their antagonists. Kluckhohn was unhappy in Anthropology. Buck may have felt the need to prevent the rising stars in those disciplines from leaving Harvard; Parsons was poised to decamp for Northwestern. Allport also cited the further urgency to reach a decision on a new framework given the end of the war and the rush of returning students.[2]

Parsons, the most ambitious among the group to establish a new social science, felt supremely confident of the prospects, if only they had the space and freedom to do so: "In the meantime a very big scientific development has been rapidly gathering force. . . . I will stake my whole professional reputation on the statement that it is one of the really great movements of modern scientific thought . . . like all really big pioneer movements it is not understood by the majority of the established high priests of social science."[3] He rolled the dice only to lose. But Parsons had not gambled away his reputation on this one wager. He remained one of the preeminent sociologists of the twentieth century. Upon his retirement in 1973, the *New York Times* wrote, "Both disciples and detractors would agree that no other living scholar has had more impact on modern social thought and theory than Professor Parsons."[4] The article continued: "Talcott Parsons achieved an almost immortal status as a man of thought. Even younger sociologists, many of whom differ with him sharply about sociology, accord him a religious-like reverence before going on to do things their own way, much the way Italian Catholics genuflect before the Pope and then vote Communist."[5] He educated three generations of sociologists, several of whom became leading scholars: Robert A. Merton, Kingsley Davis, Clifford Geertz, Robert Bellah, Neil J. Smelser, Bernard Barber, Jesse Pitts, and Renée Fox.[6] He left behind, if not a Parsons school, at least a Parsonian theory that, while controversial, remains a landmark of sociology. The article concluded: "His name weaves in and out of the literature of sociology and related disciplines like Einstein in physics and Freud in psychology."[7]

Unable to develop a unifying theory or even a common language for the different disciplines after its founding, Social Relations was left with an unwieldy structure that was eroded over time by many factors: the department's loss of its original leadership and the failure to groom new leaders believing in the mission; the withdrawal of Professor Jerome Bruner and others into their own pursuits; the uneasiness of new faculty members working outside the traditional disciplinary framework; uncongenial trends in academia, such as sociology moving away from psychology; an academic job market that continued to be organized around traditional disciplines; and the divisive effects of parochial events such as the Leary-Alpert episode, the Social Relations 148–149 controversy, and the move to William James Hall.[8] Howard Gardner, a 1971 PhD in the Social Relations Department, described the department's demise in terminology familiar to its disciplines. He noted the "psychology of ego" of the founding faculty, the "sociology of departmental power," and the "ethnography of a particular set of characters" who shared a vision but failed to build the necessary "infrastructure" to sustain it or to cultivate the younger faculty to lead it.[9]

Social Relations was not sustainable as a department because it had no theoretical foundation uniting its disciplines.[10] As Lawrence Nichols noted, essentially it was a "marriage of convenience" that ended the dysfunction in the Psychology and Sociology Departments and freed Allport, Murray, and Parsons to pursue their ideas in a department of their own.[11] Kluckhohn, who was unhappy in Anthropology, was similarly liberated. Social Relations faculty member David Riesman commended the department for providing a haven for the "beleaguered" social and clinical psychologists in the Psychology Department.[12] He cautioned critics not to underestimate the severity of the "periodic savageries of intradepartmental warfare, particularly as it involves vulnerable graduate students," that caused these marginalized professors to flee.[13] He compared them to "exiles from an oppressive regime" who concluded it was useless to stay and fight for improved conditions in their original home.[14] Despite its theoretical failings, he viewed Social Relations as a success: "I am, for example, convinced that the Social Relations Department was a creative enterprise and that the psychologists who helped make it so would not have done much to alleviate the more monolithic aspects of the Psychology Department had they remained in it."[15]

Even George Homans, the longtime critic of Parsons and his efforts to unify Social Relations around structural functionalism, eulogized the department as a "noble experiment" that had provided faculty a "rich intellectual environment" and an unusually wide latitude to pursue their interests.[16] He was grateful for the freedom to teach sociology, anthropology, social psychology, and even medieval English history.[17] As for his colleagues, however, he had mixed views:

> It put me in touch with many good and interesting men and women—as well as with some consummate asses. Some of them were both interesting and asinine at the same time. The department constrained me not at all, and ended at the right time. From my point of view—and here I can take no other—this seems a pretty good record. Let us shed a tear or two for the passing of the department, but not a flood.[18]

In reflecting on the Social Relations Department's trajectory, founder Gordon Allport likened enacting change in a university, particularly one as old as Harvard, to "a task as cumbersome as moving a cemetery."[19] He admitted the department had failed to find a formula that successfully blended interdisciplinary training and disciplinary concentration, a problem for the department since the first proseminar of 1946. Writing in 1968, he conceded defeat: "The problem of the department has been to balance the needs of specialization with a measure of desired cross-disciplinary training. Our policies have followed a wavering course between specialism and integrationism, with no satisfactory proportion yet discovered."[20] Graduate students in those early years—Birnbaum, Geertz, and Vidich, among others—testified to the lack of any meaningful interdisciplinary grounding.

Dean Buck and the Levellers underestimated the strength of the ties, emotional and professional, to the original disciplines.[21] The loyalty to one's discipline compounded the lack of theoretical integration, confounding interdisciplinary efforts.[22] David Riesman believed the nature of these attachments in academia bedeviled integration: "Anyone who thinks that vested interests are all economic knows nothing of intellectual life; investments in ideas, whether in the form of ideologies or of disciplines involve what we have made of ourselves, and this is something no dean or chancellor, acting as mediator, can easily buy off."[23] Such bonds not only hindered the pursuit of integration of research and instruction but fatally complicated the organizational arrangements of the department. Committed to the establishment of an interdisciplinary science of social relations, the founders nonetheless retained their professional identities.[24] It could scarcely be otherwise: until replaced with something new, scholarly communication depends on traditional, known methods of operation.[25] This is evident in the reliance on "wings" for intradepartmental organization, eventually evolving until they resembled departments, complete with the trappings of chairmen, "departmental" meetings, appointments, and budgetary concerns.[26] Even in the selection of subsequent members, traditional, disciplinary concerns prevailed.[27]

Each wing held fast to the desire to be a leader in its field and selected new members accordingly, thus sacrificing opportunities to bring into the enterprise potential contributors to integration.[28] Important, too, was the necessity of mounting degree programs consonant with the existing academic job market.[29] Neither aspiring students nor faculty could renounce their professional identities in favor of the label "social relationist" when no field of social relations existed to provide them with the security and rewards open to members of established disciplines.[30] Howard Gardner witnessed the phenomenon firsthand, saying that for many of his fellow graduate students, "the pull toward safe and secure traditional departments was powerful."[31] Indeed, for him this was the department's fatal flaw.

> And there, perhaps, lies the major explanation for the decline and demise of Soc Rel. Within universities, individual departments, and especially their doctoral training programs, are powerful entities. With the passage of time (and the passing of the pioneers), up-and-rising scholars wanted to be known as developmental psychologists, or sociologists of religion, or physical anthropologists—and not as experts in "Soc Rel" or even as synthesizing or qualitative social scientists.[32]

Chicken and egg—the field required practitioners, but practitioners required a field, and students felt uncomfortable pursuing an untried professional identity.[33] As early as the 1950s, David Riesman had identified—before joining the Social Relations faculty—the tendency among students in interdisciplinary ventures at the Department of Social Relations at Harvard or the Committee on Human Development at the University of Chicago to seek the security of an established discipline:

> In both cases, while the pioneering professors continued to wander at will, the students now coming along sometimes seek refuge in a disciplinary third generation identity at the first signs of nonacceptance of newly invented or marginal identities, and these departments oscillate between Balkanization and overserious straining for imperial unity. Such, I would suppose, is the dialectic of all but the most utopian culture-contact situations.[34]

He believed that students in an interdisciplinary program are torn between two competing pressures. The first is "their wish for a clear-cut departmental identity—one they would have no difficulty explaining to themselves and to all comers."[35] The second is the "pressure on them against being discipline-bound and isolationist."[36] Riesman's reference to an "overserious straining for imperial unity" was a dig at Parsons's leadership of Social Relations—although it was not enough of a drawback to keep Riesman from subsequently joining the department.[37]

By 1978, however, Riesman said he had underestimated the degree to which Social Relations was able "to recruit 'third-generation' graduate students and junior faculty who were superior to those who would have been recruited separately had there not been a joint department."[38]

> That is, because the Harvard label provided some security in what was an expanding academic market, and because the individual wings also provided sponsorship within specific disciplines, graduate students and junior faculty coming to Social Relations had the best of both worlds: they could succeed within traditional academic parameters, but they were also available for those unique and especially interesting academic opportunities which sought broadly trained people who were not undisciplined, but who had been exposed to more than a single discipline.[39]

As an example of such unique opportunities for graduates of Social Relations, Riesman cited how his son Paul's PhD in anthropology with training in sociology allowed him to secure a position in the "truly joint Sociology-Anthropology Department at Carleton College in Minnesota where the sociological and anthropological members provide a common curriculum, common examination, and steep themselves in the classics of each other's fields."[40] He noted the unique departmental needs at Carleton and stressed that financial considerations played a role. Someone with training in only one of his son's disciplines "would have been much less valuable to a small liberal arts college which cannot afford to recruit overly-specialized individuals, although it insists on scholarly and research-minded faculty."[41]

Even late in the careers of Social Relations graduates and faculty, there were unusual cross-disciplinary opportunities. Norman Birnbaum, a PhD in sociology and one of the earliest graduates of Social Relations, is a case in point. After introducing sociology to the curriculum at Oxford and serving as chairman of the Sociology Department at Amherst, among other positions at notable universities, he went on to teach for twenty-two years at Georgetown University Law Center, hardly a typical trajectory for a sociologist. Then there is Jerome Bruner, a PhD graduate in Psychology at Harvard and an early faculty member of Social Relations, who found himself teaching Lawyering Theory and a Colloquium on Culture and the Law at New York University Law School. This was at age seventy after a long and celebrated career teaching cognitive psychology at Harvard and Oxford.

The question is, however, how many cases of a career path enjoyed by Paul Riesman existed? When that scenario succeeded, it certainly validated aspects of the unique training of a social relations PhD, but it is only anecdotal evidence, and it may have been the exception rather than the rule. What about PhDs from the Departments of Psychology and Anthropology at Harvard that were made narrower in the wake of the formation of Social Relations? Were those graduates at a disadvantage vis-à-vis graduates from universities that had intact departments because the Harvard PhDs in psychology, for example, lacked—or were perceived to lack—adequate exposure to social and clinical psychology? Jerome Bruner, among others, was convinced that Social Relations harmed the discipline of psychology at Harvard and graduate students in both the Departments of Social Relations and Psychology, who needed to know more about the "other" psychology.

As the only intact discipline within the department, sociology may have fared better in some respects as a component of Social Relations than social psychology, clinical psychology, and cultural anthropology. It is difficult to assess empirically. Sociology professor David Riesman believed it was weaker after leaving Social Relations. He observed—eight years after sociology abandoned Social Relations—that students enrolling in Harvard's Sociology Department were, with notable exceptions, "inferior" to those who were attracted to the sociology wing of the Social Relations Department.[42] Of graduate students, he queried,

> Why should they come to Harvard's small Sociology Department, in spite of the halo effect Harvard itself offers, when they might go to the much larger departments, amounting to mini-universities, such as the one at Michigan where they can get a complete program, for example in social psychology, training in survey research, and urban opportunities offered by the Detroit Area Survey?[43]

As for undergraduates in the Sociology Department, Riesman expressed disappointment in 1978 at the quality of their senior honors theses. He blamed the "narrowness" of the department, however, rather than the students, stating, "It is hard for a river to rise higher than its source."[44]

Sociology remained in the shadows of History, Economics, and Government at Harvard, a recurring theme in its relatively short history. In the 1930s and 1940s, Parsons and the Levellers contended that sociology had more explanatory power for human behavior than government, history, or economics, and thus should—and could—become the preeminent discipline of the social sciences. Contrast that bold vision, however, with the observation of graduate student Norman Birnbaum in the late 1940s during the golden age of Social Relations that its "people were running twice as hard to catch up" to the big three at Harvard to have something relevant and important to contribute in the post–World War II period of American hegemony.[45] When Riesman joined the faculty in 1959, he was surprised by the defensiveness of Social Relations vis-à-vis the older social sciences.[46] By the 1970s, sociology's reality reflected Birnbaum's and Riesman's hard-eyed assessments rather than Parsons's dream.

Like a kid brother tagging along after older siblings, pestering them to play in their games, sociology continued a decades-long chase to join the team. The elder social sciences, however, simply did not want it in their clubhouse. When sociology left the Department of Social Relations, the "great powers," as Riesman called History, Economics, and Government at Harvard, refused to cooperate with the new Department of Sociology on joint appointments or in any other way.[47] He found this ironic given that one of the reasons sociology left Social Relations was because its submersion there prevented it from establishing such linkages.[48] The attitudes of the great powers toward sociology seemed to have changed little since 1950 when history professor Oscar Handlin publicly mocked the discipline as "the study of material left over from government and economics."[49]

Both faculty and students were vulnerable to the realities of an academic world stubbornly structured around traditional disciplines.[50] The failure to demonstrate that its separate components could be synthesized quickly into a viable scientific field foredoomed Social Relations.[51] Without such integration, the intended interdisciplinary character of the department sank beneath the myriad pressures of professional and disciplinary loyalties.[52] The disciplinary pressures and vested interests cited by Riesman and Gardner are elements of what social psychologist Donald Campbell called the "'ethnocentrism of the disciplines', i.e., the symptoms of tribalism or nationalism or in-group partisanship in the internal and external relations of university departments, national scientific organizations, and academic disciplines."[53] The distinct ethnocentricities of the disciplines within Social Relations impeded attempts at integration and the subsequent maintenance of an interdisciplinary program.[54] Social Relations failed to overcome such symptoms on many levels: personal, professional, theoretical, and structural.[55]

Given its ambitious goal of unifying the behavioral sciences, the failure of Social Relations stands out clearly. The department did have significant achievements in other areas, however. But what exactly is the measure of an academic department's success? Comparisons between traditional departments in terms of curriculum, graduates, and faculty yield one basis for judgment. It is difficult to formulate an objective standard of appraisal; departments are good or bad relative to each other. A unique department such as Social Relations, however, cannot be measured in a comparative fashion. Campbell warned that "a false model of departmental collaboration arises in evaluating interdisciplinary research and training programs."[56] He believed there was a biased assumption in such comparisons that all "unidisciplinary" programs or single-discipline departments are unqualified successes.[57] He argued that the fairest way to assess an interdisciplinary undertaking is to consider not only whether it met its original goals, but also to evaluate its productivity and whether it produced new methods or ideas of quality in comparison to what a single-discipline department accomplished.[58] As an example, he defended Yale's twenty-year-long interdisciplinary Institute of Human Relations against its critics:

> Perhaps it achieved less than was promised in the proposals which funded it, but certainly its record of productivity and significant innovation exceeded any unidepartmental aggregate of similar size. In like manner, unproductive or unintegrated interdisciplinary ventures are often reported as though all unidisciplinary ventures were successful, when in fact, for them too, but a minority are.[59]

Applying this standard to Social Relations, Campbell found it had succeeded in producing students and recruiting as faculty "some outstanding interdisciplinary specialists," even though its stated goal of providing competency in an interdisciplinary field proved unworkable, receiving only "lip service" after its abandonment in practice.[60] He cited the steady move toward unidisciplinary content in its graduate training programs as evidence of the return to "traditional patterns of narrowness."[61]

Since its demise in 1972, Social Relations still gets mentioned occasionally, sometimes in pedestrian ways, other times in surprising circumstances. Social Relations lost its last official Harvard vestige in 1986—forty years since its founding—when Harvard shortened the name of the Department of Psychology and Social Relations to the Department of Psychology.[62] It was an unceremonious administrative deletion, merely a rubber-stamp approval by the Faculty of Arts and Sciences.[63] A *Harvard Crimson* article attributed the move to a "decades-long drift away from an interdisciplinary approach" in Psychology and toward what one professor termed a "quasi-biological" view of the discipline.[64] Evoking the old debate within Psychology at Harvard, it cited the trend of emphasizing the hard-science biotropic areas of the discipline at the expense of the "social" aspects.[65] It was the same intellectual battle within Psychology at Harvard since William James and Hugo Munsterberg had fallen out in the 1920s, or the more consequential fracture between sociotropes and biotropes in the 1930s and 1940s.

Buoying the biotropic side of Psychology in the 1980s was the rise in studies of the biological and neurological bases of behavior, areas aligned closely with the natural sciences. The article cited the work of two young psychology professors using computers to study the biological causes of human behavior. Older professors in the department opined that such work "would not even have been recognized as psychological research 20 years ago."[66] The faculty who had been members of the Social Relations Department bemoaned the shift in academic trends and the loss of the name "Social Relations" from the Department of Psychology and Social Relations. Robert F. Bales, a social psychologist, blamed the department for not maintaining the sociotropic side of psychology: "It has been a long-time failure of our department to make sufficient appointments on the social relations side. The old guard has thinned to the point where there's no point in keeping the name."[67] David Riesman said the message to the academy was that Harvard no longer was interested in the social, less scientific side of psychology: "What they're now saying to the world is what we now are is a straight psychology department. The name change would say to an outsider, 'We don't want to deal with the dreams, the murky, the unclear anymore.'"[68] The shadowy world of the unconscious that so captivated Henry Murray, Clyde Kluckhohn, and other members of Social Relations interested in psychoanalysis was reduced to a historical footnote. Psychology at Harvard had returned to a decidedly biotropic orientation.

Although the name Social Relations had disappeared from official view, the 1990s saw a spike in public interest in one of its founders. Henry Murray's name burst into the news when his final series of disturbing experiments from 1959–1962 came to light. The world learned that Timothy Leary and Richard Alpert were not the only professors in Social Relations that had engaged in dubious research on Harvard students in that era. Murray conducted a series of mentally and emotionally brutalizing experiments on undergraduates. It started innocently enough. Harvard sophomores received an innocuous invitation, asking if they would be "willing to contribute to the solution of certain psychological problems" by serving as subjects in a series of experiments or tests averaging two hours per week.[69] The experiment's bland title, "Multiform Assessments of Personality Development among Gifted College Men," belied its harsh heritage—the test Murray had designed for the OSS in World War II to assess how well prospective spies could withstand the traumatic and severe stress of mock interrogations.[70]

It was not a one-off event: each student spent nearly two hundred hours in the experiment over the three-year period. Each student provided "hundreds of pages of information about himself, his beliefs, his family, his college life and development, his fantasies, his hopes and dreams."[71] Murray himself described that the goal of the research was focused on the "degree of anxiety and disintegration" in the individual and to design procedures to predict how subjects will "react in the course of a stressful dyadic proceeding."[72] Murray directly or through intermediaries also approached certain students who met the profile of being either exceptionally well adjusted or highly alienated. One such recruited student was a shy and alienated seventeen-year-old from a blue-collar family. To preserve the anonymity of the subjects, each was assigned a code name; Murray gave this student the code name "Lawful." Lawful was Theodore Kaczynski, who would become infamous as the "Unabomber" serial killer. He mailed or delivered sixteen package bombs, injuring twenty-three people and killing three, over a period of seventeen years. He was a student at Harvard College from 1958 to 1962, having entered when he was only sixteen years old.

Kaczynski said, "I had been talked or pressured into participating in the Murray study against my better judgment."[73] Kaczynski's attorneys obtained partial records of the Murray experiments, assembling so-called mitigating evidence for the jury to spare the defendant's life.[74] In a 1998 statement, Kaczynski said of the Murray experiments, "We were told to engage in debate about our personal philosophies, and then found that our adversary in the debate subjected us to various insults that, presumably, the psychologists helped him to concoct. It was a highly unpleasant experience."[75] He told other of his attorneys that the research "was the worst experience of my life."[76] The obvious question, of course, is why Kaczynski continued participating if the experience was so bad. His attorneys asked, "In that case, Ted, why didn't you quit? Why did you keep going back to the lab week after week, for three years?" He replied, "I wanted to prove that I could take it. That I couldn't be broken."[77] And thirty-six years later, among the few personal possessions in his tiny and austere Montana cabin, Kaczynski had kept a copy of an article Murray published on the experiment.[78] In a 1999 interview, he recalled that 1962, his final year in Murray's experiment, marked the beginning of his feeling of a "sense of disillusionment with the system."[79]

Murray had sent Kaczynski's mother a consent form for her son to participate in the research because he was only seventeen at the time. As noted, the form failed to describe the experiment in any meaningful way. She signed it, presuming that the researchers had her son's best interests at heart. Indeed, poignantly, she even thought it might help her socially awkward son adjust to life at Harvard: "At the time, I was glad to give my parental consent, feeling Teddy had some adjustment issues. I hoped these nice psychologists might help him."[80] One of Murray's research associates expressed misgivings about the ethical shortcomings of the project: "Later, I thought: We took and took and used them and what did we give them in return?"[81] And the purpose of the experiment was not clear, even to Murray's own graduate assistants. Murray sought funding to write a book based on the data collected, but there is no evidence he even started it. Another assistant, Kenneth Keniston, said he was unsure what the goals were, adding, "Murray was not the most systematic scientist."[82]

Murray's files relating to his research on Kaczynski are housed at the eponymous Henry A. Murray Research Archive at Radcliffe and, according to its director, will never be released.[83] "We have a very strong policy of maintaining the confidentiality of people who participate in studies archived here. This particular file has been permanently removed, with the reason being that we cannot protect its confidentiality anymore."[84] It is unlikely that any additional information about the Murray research and Kaczynski will ever become available, unless Kaczynski himself chooses to discuss it further.

In 2003, the *Atlantic* published an article with the sensational title, "Harvard and the Making of the Unabomber," which suggested that Murray's experiments contributed to Kaczynski's revenge fantasies and "anti-technology ideology."[85] Kaczynski's brother David drew no causal link between Murray's experiments and the bombings, but he held Murray and Harvard responsible for inflicting psychological harm on his brother:

> What I do know is that my brother was a guinea pig in an unethical and psychologically damaging research project conducted at Harvard University where he attended college in the early 1960s. While it is true my brother suffers from paranoia, it is also true that he fell victim to a conspiracy of psychological researchers who used deceptive tactics to study the emotional and psychological trauma on unwitting human subjects. My brother was harmed by psychologists who recognized—at least tangentially—that they were hurting him yet made no attempt to undo or ameliorate the harm they'd caused to their young and vulnerable subject. Thus, it would be fair to say that my brother's paranoia had a reference point in reality.[86]

This episode, of course, played no role in the dissolution of Social Relations. And even David Kaczynski stopped short of alleging any causality between Murray's experiments and Kaczynski's acts of violence. Nonetheless, it cast a shadow on Social Relations and one of its prominent founders, Henry Murray, highlighting the paucity of research standards for human subjects in the 1950s and 1960s. Murray's harsh experiments on an undergraduate without any meaningful informed consent not only tarnished the otherwise illustrious career of this towering figure in American psychology, but once again—like the Leary episode, and even the Soc Rel 149 fiasco—suggested it was a department where anything went.

The Murray-Kaczynski connection also revived interest in Murray's strange personal life. A 1993 biography of Murray described in salacious detail the forty-year sadomasochistic relationship that the married Murray maintained with Christiana Morgan, a wealthy—also married—woman who shared Murray's intense interest in Jung.[87] The revelations subjected the venerable psychologist to ridicule. A reviewer of the biography in the *New York Times* described it as a story of how the patrician, wealthy, and talented Murray "wound up in a mythologized sadomasochistic relationship replete with whips and knives."[88] She continued: "Unfortunately, the tale of Murray and Morgan's lurid relationship is by turns tiresome and comical. We see this pair relentlessly documenting their overblown version of a new psychology based on the dyad. . . . One can only wince at this middle-aged couple drawing 'drops of each other's blood into a small cup' and 'drinking to the unity of two in one.'"[89]

The publicity about Murray's experiment on Kaczynski renewed interest in Murray's sadomasochism, with one writer suggesting it had fueled in part the brutalizing nature of his experiments on Kaczynski and other subjects. In *A Mind for Murder: The Education of the Unabomber and the Origins of Modern Terrorism*, Alston Chase claims, "Murray's science was an extension of his private life."[90] Any such link is speculative, of course, but the sensational details of Murray's personal life becoming public fodder certainly dimmed the reputation of one of the founders of the Social Relations Department. Murray's biography described how his "disturbing intellectual and emotional limitations" led him to leave "a swath of damaged lives: his wife's, his lover's, his lover's husband and more."[91] Alston and others added Ted Kaczynski to the list.

Since the dissolution of Social Relations, calls to reorganize academia along interdisciplinary lines have surfaced. Critics of traditional disciplines liken them to "disconnected silos" that limit advances and innovations. Mark Taylor of Columbia University in a 2009 *New York Times* essay advocated abolishing academic departments as currently organized.[92] He argued for "problem-focused programs" with broad topics such as the mind, body, law, and information.[93] Jerry A. Jacobs of the University of Pennsylvania responded to Taylor in the *Chronicle of Higher Education*, warning against embracing "interdisciplinary hype" and "interdisciplinarity" as a panacea.[94] As a "cautionary tale from the past," Jacobs cited the Department of Social Relations and its failure "to unify anthropology, psychology and sociology."[95]

Despite failing in its grand ambition to create a new social science, Social Relations drew distinguished faculty and produced accomplished graduates.[96] Their work, while not overwhelmingly interdisciplinary, was nonetheless among the most important created anywhere and continues to stand as a significant legacy.[97] Its faculty included familiar luminaries: Gordon Allport, Henry Murray, Talcott Parsons, Clyde Kluckhohn, Florence Kluckhohn, David McClelland, George Homans, Brendan Maher, David Riesman, Jerome Bruner, Herbert Kelman, Robert F. Bales, Thomas Pettigrew, Cora DuBois, Roger Brown, George Miller, Erik Erikson, Laurence Wylie, Eleanor Maccoby, Evon Z. Vogt, Alex Inkeles, Seymour

Martin Lipset, John Whiting, Beatrice Whiting, Harrison C. White, Samuel Stouffer, and Frederick Mosteller.

Social Relations also produced graduates who became notable scholars in its constituent disciplines, and in some cases outstanding interdisciplinary specialists in keeping with the department's original ideals.[98] It is through their success that the department achieved another important legacy. It is impossible to do justice to the many accomplished PhD graduates of Social Relations, but even a small and incomplete sampling provides a sense of the department's impact on the academy: Robert N. Bellah (sociology), Stanley Milgram (social psychology), Norman Birnbaum (sociology), Renée Fox (sociology), Clifford Geertz (social anthropology), Arthur Vidich (sociology), Neil Smelser (sociology), Gardner Lindzey (social psychology), Thomas Pettigrew (sociology), Barbara Rogoff (developmental psychology), Harold Garfinkel (sociology), Charles Tilly (sociology), Ezra F. Vogel (sociology), Bertram Cohler (clinical psychology), Mark Granovetter (sociology), Richard Price (social anthropology), Michelle Zimbalist Rosaldo (cultural anthropology), Renato Rosaldo (cultural anthropology), Barry Wellman (sociology), Richard Shweder (social anthropology), Claude Fischer (sociology), and Howard Gardner (social/developmental psychology).

It is difficult to prove, as William Sims Bainbridge has claimed, that "the Soc Rel perspective still pervades the disciplines it temporarily brought together, like a stratum of bedrock, seldom noticed but always influential."[99] Some graduates of Social Relations reflected their unusual training in their cognitive styles and subsequent research, and presumably they passed elements of this on to their students. Howard Gardner—a self-described "staunch believer in the mission of the Department of Social Relations"—believed this process occurred in his own work at the Harvard Graduate School of Education as the Hobbs Professor of Cognition and Education and in that of several of his fellow graduates in Social Relations.[100] He cited as mentors three members of Social Relations, who were themselves highly interdisciplinary in their work: Jerome Bruner, David Riesman, and Erik Erikson.[101] He traced his intellectual lineage to Riesman and Erikson: "I'm still using their ideas for what I do."[102] And of Bruner, he said, "He is the person who has had the most influence both on what I do, and how I do it."[103]

To Gardner, Social Relations continues to make its unique approach felt in the academy through its graduates, who "still carry the Soc Rel banner."[104] In addition to himself, he cited classmate Rick Shweder as one who moves easily "among the social sciences" and writes in the synthesizing style of Riesman and Erikson.[105] He also cited Claude Fischer as a classmate who believed in the mission of Social Relations and applied a broad lens to his research.[106] He identified earlier graduates Robert Bellah,

Clifford Geertz, and Neil Smelser, who brought their distinctive training to bear in their work.[107] Gardner described himself and all these scholars as seeking to "tackle the big issues and to draw on the concepts and tools of several disciplines."[108] Throughout their careers, they remained "broad synthesizers in a world of disciplinarians."[109] Via such a process of transmission, the spirit of Social Relations lives on.[110] From its golden age through a gradual decline hastened by two scandals, and on to its ultimate disintegration, Homans's "noble experiment" and Riesman's "creative enterprise" endure as fitting epitaphs for the Department of Social Relations.

Notes

ABBREVIATION

HUA   Harvard University Archives

CHAPTER 1

1. Harvard University, *The Behavioral Sciences at Harvard*, faculty committee report (Cambridge, MA: Harvard University Press, 1954), 25.

2. Gordon W. Allport, *The Person in Psychology: Selected Essays* (Boston: Beacon, 1968), 398–99.

3. Ibid.

4. Ibid.

5. Talcott Parsons, *Department and Laboratory of Social Relations, Harvard University: The First Decade, 1946–1956* (chairman's report, 1956, HUA), 16 n. 1.

6. Allport, *The Person in Psychology*, 399.

7. Patrick L. Schmidt, "Towards a History of the Department of Social Relations, Harvard University, 1946–1972" (undergraduate honors thesis, Harvard University, 1978), 1.

8. David C. Engerman, "The Rise and Fall of Wartime Social Science: Harvard's Refugee Interview Project, 1950–1954," in *Cold War Social Science: Knowledge Production, Liberal Democracy, and Human Nature*, ed. Mark Solovey and Hamilton Cravens (New York: Palgrave Macmillan, 2012), 28.

9. Nils Gilman, *Mandarins of the Future: Modernization Theory in Cold War America* (Baltimore, MD: Johns Hopkins University Press, 2003), 79.

10. Schmidt, "Towards a History of the Department of Social Relations," 1–2.

11. Ibid.

12. Ibid.

13. Ibid.

14. E. L. Pattullo, "About," Department of Psychology, Harvard University, https://psychology.fas.harvard.edu/about.

15. Schmidt, "Towards a History of the Department of Social Relations," 2.

16. Jamie Cohen-Cole, *The Open Mind: Cold War Politics and the Sciences of Human Nature* (Chicago: University of Chicago Press, 2014), 83.

17. George Homans, interview by Patrick L. Schmidt and Julia Moore, October 20, 1977, tape recording, HUA; Barry V. Johnston, *Pitirim A. Sorokin: An Intellectual Biography* (Lawrence: University of Kansas Press, 1995), 313 n. 29; George Caspar Homans, *Coming to My Senses: The Autobiography of a Sociologist* (New Brunswick, NJ: Transaction, 1984), 294–96, providing background on Homans's claim and the degree to which the personal dissatisfaction of the founders of Social Relations with their original departments, and animosity between and among faculty members, was the predominant force that brought them together.

18. Schmidt, "Towards a History of the Department of Social Relations," 3.

19. Ibid.

20. Ibid.

21. Harvard University, *The Behavioral Sciences at Harvard*, 20–21.

22. Talcott Parsons, interview by Patrick L. Schmidt and Julia Moore, October 17, 1977, tape recording, HUA; Schmidt, "Towards a History of the Department of Social Relations," 4.

23. Schmidt, "Towards a History of the Department of Social Relations," 4.

24. Henry Murray, interview by Patrick L. Schmidt and Julia Moore, October 30, 1977, tape recording, HUA; Schmidt, "Towards a History of the Department of Social Relations," 5.

25. Parsons, interview, October 17, 1977; Schmidt, "Towards a History of the Department of Social Relations," 5; Johnston, *Pitirim A. Sorokin*, 137.

26. Ibid.

27. Johnston, *Pitirim A. Sorokin*, 137 n. 28.

28. Schmidt, "Towards a History of the Department of Social Relations," 5.

29. Barry V. Johnston, "The Contemporary Crisis and the Social Relations Department at Harvard: A Case Study in Hegemony and Disintegration," *American Sociologist* 29, no. 3 (Fall 1998): 30. For a description of Murray's conversion to psychoanalysis, see Rodney G. Triplet, "Henry A. Murray: The Making of a Psychologist?," *American Psychologist* 47, no. 2 (February 1992): 301–2.

30. Talcott Parsons, interview, October 17, 1977; Schmidt, "Towards a History of the Department of Social Relations," 5; Henry Murray, interview, October 30, 1977.

31. William S. Sahakian, *History and Systems of Psychology* (New York: Wiley, 1975), 302.

32. Talcott Parsons, interview, October 17, 1977; Schmidt, "Towards a History of the Department of Social Relations," 6; Edwin Newman, interview by Patrick L. Schmidt and Julia Moore, October 21, 1977, tape recording, HUA.

33. Triplet, "Henry A. Murray," 302.

34. Henry Murray, "What Should Psychologists Do about Psychoanalysis?," *Journal of Abnormal and Social Psychology* 35 (1940): 154.

35. Ibid., 152.

36. Ibid., 153.

37. Ibid.

38. Ibid.

39. Sheldon M. Stern, "William James and the New Psychology," in *Social Sciences at Harvard, 1860–1920: From Inculcation to the Open Mind*, ed. Paul H. Buck (Cambridge, MA: Harvard University Press, 1965), 180, 186.

40. Ralph B. Perry, *The Thought and Character of William James* (Boston: Little, Brown, 1936), 228.

41. Stern, "William James and the New Psychology," 217–18.

42. Ibid., 222.

43. Ibid., 219.

44. Ibid., 222.

45. Samuel Eliot Morrison, *The Development of Harvard University, 1869–1929* (Cambridge, MA: Harvard University Press, 1930), 220.

46. Schmidt, "Towards a History of the Department of Social Relations," 7.

47. Ibid.

48. Ibid.

49. Edwin G. Boring, *Psychologist at Large: An Autobiography and Selected Essays* (New York: Basic Books, 1961), 39–40.

50. Ibid., 56–57.

51. Rodney G. Triplet, "Harvard Psychology, the Psychological Clinic, and Henry A. Murray: A Case Study in the Establishment of Disciplinary Boundaries," in *Science at Harvard University: Historical Perspectives*, ed. Clark A. Elliott and Margaret W. Rossiter (Cranbury, NJ: Associated University Press, 1992), 235–36.

52. Joseph Lee, "Report of Committee to Visit the Department of Philosophy and Psychology, in Reports of the Visiting Committee of the Board of Overseers of Harvard College: For the Academic Year 1932–33," Harvard University, 151; Triplet, "Harvard Psychology," 236–37.

53. Ibid.

54. Triplet, "Harvard Psychology," 237.

55. Ibid.

56. Boring, *Psychologist at Large*, 56–57.

57. Ibid.

58. Cohen-Cole, *The Open Mind*, 74.

59. Ibid.

60. Ibid.

61. Ibid., 71.

62. Ibid.

63. Ibid.

64. Ibid.

65. Ibid., 76.

66. Ibid., 72–73.

67. Ibid., 145; Skinner, the world-renowned psychologist and author of the best-selling *Beyond Freedom and Dignity*, received a PhD in psychology at Harvard

in 1931. He remained as a researcher in the department until 1936, leaving but returning as a professor in 1948, centering his work on behavioral psychology. Skinner's greatest influence was the philosophy of behaviorist John Watson, who dismissed the concept of the mind as a "pre-scientific superstition" incapable of being studied empirically. "Historical Faculty, B. F. Skinner," Department of Psychology, Harvard University, https://psychology.fas.harvard.edu/people/b-f-skinner.

68. Cohen-Cole, *The Open Mind*, 122.

69. Ibid.

70. Ellen Herman, *The Romance of American Psychology: Political Culture in the Age of Experts* (Oakland, CA: University of California Press 1995), 8.

71. Schmidt, "Towards a History of the Department of Social Relations," 8.

72. Ibid.

73. Ibid.

74. Murray, "What Should Psychologists Do about Psychoanalysis?," 154.

75. Ibid.

76. Johnston, "The Contemporary Crisis," 30.

77. Murray, "What Should Psychologists Do about Psychoanalysis?," 154.

78. Ibid.

79. Joseph Adelson, "Against Scientism," review of *Endeavors in Psychology: Selections from the Personology of Henry A. Murray*, ed. Edwin. S. Shneidman, *New York Times*, August 9, 1981, https://www.nytimes.com/1981/08/09/books/against-scientism.html.

80. Ibid.

81. Triplet, "Harvard Psychology," 234–35.

82. Jerome Bruner, *In Search of Mind: Essays in Autobiography* (New York: Harper & Row, 1983), 35.

83. Triplet, "Harvard Psychology," 235.

84. Ibid.

85. Henry A. Murray, "Professor Murray Describes Department of Abnormal Psychology," *Harvard Crimson*, January 12, 1929, 1.

86. Ibid., 4.

87. Ibid.

88. Ibid.

89. Homans, *Coming to My Senses*, 143.

90. Triplet, "Henry A. Murray," 299.

91. Schmidt, "Towards a History of the Department of Social Relations," 9.

92. Ibid.

93. Ibid., 9–10.

94. J. F. Brown, "The Position of Psychoanalysis in the Science of Psychology," *Journal of Abnormal and Social Psychology* 35 (1940): 42–43.

95. Ibid.

96. Ibid., 30.

97. Forrest G. Robinson, *Love's Story Told: A Life of Henry A. Murray* (Cambridge, MA: Harvard University Press, 1992), 187.

98. Ibid.

99. Ibid.

100. Ibid.

101. Ibid.

102. Ibid.

103. B. F. Skinner, interview by Patrick L. Schmidt and Julia Moore, October 28, 1977, tape recording, HUA; Schmidt, "Towards a History of the Department of Social Relations," 11; Henry Murray, interview, October 30, 1977.

104. Robinson, *Love's Story Told*, 184.

105. Murray, interview, October 30, 1977; Schmidt, "Towards a History of the Department of Social Relations," 11; Skinner, interview, October 28, 1977.

106. Ibid.

107. Rodney G. Triplet, "Henry A. Murray," 303.

108. Triplet, "Harvard Psychology," 237.

109. Skinner, interview, October 28, 1977; Schmidt, "Towards a History of the Department of Social Relations," 11.

110. Schmidt, "Towards a History of the Department of Social Relations," 11.

111. Ibid.

112. Ibid.

113. Allport, *The Person in Psychology*, 391.

114. Ibid.

115. Bruner, *In Search of Mind*, 35–36.

116. Ibid., 35.

117. Ibid., 35–36.

118. Ibid., 36.

119. Ibid.

120. Allport, *The Person in Psychology*, 383.

121. Ibid.

122. Ibid.

123. Ibid.

124. Ibid.

125. Ibid., 84.

126. Ibid.

127. James William Anderson, "An Interview with Henry Murray on His Meeting with Freud," *Psychoanalytic Psychology* 34, no. 3 (2017): 325–26.

128. Ibid., 326.

129. Ibid.

130. Ibid.

131. Ibid.

132. Ibid.

133. Schmidt, "Towards a History of the Department of Social Relations," 12.

134. Ibid.

135. Allport, *The Person in Psychology*, 387–89.

136. Richard I. Evans, *Gordon Allport: The Man and His Ideas* (New York: E. P. Dutton, 1971), 18.

137. Schmidt, "Towards a History of the Department of Social Relations," 12.

138. Ibid., 13.

139. Allport, *The Person in Psychology*, 393–94.

140. Johnston, "The Contemporary Crisis," 30.

141. Triplet, "Harvard Psychology," 238–43.
142. Ibid., 238.
143. Ibid., 239.
144. Ibid., 240.
145. Ibid., 239.
146. Ibid., 240.
147. Ibid., 229.
148. Ibid., 229–30.
149. Adelson, "Against Scientism."
150. Triplet, "Harvard Psychology," 240.
151. Robinson, *Love's Story Told*, 184–85.
152. Ibid., 209.
153. Ibid., 225.
154. Ibid.
155. Ibid.
156. Ibid.
157. Gordon W. Allport to James B. Conant, January 6, 1937, HUA.
158. Ibid.
159. Ibid.
160. Karl S. Lashley to Edwin G. Boring, January 6, 1937, HUA.
161. Triplet, "Harvard Psychology," 241.
162. Ibid.
163. Ibid.
164. Ibid., 242.
165. Ibid., 243.
166. Robinson, *Love's Story Told*, 227.
167. Ibid., 226–27.
168. Ibid., 227.
169. Ibid., 227.
170. Cohen-Cole, *The Open Mind*, 83.
171. Gordon W. Allport, "The Psychologist's Frame of Reference" (presidential address delivered at the Forty-Seventh Annual Meeting of the American Psychological Association, Berkeley, California, September 7, 1939), *Psychological Bulletin* 37, no. 1 (1940): 1–28, https://www.sapili.org/subir-depois/en/ps000009.pdf.
172. Ibid., 1.
173. Ibid., 4.
174. Ibid.
175. Ibid., 9.
176. Ibid.
177. Ibid., 8.
178. Ibid.
179. Ibid., 16.
180. Ibid.
181. Ibid.
182. Ibid.
183. Ibid., 16.
184. Ibid.

185. Ibid., 6.
186. Ibid., 8.
187. Ibid., 10.
188. Ibid.
189. Ibid.
190. Allport, *The Person in Psychology*, 33–34.
191. Robert L. Church, "The Economists Study Society: Sociology at Harvard, 1891–1902," in Buck, *Social Sciences at Harvard*, 21.
192. Ibid., 18.
193. Ibid., 54.
194. Ibid., 18–21.
195. Ibid., 21.
196. Ibid.
197. Ibid.
198. Ibid., 18–19.
199. Ibid., 18.
200. David B. Potts, "Social Ethics at Harvard, 1881–1931: A Study in Activism," in Buck, *Social Sciences at Harvard*, 116.
201. Ibid., 116.
202. Ibid., 115–16.
203. Ibid.
204. Ibid., 114.
205. Ibid., 115.
206. Ibid., 119–20.
207. Ibid., 120.
208. Ibid.
209. Ibid., 121.
210. Ibid., 122.
211. Ibid.
212. Ibid., 123.
213. Johnston, *Pitirim A. Sorokin*, 58.
214. A. Lawrence Lowell to Professor Richard C. Cabot, February 9, 1926, Records of the Committee on Sociology and Social Ethics, quoted in Johnston, *Pitirim A. Sorokin*, 58.
215. Ibid., 59.
216. Ibid., 57; Schmidt, "Towards a History of the Department of Social Relations," 19.
217. Ralph Barton Perry, "Sociology and Social Ethics," n.d., 3, Records of the Committee on Sociology and Social Ethics, HUA, quoted in Johnston, *Pitirim A. Sorokin*, 57–58.
218. Johnston, *Pitirim A. Sorokin*, 55–56.
219. Potts, "Social Ethics at Harvard," 123–24.
220. Ibid., 125.
221. Ibid., 124–25.
222. Ibid., 125–26.
223. Robert K. Merton, "Remembering the Young Talcott Parsons," *American Sociologist* 15 (1980): 69, quoted in Johnston, *Pitirim Sorokin*, 62–63.

224. Johnston, *Pitirim A. Sorokin*, 62–63.
225. Schmidt, "Towards a History of the Department of Social Relations," 19.
226. Talcott Parsons, interview, November 11, 1977; Schmidt, "Towards a History of the Department of Social Relations," 19.
227. Ibid.
228. Schmidt, "Towards a History of the Department of Social Relations," 19.
229. Talcott Parsons, interview, October 17, 1977; Schmidt, "Towards a History of the Department of Social Relations," 19.
230. Ibid.
231. Johnston, *Pitirim A. Sorokin*, 70, 100.
232. Schmidt, "Towards a History of the Department of Social Relations," 20.
233. Ibid.; Johnston, *Pitirim A. Sorokin*, 93; William Sims Bainbridge, "The Harvard Department of Social Relations," in *Leadership in Science and Technology: A Reference Handbook* (Thousand Oaks, CA: Sage Publications, 2012), 498.
234. Johnston, "The Contemporary Crisis," 28–29.
235. Daniel Bell, "Talcott Parsons: Nobody's Theories Were Bigger," *New York Times*, May 13, 1979, E9.

CHAPTER 2

1. Patrick L. Schmidt, "Towards a History of the Department of Social Relations, Harvard University, 1946–1972" (undergraduate honors thesis, Harvard University, 1978), 20.
2. Talcott Parsons, "On Building Social Systems Theory: A Personal History," *Daedalus* 99, no. 4 (1970): 835.
3. Talcott Parsons, *Essays in Sociological Theory* (Glencoe, IL: Free Press, 1949), 351.
4. Schmidt, "Towards a History of the Department of Social Relations," 21.
5. Ibid.
6. Ibid.; Talcott Parsons, interview by Patrick L. Schmidt and Julia Moore, October 17, 1977, tape recording, HUA; Henry Murray, interview by Patrick L. Schmidt and Julia Moore, October 30, 1977, tape recording, HUA.
7. Schmidt, "Towards a History of the Department of Social Relations," 21.
8. Talcott Parsons, "Clyde Kluckhohn and the Integration of Social Science," in *Culture and Life: Essays in Memory of Clyde Kluckhohn*, ed. W. Taylor, J. Fischer, and E. Vogt (Carbondale: Southern Illinois University Press, 1973), 32.
9. Talcott Parsons, *Department and Laboratory of Social Relations: The First Decade, 1946–1956* (chairman's report, 1956, HUA), 11–12.
10. Parsons, "Clyde Kluckhohn," 32; Forrest Robinson, *Love's Story Told: A Life of Henry A. Murray* (Cambridge, MA: Harvard University Press, 1992), 179. For a discussion of Pareto's influence on Parsons, see Joel Isaac, *Working Knowledge: Making the Human Sciences from Parsons to Kuhn* (Cambridge, MA: Harvard University Press, 2012), 162–64. For background on Pareto and Henderson's influence on Henry Murray, see Forrest Robinson, *Love's Story Told*, 79–182.
11. Isaac, *Working Knowledge*, 32.
12. Ibid.

13. Ibid., 33.

14. Ibid.

15. Isaac, *Working Knowledge*, 164; Schmidt, "Towards a History of the Department of Social Relations," 22; Parsons, *Department and Laboratory of Social Relations*, 12.

16. Schmidt, "Towards a History of the Department of Social Relations," 22; Parsons, *Department and Laboratory of Social Relations*, 12.

17. Ibid.

18. Ibid.

19. Ibid.

20. Ibid.

21. Ibid.

22. Robert White, interview by Patrick L. Schmidt and Julia Moore, December 1, 1977, tape recording, HUA; Schmidt, "Towards a History of the Department of Social Relations," 23; Parsons, *Department and Laboratory of Social Relations*, 12; J. T. Dunlop et al., "Toward a Common Language for the Area of Social Science" (unpublished memorandum, Harvard University, 1941), in the Tozzer Library collection, Harvard University. For a summary of this attempt to develop a common conceptual scheme, see Isaac, *Working Knowledge*, 165–67.

23. Parsons, "Clyde Kluckhohn," 32.

24. Isaac, *Working Knowledge*, 165.

25. Dunlop et al., "Toward a Common Language," 4.

26. Ibid., 5.

27. Ibid.

28. Ibid., 4.

29. Ibid.

30. Isaac, *Working Knowledge*, 167.

31. Ibid.

32. Schmidt, "Towards a History of the Department of Social Relations," 23.

33. Ibid.

34. Ibid.; Henry Murray, interview by Patrick L. Schmidt and Julia Moore, October 18, 1977, tape recording, HUA; Parsons, *Essays in Sociological Theory*, 42.

35. Schmidt, "Towards a History of the Department of Social Relations," 23.

36. Ibid.

37. Ibid., 23–24.

38. Ibid.; Robert White, interview, December 1, 1977; David Riesman to Patrick L. Schmidt, May 23, 1978 (author's files), 1.

39. Gordon W. Allport, Clyde Kluckhohn, O. H. Mowrer, H. A. Murray, and Talcott Parsons to Paul H. Buck, June 10, 1943, HUA; Schmidt, "Towards a History of the Department of Social Relations," 24.

40. Allport et al. to Buck, June 10, 1943, 1.

41. Ibid.

42. Ibid.

43. Ibid., 2.

44. Paul H. Buck to G. W. Allport, C. K. M. Kluckhohn, O. H. Mowrer, H. A. Murray, and Talcott Parsons, June 11, 1943 (copy to Dean Jones, July 6, 1943), HUA.

45. Ibid.
46. G. W. Allport, C. K. M. Kluckhohn, O. H. Mowrer, H. A. Murray, and T. Parsons, "Confidential Memorandum on the Reorganization of the Social Sciences at Harvard," September 1, 1943, HUA; Schmidt, "Towards a History of the Department of Social Relations," 24.
47. Allport et al., "Confidential Memorandum," 1.
48. Ibid.
49. Ibid., 31.
50. Ibid., 5.
51. Ibid.
52. Ibid.
53. Isaac, *Working Knowledge*, 164.
54. Allport et al., "Confidential Memorandum," 31.
55. Ibid., 8.
56. Ibid., 9.
57. Ibid., 8.
58. Ibid.
59. Ibid.
60. Ibid.
61. Ibid., 6.
62. Ibid.
63. Ibid.
64. Ibid.
65. Ibid.; Parsons, *Department and Laboratory of Social Relations*, 13.
66. Allport et al., "Confidential Memorandum on the Reorganization of the Social Sciences at Harvard," 6.
67. Ibid.
68. Ibid.
69. Ibid.
70. Gordon W. Allport to Edwin G. Boring, September 27, 1944, HUA.
71. Parsons, interview, October 17, 1977; Schmidt, "Towards a History of the Department of Social Relations," 25; Gene M. Lyons, *The Uneasy Partnership: Social Science and the Federal Government in the Twentieth Century* (New York: Russell Sage Foundation, 1969), 118.
72. Parsons, *Department and Laboratory of Social Relations*, 13; Schmidt, "Towards a History of the Department of Social Relations," 25.
73. Uta Gerhardt, *Talcott Parsons: An Intellectual Biography* (Cambridge, UK: Cambridge University Press, 2002), 132; Uta Gerhardt, "A World from Brave to New: Talcott Parsons and the War Effort at Harvard University," *Journal of the History of the Behavioral Sciences* 35, no. 3 (1999): 263–64.
74. Schmidt, "Towards a History of the Department of Social Relations," 25.
75. Ibid.
76. Ibid., 26.
77. Ibid.
78. Ibid.
79. Ibid.
80. Ibid.

81. Gordon Allport to Edwin G. Boring, March 23, 1944, HUA; Schmidt, "Towards a History of the Department of Social Relations," 26–27.

82. Ibid.

83. Ibid.

84. Ibid.

85. Ibid.

86. Ibid.

87. Ibid.; Schmidt, "Towards a History of the Department of Social Relations," 25.

88. Gordon W. Allport to Paul Buck, July 24, 1944, files of E. L. Pattullo, director, Center of Behavioral Sciences, Harvard University (author's files), 1.

89. Ibid.

90. Ibid.

91. Ibid., 2.

92. Ibid.

93. Gordon W. Allport to E. G. Boring, September 27, 1944, HUA.

94. Ibid.

95. Ibid.

96. Ibid.

97. Ibid.

98. Barry V. Johnston, *Pitirim A. Sorokin: An Intellectual Biography* (Lawrence: University of Kansas Press, 1995), 151–52.

99. Ibid.

100. Talcott Parsons to Paul H. Buck, April 3, 1944, HUA, 4.

101. Ibid.

102. Ibid., 1.

103. Ibid., 2.

104. Ibid.

105. Ibid.

106. Ibid.

107. Ibid.

108. Ibid.

109. Ibid.

110. Ibid.

111. Ibid.

112. Ibid.

113. Ibid.

114. Ibid.

115. Ibid.

116. Ibid., 3.

117. George Homans, interview by Barry Johnston, March 11, 1986, cited in Johnston, *Pitirim A. Sorokin*, 316 n. 86.

118. Talcott Parsons, interview by Patrick L. Schmidt and Julia Moore, November 1, 1977, tape recording, HUA; Johnston, *Pitirim A. Sorokin*, 316 n. 86.

119. Johnston, *Pitirim Sorokin*, 163.

120. Ibid., 165.

121. Ibid., 163.

122. Ibid., 162.
123. Ibid.
124. Ibid., 164.
125. Ibid.
126. Ibid., 100 n. 66.
127. Ibid.
128. Ibid.
129. Ibid., 100.
130. Homans, *Coming to My Senses*, 131.
131. Johnston, *Pitirim A. Sorokin*, 154.
132. Ibid.
133. Ibid., 153.
134. Ibid., 153–54 n. 86.
135. Jaime Cohen-Cole, *The Open Mind: Cold War Politics and the Sciences of Human Nature* (Chicago: University of Chicago Press, 2014), 85 n. 100.
136. Paul H. Buck to E. G. Boring, 1944, quoted in Lawrence T. Nichols, "Social Relations Undone: Disciplinary Divergence and Departmental Politics at Harvard, 1946–70," *American Sociologist* 29, no. 2 (Summer 1998): 87.
137. Cohen-Cole, *The Open Mind*, 84–85. Cohen-Cole suggests that Buck's work in guiding the committee that drafted "General Education in a Free Society" at the same time that Parsons was pushing an interdisciplinary vision showed that Buck's values were aligned with those of Parsons. "Both the general education project and Parsons's vision for the social sciences placed a high value on intellectual breadth achieved through communication."
138. Ibid.
139. Isaac, *Working Knowledge*, 176.
140. Paul H. Buck, "Faculty of Arts and Sciences," *Official Register* 45 (May 20, 1948): 36–37, quoted in Isaac, *Working Knowledge*, 176.
141. Ibid.
142. Schmidt, "Towards a History of the Department of Social Relations," 41.
143. Parsons, *The Department and Laboratory of Social Relations*, 14; Ellen Condliffe Lagemann, *The Politics of Knowledge: The Carnegie Corporation, Philanthropy and Public Policy* (Chicago: University of Chicago Press, 1989), 166.
144. Riesman to Schmidt, May 23, 1978, 1.
145. Ibid.
146. Allport to Boring, September 27, 1944.
147. George Homans, interview by Patrick L. Schmidt and Julia Moore, October 20, 1977, tape recording, HUA; Schmidt, "Towards a History of the Department of Social Relations," 30; Robert White, interview, December 1, 1977; Henry Murray, interview, October 30, 1977.
148. Schmidt, "Towards a History of the Department of Social Relations," 30.
149. Ibid.; Harvard University, *The Behavioral Sciences at Harvard*, faculty committee report (Cambridge, MA: Harvard University Press, 1954), 25.
150. Schmidt, "Towards a History of the Department of Social Relations," 31.
151. Ibid.
152. Parsons, *Department and Laboratory of Social Relations*, 14; Schmidt, "Towards a History of the Department of Social Relations," 30–31.

153. Schmidt, "Towards a History of the Department of Social Relations," 31.

154. Ellen Herman, *The Romance of American Psychology: Political Culture in the Age of Experts* (Oakland: University of California Press, 1995), 18.

155. Ibid., 20.

156. Gordon W. Allport, "Psychological Service for Civilian Morale," *Journal of Consulting Psychology* 5 (September–October 1941): 235, cited in Herman, *The Romance of American Psychology*, 18 n. 11.

157. Ibid.

158. Alexander Leighton, *Human Relations in a Changing World* (New York: E. P. Dutton, 1949), 43.

159. Ibid.

160. Schmidt, "Towards a History of the Department of Social Relations," 32.

161. Ibid.

162. David C. Engerman, "Social Science in the Cold War," *Isis* 101, no. 2 (June 2010): 393–400.

163. Schmidt, "Towards a History of the Department of Social Relations," 32.

164. Engerman, "Social Science in the Cold War," 396.

165. Schmidt, "Towards a History of the Department of Social Relations," 32.

166. Ibid.

167. Lyons, *The Uneasy Partnership*, 122; Schmidt, "Towards a History of the Department of Social Relations," 33.

168. Schmidt, "Towards a History of the Department of Social Relations," 33.

169. Ibid.

170. Samuel Stouffer, *The American Soldier*, vol. 1, *Adjustment during Army Life*; vol. 2, *Combat and Its Aftermath* (Princeton, NJ: Princeton University Press, 1949), 30–31.

171. Ibid.

172. Ibid.

173. Ibid.

174. Ibid.

175. Ibid.

176. Ibid.

177. Ibid.

178. Ibid.

179. Ibid.

180. Henry Murray, interview, October 30, 1977; Schmidt, "Towards a History of the Department of Social Relations," 35; Talcott Parsons, interview, October 17, 1977; Robert White, interview, December 1, 1977.

181. Schmidt, "Towards a History of the Department of Social Relations," 35.

182. Ibid.

183. Ibid.

184. David H. Price, *Anthropological Intelligence: The Deployment and Neglect of American Anthropology in the Second World War* (Durham, NC: Duke University Press, 2008), 173.

185. Ibid., 172.

186. Ibid.

187. Ibid., 173.

188. Leighton, *Human Relations*, 295–98.

189. Ibid.

190. Ibid.

191. Ibid.

192. Ibid.

193. Schmidt, "Towards a History of the Department of Social Relations," 37.

194. Johnston, *Pitirim Sorokin*, 151.

195. Uta Gerhardt, "A World from Brave to New: Talcott Parsons and the War Effort at Harvard University," *Journal of the History of the Behavioral Sciences* 35 (Summer 1999): 263–64.

196. Schmidt, "Towards a History of the Department of Social Relations," 37.

197. Robinson, *Love's Story Told*, 278.

198. Isaac, *Working Knowledge*, 175.

199. Robinson, *Love's Story Told*, 282; Schmidt, "Towards a History of the Department of Social Relations," 37.

200. Ibid.

201. Robinson, *Love's Story Told*, 282.

202. United States Office of Strategic Services Assessment Staff, *Assessment of Men: Selection of Personnel for the Office of Strategic Services* (New York: Rhinehart, 1948); Schmidt, "Towards a History of the Department of Social Relations," 37.

203. Robinson, *Love's Story Told*, 283.

204. Ibid.

205. Ibid., 282–83.

206. Ibid., 276–78.

207. Ibid., 276–77.

208. Ibid., 277.

209. Schmidt, "Towards a History of the Department of Social Relations," 38.

210. Ibid.

211. Ibid., 32–33.

212. Leighton, *Human Relations*, 45.

213. Parsons, "Clyde Kluckhohn and the Integration of the Social Sciences," 45.

214. Ibid.

215. Schmidt, "Towards a History of the Department of Social Relations," 39.

216. Ibid.

217. Ibid.; Victor Barnouw, *Culture and Personality* (Homewood, IL: Dorsey Press, 1973), 486–87.

218. Schmidt, "Towards a History of the Department of Social Relations," 39.

219. Lagemann, *The Politics of Knowledge*, 177; Schmidt, "Towards a History of the Department of Social Relations," 40; Samuel Stouffer, *Social Research to Test Ideas* (Glencoe, IL: Free Press, 1962), xv.

220. Ibid.; Paul Lazarsfeld, cited in Samuel Stouffer, *Social Research to Test Ideas* (Glencoe, IL: Free Press, 1962), xv.

221. Herman, *The Romance of American Psychology*, 5–6, 304–6.

222. Charles William Bray, *Psychology and Military Proficiency: A History of the Applied Psychology Panel of the National Defense Research Committee* (Princeton, NJ: Princeton University Press, 1948), v, quoted in Herman, *The Romance of American Psychology*, 19 n. 15.

223. Herman, *The Romance of American Psychology*, 19.
224. Ibid.
225. David C. Engerman, "The Rise and Fall of Wartime Social Science: Harvard's Refugee Interview Project, 1950–1954," in *Cold War Social Science: Knowledge Production, Liberal Democracy, and Human Nature*, Mark Solovey and Hamilton Cravens (New York: Palgrave Macmillan, 2012), 28.
226. Ibid.
227. Isaac, *Working Knowledge*, 172.
228. Ibid.
229. Ibid.
230. Ibid., 173.
231. Ibid.
232. Ibid., 173–75.
233. Ibid., 174.
234. Parsons, *Department and Laboratory of Social Relations*, 14; Lagemann, *The Politics of Knowledge*, 166; Schmidt, "Towards a History of the Department of Social Relations," 41.
235. Parsons, *Department and Laboratory of Social Relations*, 14; Schmidt, "Towards a History of the Department of Social Relations," 41.
236. Ibid.
237. Gordon W. Allport, *The Person in Psychology: Selected Essays* (Boston: Beacon, 1968), 399–400.
238. Ibid.

CHAPTER 3

1. Patrick L. Schmidt, "Towards a History of the Department of Social Relations, Harvard University, 1946–1972" (undergraduate honors thesis, Harvard University, 1978), 41.
2. Ibid.
3. Ibid.
4. "The Place of Psychology in an Ideal University: The Report of the University Commission on the Future of Psychology at Harvard," Harvard University, 1947, ix.
5. Ibid., 35–36.
6. Schmidt, "Towards a History of the Department of Social Relations," 42–43.
7. Ibid., 43.
8. Gordon Allport, Crane Britton, Clyde Kluckhohn, Edward Mason, Talcott Parsons, and Payson Wild to President Conant, October 16, 1945, HUA.
9. Ibid.
10. Ibid.
11. Ibid., 2.
12. Ibid.
13. Paul H. Buck to Talcott Parsons, October 16, 1945, HUA.
14. Paul H. Buck to Payson S. Wild et al., November 14, 1945, HUA.

15. Ibid.

16. Ibid.

17. Ibid.

18. Ibid.

19. Talcott Parsons to Paul H. Buck, November 16, 1945, HUA.

20. Gordon W. Allport to Paul H. Buck, November 16, 1945, HUA.

21. O. Hobart Mowrer to Paul H. Buck, November 16, 1945, HUA.

22. Ibid.

23. Clyde Kluckhohn to Paul H. Buck, November 18, 1945, HUA.

24. Ibid.

25. Ibid.

26. Kluckhohn to Buck, November 18, 1945.

27. Ibid.

28. Allport to Buck, November 16, 1945.

29. Barry V. Johnston, *Pitirim Sorokin: An Intellectual Biography* (Lawrence: University of Kansas Press, 1995), 157.

30. Kluckhohn to Buck, November 18, 1945.

31. Ibid.

32. E. G. Boring to Paul H. Buck, November 19, 1945, HUA.

33. "Social Anthropology, Comment by E. G. Boring," November 19, 1945, HUA.

34. Ibid.

35. Ibid.

36. Ibid.

37. Ibid.

38. Ibid.

39. David Riesman to Patrick L. Schmidt, May 23, 1978 (author's files).

40. Ibid.

41. Ibid., 1.

42. Ibid., 2.

43. Ibid.

44. Ibid.

45. Paul H. Buck to E. G. Boring, November 20, 1945, HUA.

46. Ibid.

47. Ibid.

48. Boring to Buck, November 27, 1945.

49. Ibid.

50. Ibid.

51. J. G. Beebe-Center to Dean Paul H. Buck, November 26, 1945, HUA.

52. Ibid.

53. Ibid.

54. Ibid.

55. Ibid.

56. Ibid.

57. Jamie Cohen-Cole, *The Open Mind: Cold War Politics and the Sciences of Human Nature* (Chicago: University of Chicago Press, 2014), 85.

58. Ibid.; Schmidt, "Towards a History of the Department of Social Relations," 43.

59. Schmidt, "Towards a History of the Department of Social Relations," 43; Talcott Parsons, *Department and Laboratory of Social Relations, Harvard University: The First Decade, 1946–1956* (chairman's report, 1956, HUA), 15.

60. Ibid.

61. Ibid.

62. Ibid.

63. Talcott Parsons, *Department and Laboratory of Social Relations,* 15–16.

64. Schmidt, "Towards a History of the Department of Social Relations," 43.

65. Ibid., 43–44.

66. Talcott Parsons, interview by Patrick L. Schmidt and Julia Moore, October 17, 1977, tape recording, HUA; Henry Murray, interview by Patrick L. Schmidt and Julia Moore, November 30, 1977, tape recording, HUA; Schmidt, "Towards a History of the Department of Social Relations," 44.

67. Talcott Parsons, *Department and Laboratory of Social Relations,* 15–16; Schmidt, "Towards a History of the Department of Social Relations," 44.

68. Ibid.

69. Minutes from Faculty of Arts and Sciences Meeting, January 29, 1946, Harvard University, HUA; Schmidt, "Towards a History of the Department of Social Relations," 44–45.

70. Parsons, *Department and Laboratory of Social Relations,* 16 n. 1.

71. Gordon W. Allport, *The Person in Psychology: Selected Essays* (Boston: Beacon, 1968), 398–99.

72. University News Office, 1946–71, Friday Afternoon Papers, Harvard University, February 1, 1946, HUA.

73. Allport, *The Person in Psychology,* 399.

74. Gordon Allport and Edwin G. Boring, "Psychology and Social Relations at Harvard University," *American Psychologist* 1, no. 4 (April 1946): 119–22.

75. Ibid.

76. Edwin G. Boring, *Psychologist at Large: An Autobiography and Select Essays* (New York: Basic Books, 1961), 65.

77. Ibid.

78. Allport and Boring, "Psychology and Social Relations," 119.

79. Ibid.

80. Ibid.

81. Ibid.

82. Ibid.

83. Ibid., 119.

84. Ibid., 120.

85. Ibid.

86. Ibid.

87. Ibid.

88. Ibid.

89. Ibid.

90. Ibid.

91. Ibid.

92. Ibid., 121.
93. Ibid.
94. Ibid.
95. Ibid.
96. Ibid.
97. Ibid.
98. Ibid.
99. Ibid.
100. Ibid.
101. Schmidt, "Towards a History of the Department of Social Relations," 48.
102. Ibid.

CHAPTER 4

1. Jamie Cohen-Cole, *The Open Mind: Cold War Politics and the Sciences of Human Nature* (Chicago: University of Chicago Press, 2014), 85; Joel Isaac, *Working Knowledge: Making the Human Sciences from Parsons to Kuhn* (Cambridge, MA: Harvard University Press, 2012), 167–75.
2. Cohen-Cole, *The Open Mind*, 85.
3. Ibid., 65.
4. Ibid., 65.
5. Ibid., 93.
6. Ibid., 65.
7. David Riesman, *Constraint and Variety in American Education* (Garden City, NY: Doubleday, 1958), 66–67.
8. Cohen-Cole, *The Open Mind*, 65.
9. Ibid., 101.
10. Ibid., 100–101.
11. Ibid.
12. Talcott Parsons, *Department and Laboratory of Social Relations, Harvard University: The First Decade, 1946–1956* (chairman's report, 1956, HUA), 16–18; Patrick L. Schmidt, "Towards a History of the Department of Social Relations, Harvard University, 1946–1972" (undergraduate honors thesis, Harvard University, 1978), 49–50.
13. Ibid.
14. Ibid.
15. Parsons, *Department and Laboratory of Social Relations*, 16–17.
16. *Official Register of Harvard University, Department of Social Relations* (Cambridge, MA: Harvard University Press, 1946), 8–14; Schmidt, "Towards a History of the Department of Social Relations," 50.
17. Schmidt, "Towards a History of the Department of Social Relations," 50.
18. Ibid.; *Official Register of Harvard University, Department of Social Relations*.
19. William Sims Bainbridge, "The Harvard Department of Social Relations," in *Leadership in Science and Technology: A Reference Handbook* (Thousand Oaks, CA: Sage Publications, 2012), 499.

20. Parsons, *Department and Laboratory of Social Relations*, 19.

21. Ibid.

22. Ibid.

23. Ibid.

24. George Caspar Homans, *Coming to My Senses: The Autobiography of a Sociologist* (New Brunswick, NJ: Transaction, 1984), 305.

25. Schmidt, "Towards a History of the Department of Social Relations," 51.

26. Ibid., 52.

27. Ibid.

28. Ibid.

29. Ellen Condliffe Lagemann, *The Politics of Knowledge: The Carnegie Corporation, Philanthropy, and Public Policy* (Chicago: University of Chicago Press, 1989), 166.

30. Ibid., 166. Dollard wrote to Kluckhohn in 1939, "We need some good solid observers in anthropology who have more than the Culture-Personality pattern than is current at the present time."

31. Ibid.

32. Ibid.

33. Schmidt, "Towards a History of the Department of Social Relations," 52.

34. Ibid.

35. Ibid.

36. Ibid.

37. Ibid.

38. Ibid.

39. Talcott Parsons, interview by Patrick L. Schmidt and Julia Moore, October 1, 1977, tape recording, HUA; Schmidt, "Towards a History of the Department of Social Relations," 52–53.

40. Lagemann, *The Politics of Knowledge*, 169.

41. Ibid.

42. Ibid.

43. Cohen-Cole, *The Open Mind*, 89.

44. Harvard University, *The Behavioral Sciences at Harvard*, faculty committee report (Cambridge, MA: Harvard University, 1954); Cole-Cohen, *The Open Mind*, 89 n. 122.

45. Clifford Geertz, *After the Fact: Two Countries, Four Decades, One Anthropologist* (Cambridge, MA: Harvard University Press, 1995), 99–100.

46. Cohen-Cole, *The Open Mind*, 89–90.

47. Ibid.

48. Parsons, *Department and Laboratory of Social Relations*, 80.

49. Ibid.

50. Ibid.

51. Ibid.

52. Ibid., 80–81.

53. Ibid., 81.

54. Ibid.

55. Ibid., 19.

56. Ibid.; Schmidt, "Towards a History of the Department of Social Relations," 55.

57. Schmidt, "Towards a History of the Department of Social Relations," 55.

58. Ibid.

59. Ibid.

60. Ibid.; Parsons, *Department and Laboratory of Social Relations*, 20.

61. Ibid.

62. Parsons, *Department and Laboratory of Social Relations*, 53–54; Schmidt, "Towards a History of the Department of Social Relations," 56.

63. Ibid.

64. Parsons, *Department and Laboratory of Social Relations*, 55.

65. Ibid.; Edwin G. Boring and Gardner Lindzey, eds., *A History of Psychology in Autobiography*, vol. 5 (New York: Appleton-Century-Crofts, 1967), 18.

66. Parsons, *Department and Laboratory of Social Relations*, 55.

67. Ibid., 56–57; Thelma Alper, interview by Patrick L. Schmidt and Julia Moore, October 28, 1977, tape recording, HUA; Schmidt, "Towards a History of the Department of Social Relations," 69.

68. Riesman, *Constraint and Variety*, 78.

69. Homans, *Coming to My Senses*, 303.

70. Ibid.

71. Allport, *The Person in Psychology*, 399.

72. Parsons, *Department and Laboratory of Social Relations*, 54.

73. Ibid., 54–55.

74. Ibid., 34.

75. Ibid.

76. Ibid.

77. Ibid.; Schmidt, "Towards a History of the Department of Social Relations," 57.

78. Parsons, *Department and Laboratory of Social Relations*, 34.

79. Ibid., 34–35.

80. Ibid., 35.

81. Ibid., 35–36.

82. Ibid., 36.

83. Schmidt, "Towards a History of the Department of Social Relations," 59.

84. Ibid.

85. Ibid.

86. Ibid., 60.

87. Ibid., 61.

88. Ibid.

89. Ibid.

90. Ibid.

91. Ibid., 62.

92. Ibid.

93. Isaac, *Working Knowledge*, 177.

94. Ibid., 177–78.

95. Ibid.

96. Lagemann, *The Politics of Knowledge*, 171.

97. Ibid.
98. David Riesman to Patrick Schmidt, May 23, 1978 (author's files), 3.
99. Ibid.
100. Ibid.
101. Isaac, *Working Knowledge*, 178.
102. Homans, *Coming to My Senses*, 305.
103. Ibid., 301.
104. Clyde Kluckhohn and Henry Murray, eds., *Personality in Nature, Society, and Culture* (New York: Knopf, 1948); Thomas Blass, *The Man Who Shocked the World: The Life and Legacy of Stanley Milgram* (New York: Basic Books, 2004), 20.
105. "Personality and Its Functions; Personality in Nature, Society and Culture," *New York Times*, November 21, 1948.
106. Kluckhohn and Murray, *Personality in Nature, Society, and Culture*.
107. Isaac, *Working Knowledge*, 179.
108. Schmidt, "Towards a History of the Department of Social Relations," 62.
109. Ibid.
110. "Social Relations Dep. Will Study Its Program," *Harvard Crimson*, October 18, 1949.
111. Ibid.
112. Isaac, *Working Knowledge*, 177.
113. Schmidt, "Towards a History of the Department of Social Relations," 62–63.
114. Ibid.
115. Ibid.; Talcott Parsons and Edward Shils, eds., *Toward a General Theory of Action* (Cambridge, MA: Harvard University Press, 1951), v.
116. Isaac, *Working Knowledge*, 181.
117. Ibid.; Lagemann, *The Politics of Knowledge*, 170.
118. Joel Isaac, "Theorist at Work: Talcott Parsons and the Carnegie Project on Theory, 1949–1951," *Journal of the History of Ideas* 71, no. 2 (April 2010): 300–301.
119. Parsons and Shils, *Toward a General Theory of Action*, v–vi; Schmidt, "Towards a History of the Department of Social Relations," 63.
120. Lagemann, *The Politics of Knowledge*, 169.
121. Ibid.
122. Isaac, *Working Knowledge*, 181.
123. Isaac, "Theorist at Work," 302; Isaac, *Working Knowledge*, 182.
124. David M. Schneider, *Schneider on Schneider: The Conversion of the Jews and Other Anthropological Stories*, ed. Richard Handler (Durham, NC: Duke University Press, 1995), 81–82.
125. Isaac, *Working Knowledge*, 182.
126. Ibid.; Bainbridge, "The Harvard Department of Social Relations," 500.
127. Ibid.
128. Isaac, "Theorist at Work," 302–3; Isaac, *Working Knowledge*, 182. As Isaac pointed out based on his review of the minutes of the seminar: "A report on the meeting of 'Group 2' (the general seminar) held on October 3, 1949, noted a 'feeling of uneasiness about the term 'functional': Ordinarily by the term 'functional' is meant that actions produce consequences which will maintain structure. An

empirical question immediately presents itself: Are all actions functional? Do they maintain the system?"

129. Ibid.
130. Ibid.
131. Ibid.
132. Homans, *Coming to My Senses*, 302.
133. Isaac, *Working Knowledge*, 184.
134. Ibid., 188.
135. Ibid., 188.
136. Talcott Parsons to John W. Gardner, December 13, 1949, cited in Isaac, *Working Knowledge*, 188.
137. Isaac, *Working Knowledge*, 189.
138. Parsons and Shils, *Toward a General Theory of Action*, v–vi.
139. Ibid.
140. Ibid.; Isaac, *Working Knowledge*, 184.
141. Ibid.
142. Isaac, *Working Knowledge*, 184.
143. Parsons and Shils, *Toward a General Theory of Action*, 3–27.
144. Ibid., 26 n. 31.
145. Ibid.
146. Ibid.
147. Ibid., 7 n. 9.
148. Gordon Allport to Talcott Parsons, September 10, 1950, HUA.
149. Parsons and Shils, *Toward a General Theory of Action*, 3.
150. Nils Gilman, *Mandarins of the Future: Modernization Theory in Cold War America* (Baltimore, MD: Johns Hopkins University Press, 2003), 84.
151. Parsons and Shils, *Toward a General Theory of Action*, 27.
152. Ibid.
153. Ibid.
154. Ibid., vii–viii.
155. Ibid., vii.
156. Ibid., vii–viii.
157. Ibid.
158. Isaac, *Working Knowledge*, 186–87.
159. Ibid., 48, 77; Bainbridge, "The Harvard Department of Social Relations," 500.
160. Parsons and Shils, *Toward a General Theory of Action*, 48.
161. Gilman, *Mandarins of the Future*, 86.
162. Isaac, "Theorist at Work," 309.
163. E. L. Pattullo, director of the Center for Behavioral Sciences, Harvard University, personal communication, November 1977.
164. Robert Reinhold, "A Mentor of Sociologists Retires after 42 Years at Harvard Post," *New York Times*, June 14, 1973.
165. Ibid.
166. Daniel Bell, "Talcott Parsons: Nobody's Theories Were Bigger," *New York Times*, May 13, 1979.
167. Ibid.

168. Ibid.

169. Ibid.

170. Ibid.

171. Geertz, *After the Fact*, 100.

172. Parsons and Shils, *Toward a General Theory of Action*, 286–87.

173. Ibid., 305–16.

174. Ibid., 247–75.

175. Isaac, *Working Knowledge*, 190–91.

176. Robert W. White, interview by Patrick L. Schmidt and Julia Moore, December 7, 1977, tape recording, HUA; David McClelland, interview by Patrick L. Schmidt and Julia Moore, November 16, 1977, tape recording, HUA; Schmidt, "Towards a History of the Department of Social Relations," 64.

177. David Riesman to Patrick L. Schmidt, May 23, 1978, 2.

178. Ibid.

179. Cohen-Cole, *The Open Mind*, 79.

180. B. Robert Owens, "Producing Parsons' Reputation: Early Critiques of Talcott Parsons' Social Theory and the Making of a Caricature," *Journal of the History of the Behavioral Sciences* 46, no. 2 (2010): 174.

181. M. B. Smith, review of *Toward a General Theory of Action*, ed. T. Parsons, E. A. Shils, E. C. Tolman, G. W. Allport, C. Kluckhohn, H. A. Murray, R. R. Sears, R. C. Sheldon, and S. A. Stouffer, *Journal of Abnormal and Social Psychology* 48, no. 2 (1953): 315–18.

182. Ibid., 315.

183. Ibid.

184. Ibid.

185. Ibid.

186. Schmidt, "Towards a History of the Department of Social Relations," 65; Homans, *Coming to My Senses*, 302.

187. George C. Homans, interview by Patrick L. Schmidt and Julia Moore, October 20, 1977, tape recording, HUA; Schmidt, "Towards a History of the Department of Social Relations," 65 n. 96.

188. Isaac, *Working Knowledge*, 189.

189. Homans, *Coming to My Senses*, 303.

190. Ibid.

191. Ibid.

192. Ibid.

193. Lagemann, *The Politics of Knowledge*, 170.

194. Isaac, *Working Knowledge*, 190.

195. Bainbridge, "The Harvard Department of Social Relations," 502.

196. Parsons, *Department and Laboratory of Social Relations*, 34.

197. Homans, *Coming to My Senses*, 303.

198. Ibid.

199. Gilman, *Mandarins of the Future*, 84.

200. David C. McClelland, *Motives, Personality, and Society: Selected Papers* (New York: Praeger, 1984), 522, quoted in Gilman, *Mandarins of the Future*, 79 n. 16.

201. Talcott Parsons to Paul H. Buck, April 3, 1944, HUA.

202. Gilman, *Mandarins of the Future*, 78.

203. Richard Handler, "An Interview with Clifford Geertz," *Current Anthropology* 32, no. 5 (December 1991): 603–13.

204. Clifford Geertz, *Available Light: Anthropological Reflections on Philosophical Topics* (Princeton, NJ: Princeton University Press, 2000), 8.

205. Isaac, *Working Knowledge*, 178.

206. Geertz, *After the Fact*, 101.

207. Ibid.

208. Geertz, *Available Light*, 8.

209. Ibid., 101.

210. Benton Johnson and Miriam Johnson, "The Integrating of the Social Sciences: Theoretical and Empirical Research and Training in the Department of Social Relations at Harvard," in Samuel Z. Klausner and Victor M. Lidz, eds., *The Nationalization of the Social Sciences* (Philadelphia: University of Pennsylvania Press, 1986), 132.

211. Arthur J. Vidich, *With a Critical Eye: An Intellectual and His Times* (Knoxville, TN: Newfound Press, 2009), 231.

212. Ibid.

213. Ibid.

214. Ibid., 230.

215. Ibid., 232.

216. Ibid., 232–33.

217. Ibid., 233.

218. Ibid.

219. Ibid., 233–34.

220. Norman Birnbaum, interview by Patrick L. Schmidt, August 10, 2015, Washington, DC.

221. Ibid.

222. Norman Birnbaum, *From the Bronx to Oxford and Not Quite Back* (Washington, DC: New Academia, 2017), 104.

223. Ibid.

224. Ibid.

225. Ibid.

226. Ibid., 105.

227. Ibid.

228. Norman Birnbaum, interview, August 10, 2015.

229. Ibid.

230. David M. Schneider, *Schneider on Schneider: The Conversion of the Jews and Other Anthropological Stories*, ed. Richard Handler (Durham, NC: Duke University Press, 1995), 79.

231. Ibid.

232. Gilman, *Mandarins of the Future*, 72.

233. Ibid.

234. Ibid.

235. Schneider, *After the Fact*, 99.

236. Gilman, *Mandarins of the Future*, 72. "For the first time, American intellectuals raised in the tradition of pragmatic, theoretical modesty faced a cognitive

crisis that would propel them into embracing avant-garde European social theory as a basis for understanding the third world."

237. Ibid.

238. Ibid.

239. Ibid.

240. Ibid.

241. Ibid., 3, 73.

242. Ibid., 3–4.

243. Ibid., 77.

244. Charles Wagley, *Area Research and Training: A Conference Report on the Study of World Areas* (Columbia University and SSRRC, 1947), 5, quoted in Gilman, *Mandarins of the Future*, 77 n. 6.

245. Bainbridge, "The Harvard Department of Social Relations," 500.

246. Gilman, *Mandarins of the Future*, 76.

247. Ibid.

248. Ibid., 89.

249. Ibid., 3.

250. Lagemann, *The Politics of Knowledge*, 173.

251. Ibid., 174.

252. Ibid., 169.

253. Ibid., 173.

254. David C. Engerman, "The Rise and Fall of Wartime Social Science: Harvard's Refugee Interview Project," in *Cold War Science: Knowledge, Liberal Democracy, and Human Nature*, ed. Mark Solovey and Hamilton Cravens (New York: Palgrave Macmillan, 2012), 29.

255. Robert A. McCaughey, *International Studies and Academic Enterprise: A Chapter in the Enclosure of American Learning* (New York: Columbia University Press, 1984), quoted in Lagemann, *The Politics of Knowledge*, 175 n. 91.

256. Ibid.

257. Ibid.

258. Ibid., 173 n. 82.

259. Ibid., 175.

260. Talcott Parsons, "Clyde Kluckhohn and the Integration of Social Science," in *Culture and Life: Essays in Memory of Clyde Kluckhohn*, ed. Walter W. Taylor, John L. Fischer, and Evon Z. Vogt (Carbondale: Southern Illinois University Press, 1973), 35.

261. Birnbaum, *From the Bronx to Oxford*, 109.

262. Lagemann, *The Politics of Knowledge*, 174.

263. Ibid.

264. Ibid.; Margaret Mead and Rhoda Metraux, eds., *The Study of Western Cultures*, vol. 1, *The Study of Culture at a Distance* (Chicago: University of Chicago Press, 1953), 3.

265. Talcott Parsons, "Clyde Kluckhohn and the Integration of Social Science," in Taylor et al., *Culture and Life*, 36.

266. Andrew L. Yarrow, "Nathan Pusey, Harvard President through Growth and Turmoil Alike, Dies at 94," *New York Times*, October 15, 2001, http://

mobile.nytimes.com/2001/11/15/us/nathan-pusey-harvard-president-through-growth-and-turmoil-dies-at-94.html.

267. Parsons, "Clyde Kluckhohn," 36.

268. David H. Price, *Cold War Anthropology: The CIA, the Pentagon, and the Growth of Dual Use Anthropology* (Durham, NC: Duke University Press, 2016), 86.

269. Ibid.

270. Engerman, "The Rise and Fall of Wartime Social Science," 29.

271. Ibid.

272. Sigmund Diamond, *Compromised Campus: The Collaboration of Universities with the Intelligence Community, 1945–1955* (New York: Oxford University Press, 1992), 58–59; Price, *Cold War Anthropology*, 84–85.

273. Ibid.

274. Price, *Cold War Anthropology*, 85.

275. Ibid.

276. Diamond, *Compromised Campus*, 58.

277. Ibid., 59 n. 9.

278. Ibid.

279. Ibid.

280. Ibid.

281. Ibid.

282. Ibid.

283. David C. Engerman, "Social Science in the Cold War," *Isis* 101 (2010), 398.

284. Ibid.

285. Ibid.

286. Ibid., 399.

287. Ibid.; Alex Inkeles, "Clyde Kluckhohn's Contribution to Studies of Russia and the Soviet Union," in Taylor et al., *Culture and Life*, 66–68.

288. Engerman, "The Rise and Fall of Wartime Social Science," 32.

289. Ibid., 30.

290. Ibid., 31.

291. Ibid.

292. Ibid., 32.

293. Ibid.

294. Ibid., 32–33.

295. Ibid., 33.

296. Ibid.

297. Ibid., 35.

298. Ibid.

299. Ibid.

300. Ibid.

301. Ibid., 35.

302. Ibid., 31.

303. Mark Solovey, "Cold War Social Science: Specter, Reality, or Useful Concept?," in *Cold War Science: Knowledge, Liberal Democracy, and Human Nature*, ed. Mark Solovey and Hamilton Cravens (New York: Palgrave Macmillan, 2012), 14.

304. Engerman, "The Rise and Fall of Wartime Social Science," 31.

305. Ibid.

306. Ibid.
307. Engerman, "Social Science in the Cold War," 399–400.
308. Price, *Cold War Anthropology*, 359.
309. Engerman, "The Rise and Fall of Wartime Social Science," 35–37.
310. Ibid., 36.
311. Ibid., 35–36.
312. Ibid., 36.
313. Ibid.
314. Ibid., 36 n. 67.
315. Ibid., 37.
316. Ibid., 38.
317. Inkeles, "Clyde Kluckhohn's Contribution," 61.
318. Ibid.
319. Ibid.
320. Lagemann, *The Politics of Knowledge*, 176.
321. Ibid.
322. Ibid.
323. Ibid.
324. Ibid.
325. Engerman, "The Rise and Fall of Wartime Social Science," 28.
326. Quoted in Roger Greiger, *American Higher Education after World War II* (Princeton, NJ: Princeton University Press, 2019), 99.
327. Jerome Bruner, *In Search of Mind: Essays in Autobiography* (New York: Harper & Row, 1983), 63.
328. Harvard University, *The Behavioral Sciences at Harvard*, 12.
329. Cohen-Cole, *The Open Mind*, 91.
330. Ibid.
331. "Social Relations 'Correction,'" *Harvard Crimson*, May 3, 1949.
332. Ibid.
333. Ibid.
334. "Soc Rel Criticized at Adams Forum," *Harvard Crimson*, March 22, 1950.
335. Ibid.
336. Parsons, *Department and Laboratory of Social Relations*, 17.
337. Ibid.
338. "Soc Rel Criticized at Adams Forum," *Harvard Crimson*, March 22, 1950.
339. Riesman, *Constraint and Variety*, 79.
340. Ibid.
341. Ibid.

CHAPTER 5

1. Patrick L. Schmidt, "Towards a History of the Department of Social Relations: Harvard University, 1946–1972" (undergraduate honors thesis, Harvard University, 1978), 73–74.
2. Jerome Bruner, *In Search of Mind: Essays in Autobiography* (New York: Harper & Row, 1983), 63.

3. Ibid.

4. Ibid.

5. Jerome Bruner to James C. Miller, November 1, 1948, HUA.

6. Ibid., 1.

7. Ibid.

8. Jerome Bruner to Gordon Allport, April 11, 1950, HUA.

9. Ibid.

10. Ibid.

11. Jerome Bruner to E. G. Boring, May 10, 1951 (marked "letter never sent"), HUA.

12. Ibid., 1.

13. Ibid., 2.

14. Ibid., 1.

15. Ibid.

16. Ibid., 1.

17. Ibid.

18. Benedict Carey, "Jerome Bruner, Who Shaped Understanding of the Young Mind, Dies at 100," *New York Times*, June 9, 2016.

19. Ibid.

20. Ibid.

21. Seymour Martin Lipset and David Riesman, *Education and Politics at Harvard* (New York: McGraw-Hill, 1971), 349.

22. Ibid.

23. Bruner to Boring, May 10, 1951, 1.

24. Ibid.

25. Ibid., 2.

26. Ibid.

27. Ibid.

28. Ibid.

29. Ibid.

30. E. G. Boring to Jerome Bruner, May 21, 1951, HUA.

31. Ibid.

32. Ibid.

33. Gordon Allport to Jerome Bruner, October 29, 1951, HUA, 1.

34. Ibid., 2.

35. Ibid., 3.

36. Ibid., 4.

37. Jerome Bruner to Gordon Allport, December 23, 1951, HUA, 1.

38. Ibid.

39. Ibid., 1.

40. Ibid., 1–2.

41. Bruner, *In Search of Mind*, 63–64.

42. Ibid., 64.

43. Jamie Cohen-Cole, *The Open Mind: Cold War Politics and the Sciences of Human Nature* (Chicago: University of Chicago Press, 2014), 94.

44. Robert White, interview by Patrick L. Schmidt and Julia Moore, December 1, 1977, tape recording, HUA; Schmidt, "Towards a History of the Department of Social Relations," 86.

45. Ibid.

46. Joel Isaac, *Working Knowledge: Making the Human Sciences from Parsons to Kuhn* (Cambridge, MA: Harvard University Press, 2012), 178.

47. Lawrence T. Nichols, "Social Relations Undone: Disciplinary Divergence and Departmental Politics at Harvard, 1946–1970," *American Sociologist* 29, no. 2 (Summer 1998): 94.

48. Ibid.

49. Quoted in Nichols, "Social Relations Undone," 94.

50. Arthur J. Vidich, *With a Critical Eye: An Intellectual and His Times* (Knoxville, TN: Newfound Press, 2009), 226.

51. Ibid., 226, 230; Forrest G. Robinson, *Love's Story Told: A Life of Henry A. Murray* (Cambridge, MA: Harvard University Press, 1992), 151.

52. Vidich, *With a Critical Eye*, 230–31.

53. Gordon W. Allport, *The Person in Psychology: Selected Essays* (Boston: Beacon, 1968), 399.

54. Nichols, "Social Relations Undone," 90.

55. Ibid.

56. Ibid.

57. Schmidt, "Towards a History of the Department of Social Relations," 66.

58. Ibid.

59. Talcott Parsons, *Department and Laboratory of Social Relations, Harvard University: The First Decade, 1946–1956* (chairman's report, 1956, HUA), 28–29.

60. Schmidt, "Towards a History of the Department of Social Relations," 66–67.

61. Ibid.; Robert White, interview by Patrick L. Schmidt and Julia Moore, December 1, 1977, tape recording, HUA; Gardner Lindzey, interview by Patrick L. Schmidt and Julia Moore, December 10, 1977, tape recording, HUA; Roger Brown, interview by Patrick L. Schmidt and Julia Moore, October 20, 1977, tape recording, HUA; Laurence Wylie, interview by Patrick L. Schmidt and Julia Moore, October 20, 1977, tape recording, HUA.

62. David Riesman to Patrick L. Schmidt, May 23, 1978 (author's files).

63. Ibid.

64. Ibid., 3.

65. George C. Homans, *Coming to My Senses: The Autobiography of a Sociologist* (New Brunswick, NJ: Transaction, 1984), 306.

66. Ibid.

67. Ibid.

68. John Whiting, interview by Patrick L. Schmidt and Julia Moore, October 27, 1977, tape recording, HUA; Patrick L. Schmidt, "Towards a History of the Department of Social Relations," 67; David McClelland, interview by Patrick L. Schmidt and Julia Moore, October 8, 1977, tape recording, HUA; "Survey of Harvard Ph.D.'s from Department of Social Relations 1950–54," Department of Social Relations file, Harvard University, HUA, cited in Schmidt, "Towards a History of the Department of Social Relations," 67.

69. Parsons, *Department and Laboratory of Social Relations*, 39.

70. Ibid; McClelland, interview, October 8, 1977; Schmidt, "Towards a History of the Department of Social Relations," 67–68.

71. Schmidt, "Towards a History of the Department of Social Relations," 68.

72. Ibid.; Thelma Alper, interview by Patrick L. Schmidt and Julia Moore, October 28, 1977, tape recording, HUA; Sheldon White, interview by Patrick L. Schmidt and Julia Moore, November 14, 1977, tape recording, HUA; David McClelland, interview by Patrick L. Schmidt and Julia Moore, October 16, 1977, tape recording, HUA; Parsons, *Department and Laboratory of Social Relations*, 56.

73. Thomas Pettigrew, interview by Patrick L. Schmidt and Julia Moore, October 28, 1977, tape recording, HUA; Schmidt, "Towards a History of the Department of Social Relations," 69.

74. Riesman to Schmidt, May 23, 1978, 3.

75. Schmidt, "Towards a History of the Department of Social Relations," 69.

76. Ibid.

77. Quoted in Nichols, "Social Relations Undone," 96.

78. Talcott Parsons to McGeorge Bundy, November 8, 1955, HUA, 1.

79. Ibid.

80. Ibid., 2.

81. Ibid., 4.

82. Ibid., 3.

83. Ibid., 3–4.

84. Ibid., 4.

85. Ibid., 3.

86. Nichols, "Social Relations Undone," 96.

87. Ibid.

88. Ibid.

89. Quoted in Nichols, "Social Relations Undone," 96.

90. Ibid.

91. Parsons, *Department and Laboratory of Social Relations*.

92. Ibid., 3–4.

93. Ibid., 5.

94. Ibid.

95. Ibid.

96. Ibid.

97. Ibid., 5-6.

98. Ibid., 6.

99. Ibid.

100. Ibid.

101. Ibid., 6-7.

102. Ibid., 33.

103. Ibid., 34.

104. Ibid.

105. Ibid., 38.

106. Ibid., 38–39.

107. Ibid., 39.

108. David McClelland, interview by Patrick L. Schmidt and Julia Moore, November 16, 1977, tape recording, HUA.

109. Ibid.

110. Ibid.

111. Ibid., 39–40.

112. Ibid., 40.

113. Ibid., 40 n. 1.

114. Harvard University, *The Behavioral Sciences at Harvard*, faculty committee report (Cambridge, MA: Harvard University Press, 1954), 300–301.

115. Ibid., 300.

116. Ibid., 300–301.

117. Ibid.

118. Allport, *The Person in Psychology*, 400.

119. Schmidt, "Towards a History of the Department of Social Relations," 69–70.

120. Ibid., 70.

121. Ibid.

122. Riesman and Lipset, *Education and Politics at Harvard*, 354; E. L. Pattullo, interview by Patrick L. Schmidt and Julia Moore, October 28, 1977, tape recording, HUA: Schmidt, "Towards a History of the Department of Social Relations," 70.

123. David Riesman, with Reuel Denney and Nathan Glazer, "Storytellers as Tutors in Technique: From *The Lonely Crowd*," in *Mass Communication and American Social Thought: Key Texts, 1919–1968*, ed. John Durham Peters and Peter Simonson (Lanham, MD: Rowman & Littlefield, 2004), 293.

124. Ibid.

125. Orlando Patterson, "The Last Sociologist," *New York Times*, May 19, 2002. Despite this and other achievements, Riesman had, according to Patterson, "died discarded and forgotten by his discipline." He wrote, "The dishonoring of David Riesman, and the tradition of sociology for which he stood, is not a reflection of their insignificance. It is merely a sign of the rise in professional sociology of a style of scholarship that mimics the methodology and language of the natural sciences—in spite of their inappropriateness for the understanding of most areas of the world."

126. Charles McGrath, "The Lives They Lived; Big Thinkster," *New York Times Magazine*, December 29, 2002.

127. Ibid.

128. Paul Buhle, "David Riesman: Radical American Sociologist Whose Landmark Book, *The Lonely Crowd*, First Challenged the Values of the Consumer Society," *Guardian*, May 13, 2002.

129. "David Riesman, Author of *The Lonely Crowd*," Memorial Minute, *Harvard Gazette*, November 13, 2003, https://news.harvard.edu/gazette/story/2003/11/memorial-minute-david-riesman-author-of-the-lonely-crowd.

130. Riesman to Schmidt, May 23, 1978.

131. David Riesman, *Constraint and Variety in American Education* (Garden City, NY: Doubleday, 1958), 84–85.

132. "Erik Erikson, 91, Psychoanalyst Who Reshaped Views of Human Growth, Dies," *New York Times*, May 13, 1994.

133. Ibid.

134. Ibid.

135. Ibid.

136. Corydon Ireland, "Howard Gardner: A Blessing of Influences," *Harvard Gazette*, October 17, 2013, http://news.harvard.edu/gazette/story/2013/10/the -mentors-of-howard-gardner.

137. Ibid.

138. Ibid.

139. Morton Keller and Phyllis Keller, *Making Harvard Modern: The Rise of America's University* (New York: Oxford University Press, 2001), 218.

140. Ibid.

141. Ibid.

142. Ibid.

143. "Un Original," *Harvard Magazine*, March 1, 2000.

144. Ibid.

145. Riesman to Schmidt, May 23, 1978.

146. Ireland, "Howard Gardner."

147. Howard Gardner, "A Requiem for 'Soc Rel': Here's to Synthesizing Social Science" (blog of Howard Gardner, Hobbs Professor of Cognition and Education, Harvard Graduate School of Education, October 4, 2018), https://www.thereal worldofcollege.com/blog/a-requiem-for-soc-rel-heres-to-synthesizing-social -science.

148. "David Riesman, Author of *The Lonely Crowd*," Memorial Minute, *Harvard Gazette*, November 13, 2003.

149. Howard Gardner, *A Synthesizing Mind: A Memoir from the Creator of Multiple Intelligence Theory* (Cambridge, MA: MIT Press, 2020), 51, 213.

150. Schmidt, "Towards a History of the Department of Social Relations," 70–71.

151. Ibid.

152. Ibid.

153. Ibid.; Whiting, interview, October 27, 1977; Talcott Parsons, interview by Patrick L. Schmidt and Julia Moore, November 15, 1977, tape recording, HUA.

154. Ibid.

155. Riesman to Schmidt, May 23, 1978.

156. Schmidt, "Towards a History of the Department of Social Relations," 70–71.

157. Ibid.

158. Ibid.; Parsons, *Department and Laboratory of Social Relations*, 52.

159. Ibid.

160. Ibid.

161. Allport, *The Person in Psychology*, 393; Robert White, interview, December 1, 1977; Schmidt, "Towards a History of the Department of Social Relations," 71; David McClelland, interview by Patrick L. Schmidt and Julia Moore, November 8, 1977, tape recording, HUA.

162. Ibid., 71.

163. Ibid.

164. Ibid.

165. Ibid., 71–72.

166. Ibid. 72.

167. Franz Brotzen, "Social Sciences Marks 30th Anniversary," *Rice University News & Media*, March 19, 2010.

Davidson recalled that when he arrived at Rice in 1966, most of the departments that later became the School of Social Sciences were quite small. They offered an interdisciplinary doctoral program that was modeled on Harvard's Department of Social Relations. "Any of us social scientists at Rice could oversee a doctoral dissertation in our department," Davidson said, "and the rest of the dissertation committee typically consisted of people both in that department and in the other social science departments." However, Davidson acknowledged that the Ph.D. program "was seen by faculty in the program as less than competitive." When Harvard began to take steps to disaggregate Social Relations into its component departments, it led to a similar move at Rice. Each department would eventually be given enough faculty members to sustain its own Ph.D. program, Davidson said.

168. Schmidt, "Towards a History of the Department of Social Relations," 72.
169. Ibid.

CHAPTER 6

1. Brendan Maher, interview by Patrick L. Schmidt and Julia Moore, December 1, 1977, tape recording, HUA; Roger Brown, interview by Patrick L. Schmidt and Julia Moore, October 20, 1977, tape recording, HUA; Robert White, interview by Patrick L. Schmidt and Julia Moore, December 1, 1977, tape recording, HUA; David McClelland, interview by Patrick L. Schmidt and Julia Moore, November 8, 1977, tape recording, HUA; Patrick L. Schmidt, "Towards a History of the Department of Social Relations, Harvard University, 1946–1972" (undergraduate honors thesis, Harvard University, 1978), 73.

2. Edward L. Pattullo, interview by Patrick L. Schmidt and Julia Moore, October 28, 1977, tape recording, HUA: Schmidt, "Towards a History of the Department of Social Relations," 74.

3. Schmidt, "Towards a History of the Department of Social Relations," 74.

4. Ibid.

5. Ibid.

6. Ibid.

7. Ibid.; Jamie Cohen-Cole, *The Open Mind: Cold War Politics and the Sciences of Human Nature* (Chicago: University of Chicago Press, 2014), 170.

8. Ibid.; E. J. Kahn Jr., *Harvard: Through Change and through Storm* (New York: Norton, 1969), 82.

9. "Annual Report of the Center for Cognitive Study, 1961," Harvard University; Schmidt, "Towards a History of the Department of Social Relations," 74.

10. Cohen-Cole, *The Open Mind*, 169.

11. Ibid., 169 n. 20, citing letter from Jerome S. Bruner and George A. Miller to Nathan Pusey, January 4, 1962.

12. Cohen-Cole, *The Open Mind*, 169.

13. Ibid.

14. Ibid.

15. Ibid., 170, citing Center for Cognitive Studies, *First Annual Report, 1960–1961*, 1–2.

16. Ibid., 168.

17. Schmidt, "Towards a History of the Department of Social Relations," 74.

18. Ibid.

19. Ibid.

20. Ibid.

21. Ibid.; Victor Barnouw, *Culture and Personality* (Homewood, IL: Dorsey Press, 1973), 487–88.

22. David Riesman, *Constraint and Variety in American Education* (Garden City, NY: Doubleday, 1958), 95.

23. Schmidt, "Towards a History of the Department of Social Relations," 75.

24. Ibid.

25. Ibid.; McClelland, interview by Patrick L. Schmidt and Julia Moore, November 16, 1977, tape recording, HUA.

26. Harrison White, interview by Patrick L. Schmidt and Julia Moore, November 19, 1977, tape recording, HUA; David Riesman, interview by Patrick L. Schmidt and Julia Moore, November 6, 1977, tape recording, HUA; Schmidt, "Towards a History of the Department of Social Relations," 75.

27. Schmidt, "Towards a History of the Department of Social Relations," 75.

28. Ibid.

29. Ibid.

30. Ibid.

31. Ibid.

32. Ibid.

33. Ibid.

34. Ibid.

35. Ibid.

36. Ibid.

37. Ibid.; Frederick Mosteller, interview by Patrick L. Schmidt and Julia Moore, November 25, 1977, tape recording, HUA.

38. Schmidt, "Towards a History of the Department of Social Relations," 76–77.

39. Ibid., 77.

40. Ibid.

41. Ibid.

42. Don Lattin, *The Harvard Psychedelic Club: How Timothy Leary, Ram Dass, Huston Smith, and Andrew Weil Killed the Fifties and Ushered in a New Age for America* (New York: HarperCollins, 2010), 20.

43. "David Clarence McClelland, Faculty of Arts and Sciences," Memorial Minute, *Harvard Gazette*, November 8, 2007, https://news.harvard.edu/gazette/story/2007/11/david-clarence-mcclelland.

44. Ibid.

45. Robert Greenfield, *Timothy Leary: A Biography* (Orlando, FL: Harcourt, 2006), 104.

46. Ibid., 104–5.

47. Timothy Leary, *Flashbacks: An Autobiography* (Los Angeles: J. P. Tarcher, 1983), 19.

48. Ibid.

49. Ibid.

50. Ibid., 20.

51. Greenfield, *Timothy Leary*, 106.

52. Ibid., 106–7.

53. Ibid., 107.

54. Leary, *Flashbacks*, 21.

55. Ibid.

56. Ibid.

57. Lattin, *The Harvard Psychedelic Club*, 41.

58. Noah Gordon, "The Hallucinogenic Drug Cult," *The Reporter*, August 15, 1963, 36, https://bibliography.maps.org/bibliography/default/resource/13433.

59. Greenfield, *Timothy Leary*, 145–53; Leary, *Flashbacks*, 78–79.

60. Greenfield, *Timothy Leary*, 180–81.

61. Ibid., 117–18.

62. Ibid., 118; Leary, *Flashbacks*, 41.

63. Ibid.

64. Ibid.

65. Greenfield, *Timothy Leary*, 118–19; Leary, *Flashbacks*, 41–42.

66. Ibid., 142.

67. Leary, *Flashbacks*, 61.

68. Greenfield, *Timothy Leary*, 137.

69. Ibid., 138.

70. Ibid.

71. Ibid., 139.

72. Ibid., 138.

73. Ibid., 139.

74. Ibid.

75. Ibid., 154.

76. Leary, *Flashbacks*, 51. Leary credited Ginsberg for opening doors: "Because of Allen Ginsberg the existence of our drug research project came to the attention of the Beatnik network."

77. Greenfield, *Timothy Leary*, 154.

78. Ibid., 116–17.

79. Ibid., 117.

80. Ibid., 160.

81. Lattin, *The Harvard Psychedelic Club*, 133.

82. Ibid., 61; Schmidt, "Towards a History of the Department of Social Relations," 77.

83. Schmidt, "Towards a History of the Department of Social Relations," 77.

84. Gordon, "The Hallucinogenic Drug Cult," 36.

85. Ibid.; John Spiegel, interview by Patrick L. Schmidt and Julia Moore, November 17, 1977, tape recording, HUA: Schmidt, "Towards a History of the Department of Social Relations," 77.

86. Peter Owen Whitmer, *Aquarius Revisited*, quoted in Greenfield, *Timothy Leary*, 177.

87. Leary, *Flashbacks*, 121.

88. Ibid., 158.

89. Andrew T. Weil, "The Strange Case of the Harvard Drug Scandal," *Look*, November 5, 1963, https://bibliography.maps.org/bibliography/default/resource/15046.

90. Leary, *Flashbacks*, 159.

91. Ibid.

92. Ibid.

93. Schmidt, "Towards a History of the Department of Social Relations," 78.

94. Leary, *Flashbacks*, 159; Lattin, *The Harvard Psychedelic Club*, 88–89.

95. Ibid.

96. Lattin, *The Harvard Psychedelic Club*, 89.

97. Herbert Kelman, interview by Patrick L. Schmidt and Julia Moore, January 27, 1978, tape recording, HUA; Schmidt, "Towards a History of the Department of Social Relations," 78.

98. Weil, "The Strange Case," 44.

99. Greenfield, *Timothy Leary*, 174.

100. Kelman, interview, January 27, 1978; Schmidt, "Towards a History of the Department of Social Relations," 78.

101. Leary, *Flashbacks*, 122.

102. Ibid., 121.

103. Ibid.

104. Lattin, *The Harvard Psychedelic Club*, 90.

105. Ibid., 90.

106. Leary, *Flashbacks*, 116–22.

107. Ibid., 122.

108. Andrew Weil, "The Strange Case," 44.

109. Ibid.

110. Ibid; Schmidt, "Towards a History of the Department of Social Relations," 78.

111. Weil, "The Strange Case," 44; Gordon, "The Hallucinogenic Drug Cult," 37.

112. Gordon, "The Hallucinogenic Drug Cult," 38.

113. Fred Hechinger, "Use of 'Mind-Distorting' Drugs Rising at Harvard, Dean Says," *New York Times*, December 11, 1962, 1, 3.

114. Ibid.

115. Timothy Leary and Richard Alpert, letter to the editor, *Harvard Crimson*, December 13, 1962; Fred M. Hechinger, "Harvard Debates Mind-Drug Peril, Psychologists Say Dean Errs on 'Danger' of Stimulants," *New York Times*, December 14, 1962, 7.

116. Leary and Alpert, letter to the editor, December 13, 1962.

117. Ibid.

118. Ibid.

119. Gordon, "The Hallucinogenic Drug Cult," 39.

120. Ibid; Andrew Weil, *Dying to Know: Ram Dass & Timothy Leary—Extras* (directed by Gay Dillingham, August 26, 2016). Weil contends that Harvard never formally fired Leary.

121. Greenfield, *Timothy Leary*, 196.

122. Schmidt, "Towards a History of the Department of Social Relations," 81.

123. Ibid.; Robert Freed Bales, interview by Patrick L. Schmidt and Julia Moore, December 9, 1977, tape recording, HUA.

124. Ibid.

125. Greenfield, *Timothy Leary*, 199, citing David C. McClelland to Timothy Leary, June 10, 1963.

126. Ibid.

127. Ibid.

128. Gordon, "The Hallucinogenic Drug Cult," 39.

129. Ibid.

130. Ibid., 197.

131. Gordon, "The Hallucinogenic Drug Cult," 40.

132. Lattin, *The Harvard Psychedelic Club*, 93–94.

133. Ibid.

134. Ibid.

135. Weil, *Dying to Know*, remarks of Andrew Weil on his role in the dismissal of Alpert.

136. Lattin, *The Harvard Psychedelic Club*, 56–60, 94–96.

137. Ibid.

138. Weil, *Dying to Know*.

139. Lattin, *The Harvard Psychedelic Club*, 59, 94.

140. Ibid.

141. Ibid., 94–96; Greenfield, *Timothy Leary*, 177.

142. Lattin, *The Harvard Psychedelic Club*, 93–94.

143. Ibid., 94–95.

144. Ibid.

145. James Penner, ed., *Timothy Leary: The Harvard Years* (Rochester, Vermont: Park Street Press, 2014), 2.

146. Greenfield, *Timothy Leary*, 196–97.

147. Joseph M. Russin and Andrew T. Weil, "The *Crimson* Takes Leary, Alpert to Task: 'Roles' & 'Games' In William James," *Harvard Crimson*, May 28, 1963. https://www.thecrimson.com/article/1973/1/24/the-crimson-takes-leary-alpert-to.

148. Ibid.

149. "Harvard Ousting Aide in Drug Case," *New York Times*, May 27, 1963, 41; "Ousted Educator Rebuts Harvard," *New York Times*, May 28, 1963, 13.

150. Ibid.; Weil, *Dying to Know*.

151. Weil, "The Strange Case"; Gordon, "The Hallucinogenic Drug Cult."

152. Penner, ed., *Timothy Leary: The Harvard Years*, 322.

153. Lattin, *The Harvard Psychedelic Club*, 95.

154. Weil, "The Strange Case," 46.

155. Lattin, *The Harvard Psychedelic Club*, 199.

156. Ibid.

157. Brendan Maher, interview by Patrick L. Schmidt and Julia Moore, December 1, 1977, tape recording, HUA; Schmidt, "Towards a History of the Department of Social Relations," 81.

158. Greenfield, *Timothy Leary*, 172.

159. Ibid., 172.
160. Ibid.
161. Ibid., 171.
162. Ibid.
163. Ibid.
164. Leary, *Flashbacks*, 159.
165. Ibid.
166. Greenfield, *Timothy Leary*, 158–59.
167. Ibid.
168. Ibid., 159.
169. Ibid.
170. Ibid.
171. Ibid.
172. Ibid.
173. Ibid.
174. Ibid., 160.
175. Schmidt, "Towards a History of the Department of Social Relations," 81.
176. "Final Report to Dean Ford from David C. McClelland, Chairman, Dean's *Ad Hoc* Committee on the Future of the Behavioral Sciences at Harvard," May 1963, HUA.
177. Ibid., 2.
178. Ibid.
179. Ibid.
180. Ibid.
181. Ibid., 3.
182. Ibid.
183. Ibid.
184. Ibid.
185. Ibid., 2.
186. Ibid., 1.
187. Ibid, 4–5.
188. Ibid., 4.
189. Ibid.
190. Ibid.
191. Ibid., 3.
192. Ibid., 1.
193. Ibid.
194. Andrew T. Weil, "Social Relations at Harvard after Seventeen Years: Problems, Successes and a Highly Uncertain Future," *Harvard Crimson*, June 13, 1963.
195. Ibid.
196. Ibid.
197. Ibid.
198. Ibid.
199. Schmidt, "Towards a History of the Department of Social Relations," 81.
200. Ibid.
201. Ibid.
202. Allport, *The Person in Psychology*, 404.

203. Schmidt, "Towards a History of the Department of Social Relations," 81.
204. Ibid.
205. Ibid.; Pattullo, interview, October 28, 1977.
206. Schmidt, "Towards a History of the Department of Social Relations," 82.
207. Ibid.
208. Allport, *The Person in Psychology*, 406.
209. Gordon W. Allport, "William James and the Behavioral Sciences—Remarks at the Installation of the Ellen Emmet Rand Portrait of William James in William James Hall, Harvard University, November 5, 1965," *Journal of the History of the Behavioral Sciences* 2, no. 2 (April 1966): 145–47.
210. Ibid., 145.
211. Ibid.
212. Ibid.
213. Ibid.
214. Ibid.
215. Allport, *The Person in Psychology*, 406.
216. Juliet E. Isselbacher, "The Lingering Spirit of William James," *Harvard Crimson*, October 16, 2019.
217. Pattullo, interview, October 28, 1977; Schmidt, "Towards a History of the Department of Social Relations," 83.
218. Allport, *The Person in Psychology*, 404.
219. Gregory A. Briker, "B. F. Skinner at Harvard," *Harvard Crimson*, October 16, 2014.
220. Ibid.
221. Homans, *Coming to My Senses*, 304.
222. Dale Allen Gyure, *Minoru Yamasaki: Humanist Architecture for a Modernist World* (New Haven, CT: Yale University Press, 2017), 182.
223. James McCown, "For a Time, Jose Lluís Sert's Brawny Buildings Defined Modern Boston," *Metropolis*, September 23, 2019.
224. "Modern Monday: William James Hall," Cambridge Historical Commission, December 11, 2018.
225. Ibid.
226. Ibid.
227. Gyure, *Minoru Yamasaki*, 182.
228. Schmidt, "Towards a History of the Department of Social Relations," 83.
229. Homans, *Coming to My Senses*, 304.
230. Cohen-Cole, *The Open Mind*, 184 n. 65.
231. Pattullo, interview, October 28, 1977; Schmidt, "Towards a History of the Department of Social Relations," 83.
232. Michael D. Nolan, "PSR Simplifies Moniker, Forsakes SR to Become P," *Harvard Crimson*, February 7, 1986.
233. William James, *The Will to Believe: And Other Essays in Popular Philosophy* (New York: Longmans Green, 1907), 216.
234. Allport, "William James and the Behavioral Sciences," 146.
235. Pattullo, interview, October 28, 1977; Schmidt, "Towards a History of the Department of Social Relations," 83: Edwin Newman, interview by Patrick L. Schmidt and Julia Moore, November 4, 1977, tape recording, HUA.

236. Ibid.

237. Thomas Blass, *The Man Who Shocked the World: The Life and Legacy of Stanley Milgram* (New York: Basic Books, 2004), 148.

238. Pattullo, interview, October 28, 1977; Schmidt, "Towards a History of the Department of Social Relations," 83.

239. Schmidt, "Towards a History of the Department of Social Relations," 84.

240. Ibid.

241. Ibid.

242. Ibid.; Robert White, interview, December 1, 1977.

243. Schmidt, "Towards a History of the Department of Social Relations," 84.

244. Ibid.

245. Ibid.; McClelland, interview, November 8, 1977.

246. Schmidt, "Towards a History of the Department of Social Relations," 84.

247. Ibid., 84–85.

248. Ibid., 85.

249. Ibid.

250. Ibid.

251. Ibid.

252. "Garmezy Attacks Soc Rel Dept," *Harvard Crimson*, April 15, 1967.

253. Ibid.

254. Ibid.

255. "Soc Rel Votes to Drop Clinical Psychology," *Harvard Crimson*, March 2, 1967, 1, 4; Maher, interview, December 1, 1977; Schmidt, "Towards a history of the Department of Social Relations," 85.

256. Ibid., 85–86; Benjamin Sendor, "Clinical Psychology at Harvard: Case History of In [*sic*] Institutional Identity Crisis," *Harvard Crimson*, May 23, 1973, https://www.thecrimson.com/article/1973/5/23/clinical-psychology-at-harvard-pbabt-the.

257. Ibid.; McClelland, interview, December 8, 1977.

258. Schmidt, "Towards a History of the Department of Social Relations," 86.

259. Allport, *The Person in Psychology*, 406.

260. Ibid.

261. Marshall J. Getz, "Henry Murray: Brief Life of a Personality Psychologist: 1893–1988," *Harvard Magazine*, March–April 2014, https://harvardmagazine.com/2014/03/henry-a-murray.

262. George C. Homans, "Bringing Men Back In," *American Sociological Review* 25, no. 5 (December 1964): 809.

263. Ibid.

264. Ibid., 817.

265. Ibid., 814.

266. William Sims Bainbridge, "The Harvard Department of Social Relations," in *Leadership in Science and Technology: A Handbook* (Thousand Oaks, CA: Sage Publications, 2011), 502.

267. Homans, "Bringing Men Back In," 817.

268. Ibid., 815–16.

269. Ibid., 818.

270. Bainbridge, "The Harvard Department of Social Relations," 502.

271. Ibid., 502.
272. Schmidt, "Towards a History of the Department of Social Relations," 86; Roger Brown and Richard Herrnstein to Talcott Parsons, September 25, 1967, HUA.
273. Ibid.
274. Schmidt, "Towards a History of the Department of Social Relations," 86–87.
275. Ibid., 87.
276. Roger Brown and Richard Herrnstein, "Reorganization Plan," Department of Psychology and Social Relations files, Harvard University; Schmidt, "Towards a History of the Department of Social Relations," 87.
277. Ibid.
278. Pattullo, interview, October 28, 1977; Schmidt, "Towards a History of the Department of Social Relations," 87.
279. Ibid.
280. Ibid.
281. Ibid., 88.
282. Ibid.
283. Ibid.
284. Ibid.; Gary Fine, "The Dissolution of Social Relations at Harvard: A Social History" (unpublished paper, n.d.), 5–6.
285. Schmidt, "Towards a History of the Department of Social Relations," 88.
286. Ibid.
287. Ibid.
288. Ibid.
289. Homans, *Coming to My Senses*, 306.
290. Ibid.
291. Ibid.
292. Fine, "The Dissolution of Social Relations at Harvard," 6–7; Schmidt, "Towards a History of the Department of Social Relations," 89.

CHAPTER 7

1. Patrick L. Schmidt, "Towards a History of the Department of Social Relations" (undergraduate honors thesis, Harvard University, 1978), 89–90.
2. Morton Keller and Phyllis Keller, *Making Harvard Modern: The Rise of America's University* (New York: Oxford University Press, 2001), 311.
3. Ibid., 309.
4. Ibid., 313.
5. Bernard D. Nossiter, "Student-Led Course Shatters Tradition at Harvard," *Washington Post*, May 30, 1969, A6; Tom Christoffel, David Finkelhor, and Dan Gilbarg, eds., *Up Against the American Myth: A Radical Critique of Corporate Capitalism Based upon the Controversial Harvard College Course, Social Relations 148–149* (New York: Holt, Rinehart & Winston, 1970), iv.
6. Nossiter, "Student-Led Course Shatters Tradition at Harvard."

7. Ibid.

8. Ibid.; Schmidt, "Towards a History of the Department of Social Relations," 90–91; Seymour Martin Lipset and David Riesman, *Education and Politics at Harvard* (New York: McGraw-Hill, 1975), 217–18.

9. Lipset and Riesman, *Education and Politics at Harvard*, 217–18.

10. Ibid.

11. William M. Kutik, "Black Leader Plans Lecture Here Monday," *Harvard Crimson*, September 24, 1968; George Howe Colt, *The Game: Harvard, Yale, and America in 1968* (New York: Scribner, 2018), 43–44.

12. Kutik, "Black Leader Plans Lecture Here Monday."

13. Ibid.; Colt, *The Game*, 43.

14. Bernard D. Nossiter, "Radicalism Course Splits Harvard," *Washington Post*, May 29, 1969, A8.

15. Schmidt, "Towards a History of the Department of Social Relations," 90.

16. Kutik, "Black Leader Plans Lecture Here Monday."

17. Ibid.

18. Schmidt, "Towards a History of the Department of Social Relations," 90.

19. Keller and Keller, *Making Harvard Modern*, 312.

20. Ibid.

21. Ibid.

22. Colt, *The Game*, 44.

23. Nossiter, "Student-Led Course Shatters Tradition at Harvard."

24. Schmidt, "Towards a History of the Department of Social Relations," 90.

25. Nossiter, "Student-Led Course Shatters Tradition at Harvard."

26. Nossiter, "Radicalism Course Splits Harvard."

27. Roger Brown, "Social Relations 148–149, Report to the Faculty," June 9, 1969, Department of Psychology and Social Relations files, Harvard University, 1–3; Schmidt, "Towards a History of the Department of Social Relations," 90–91.

28. Ibid.

29. Keller and Keller, *Making Harvard Modern*, 312.

30. Ibid., 313.

31. Ibid.

32. Ibid., 314–15.

33. Ibid., 316; Andrew L. Yarrow, "Nathan Pusey, Harvard President through Growth and Turmoil Alike, Dies at 94," *New York Times*, October 15, 2001, http://mobile.nytimes.com/2001/11/15/us/nathan-pusey-harvard-president-through-growth-and-turmoil-dies-at-94.html.

34. Yarrow, "Nathan Pusey."

35. Ibid.

36. Ibid.; "Harvard Conspiracy Seeks New Education," *Harvard Crimson*, March 20, 1969, https://www.thecrimson.com/article/1969/3/20/harvard-conspiracy-seeks-new-education-pa.

37. Ibid.

38. "Harvard Conspiracy Seeks New Education."

39. "Are You Unhappy?," *Harvard Crimson*, March 24, 1969, https://www.thecrimson.com/article/1969/3/24/are-you-unhappy-with-the-education.

40. Lipset and Riesman, *Education and Politics at Harvard*, 21.

41. Nossiter, "Student-Led Course Shatters Tradition at Harvard."

42. David Finkelhor, quoted in Lipset and Riesman, *Education and Politics at Harvard*, 218.

43. Steven Kelman, quoted in Lipset and Riesman, *Education and Politics at Harvard*, 218.

44. Nossiter, "Student-Led Course Shatters Tradition at Harvard."

45. Nossiter, "Radicalism Course Splits Harvard."

46. Schmidt, "Towards a History of the Department of Social Relations," 91.

47. Ibid.; Nossiter, "Student-Led Course Shatters Tradition at Harvard."

48. Keller and Keller, *Making Harvard Modern*, 312: "The department [Social Relations]—one in which not everything, but a lot went—readily agreed."

49. Nossiter, "Radicalism Course Splits Harvard."

50. Schmidt, "Towards a History of the Department of Social Relations," 91.

51. Ibid.; Nossiter, "Student-Led Course Shatters Tradition at Harvard"; Brown, "Social Relations 148–149," 2.

52. Schmidt, "Towards a History of the Department of Social Relations," 92.

53. Nossiter, "Student-Led Course Shatters Tradition at Harvard."

54. Nossiter, "Radicalism Course Splits Harvard."

55. Nossiter, "Student-Led Course Shatters Tradition at Harvard."

56. Ibid.

57. Ibid.

58. Ibid.

59. Ibid.

60. Telephone conversation with Daniel P. Sorensen, who was a student in the section, December 26, 2019.

61. Nossiter "Student-Led Course Shatters Tradition."

62. Ibid.

63. Schmidt, "Towards a History of the Department of Social Relations," 92.

64. Ibid.

65. Keller and Keller, *Making Harvard Modern*, 326.

66. Ibid.

67. Ibid.

68. Keller and Keller, *Making Harvard Modern*, 313; Roger Brown, interview by Patrick L. Schmidt and Julia Moore, October 20, 1977, tape recording, HUA; Schmidt, "Towards a History of the Department of Social Relations," 92.

69. Keller and Keller, *Making Harvard Modern*, 313.

70. Brown, interview, October 20, 1977; Schmidt, "Towards a History of the Department of Social Relations," 92.

71. Schmidt, "Towards a History of the Department of Social Relations," 92.

72. Ibid., 92–93.

73. Ibid.

74. Ibid., 93.

75. Keller and Keller, *Making Harvard Modern*, 311–12.

76. Schmidt, "Towards a History of the Department of Social Relations," 92–93.

77. Ibid.

78. Ibid.; Gary Fine, "The Dissolution of Social Relations at Harvard: A Social History" (unpublished paper, n.d.), 9. A newspaper article identified Thomas

Pettigrew, professor of social psychology, as having received threatening phone calls. Nossiter, "Student-Led Course Shatters Tradition at Harvard."

79. Homans, *Coming to My Senses: The Autobiography of a Sociologist* (New Brunswick, NJ: Transaction, 1984), 306.

80. Ibid. Homans criticized the department for allowing the "famous student-organized radical course called Social Relations 129," but it is clear from the context he is referring to Social Relations 148–149.

81. Ibid.

82. Schmidt, "Towards a History of the Department of Social Relations," 93.

83. Fine, "The Dissolution of Social Relations," 8–9.

84. Homans, *Coming to My Senses*, 306.

85. Ibid.

86. Ibid.

87. Ibid., 307.

88. Ibid.

89. Ad hoc committee letter to Dean Franklin Ford, October 1, 1968, Department of Psychology and Social Relations, Harvard University.

90. Ibid., 1.

91. Ibid.

92. Ibid.

93. Ibid.

94. Ibid.

95. James A. Davis to Franklin Ford, October 1, 1968, HUA, 1.

96. Ibid.

97. Ibid.

98. Ibid.

99. Ibid.

100. Ibid.

101. Ibid.

102. Ibid.

103. Ibid., 2.

104. Fine, "The Dissolution of Social Relations," 8; Schmidt, "Towards a History of the Department of Social Relations," 94.

105. Schmidt, "Towards a History of the Department of Social Relations," 94.

106. Ibid.; Steven Kelman, interview by Patrick L. Schmidt and Julia Moore, January 27, 1978, tape recording, HUA.

107. R. Freed Bales, "Graduate Training of Social Psychologist at Harvard University," cited in Sven Lundstedt, *Higher Education in Social Psychology* (Cleveland, OH: Press of Case Western Reserve University, 1968), 109.

108. Davis to Ford, October 1, 1968, 2.

109. Talcott Parsons to Roger Brown, September 25, 1968, HUA, 1.

110. Ibid.

111. Ibid.

112. Ibid.

113. Ibid.

114. Ibid., 2.

115. Ibid.

116. Saniel B. Bonder, "Sociology Faculty Wants Independent Department; Committee to Lay Plans," *Harvard Crimson*, December 8, 1969.

117. Ibid.

118. Ibid.

119. Ibid.

120. Ibid.

121. Schmidt, "Towards a History of the Department of Social Relations," 95.

122. Ibid.

123. Ibid.

124. Ibid.; Harrison White, interview by Patrick L. Schmidt and Julia Moore, October 19, 1977, tape recording, HUA; Schmidt, "Towards a History of the Department of Social Relations," 95.

125. Fine, "The Dissolution of Social Relations," 10.

126. Schmidt, "Towards a History of the Department of Social Relations," 95.

127. Ibid., 96.

128. Ibid.

129. Ibid.

130. Fine, "The Dissolution of Social Relations," 11, citing Harrison White, "Annual Report of the Department of Social Relations 1969–70."

131. Schmidt, "Towards a History of the Department of Social Relations," 96.

132. Ibid.

133. Ibid., 97; Harrison White, "Directions for Sociology," April 21, 1970 (unpublished memorandum in files of E. L. Pattullo, Center for the Behavioral Sciences, Department of Psychology and Social Relations, Harvard University).

134. White, "Directions for Sociology."

135. Saniel B. Bonder, "Social Relations Department Meeting Yields No Conclusion on Reorganization," *Harvard Crimson*, February 28, 1970.

136. Ibid.

137. Fine, "The Dissolution of Social Relations," 11.

138. Ibid.

139. Ibid.

140. Ibid.

141. Schmidt, "Towards a History of the Department of Social Relations," 97.

142. Ibid.

143. Jeff Magalif, "Professors Seek Autonomy for Social Psychologists," *Harvard Crimson*, April 6, 1970.

144. Ibid.

145. Ibid.

146. Ibid.

147. Ibid.

148. Robert Reinhold, "Harvard Changes Sociology's Role," *New York Times*, June 1, 1970, https://www.nytimes.com/1970/06/01/archives/harvard-changes-sociologys-role-reestablishes-department-after.html.

149. Ibid.

150. Ibid.

151. Ibid.

152. Ibid.

153. Ibid.

154. John Leonard, "Rent a Liberal Technologue, Cheap," Books of the Times, *New York Times*, June 3, 1970, https://www.nytimes.com/1970/06/03/archives/books-of-the-times-sociology-2-rent-a-liberal-technologue-cheap.html.

155. Schmidt, "Towards a History of the Department of Social Relations," 97.

156. Ibid.

157. Ibid.; John Whiting, interview by Patrick L. Schmidt and Julia Moore, October 20, 1977, tape recording, HUA.

158. Roger Brown, interview, October 20, 1977; Schmidt, "Towards a History of the Department of Social Relations," 97–98.

159. Schmidt, "Towards a History of the Department of Social Relations," 98.

160. Ibid.

161. Ibid.

162. Ibid.

163. Ibid.

164. George Goethals, memorandum containing plans submitted by Messrs: Pattullo, Bales, DeVore, Whiting, Newman, Homans, and Lamberg-Karlovsky, November 18, 1970, Department of Psychology and Social Relations files, Harvard University; Schmidt, "Towards a History of the Department of Social Relations," 98.

165. Schmidt, "Towards a History of the Department of Social Relations," 98–99.

166. Ibid.; E. L. Pattullo, note to file, Department of Psychology and Social Relations, Harvard University.

167. Schmidt, "Towards a history of the Department of Social Relations," 99.

168. Pattullo, interview by Patrick L. Schmidt and Julia Moore, October 28, 1977, tape recording, HUA; Schmidt, "Towards a History of the Department of Social Relations," 99.

169. Ibid.

170. Schmidt, "Towards a History of the Department of Social Relations," 99–100.

171. Ibid.; Kelman, interview, January 27, 1978; McClelland, interview, November 8, 1977.

172. "It has been my observation over many years that innovation seldom comes from a faculty group, or rather an administrator finds a faculty minority whom he backs if he has courage and power enough and resources enough and whom he protects in formative years." David Riesman letter to Everett C. Hughes and Talcott Parsons, July 3, 1970, quoted in Lawrence T. Nichols, "Social Relations Undone: Disciplinary Divergence and Departmental Politics at Harvard, 1946–70," *American Sociologist* 29, no. 2 (Summer 1998): 104.

173. J. T. Dunlop et al., "Toward a Common Language for the Area of Social Science" (unpublished memorandum, Harvard University, 1941), in the Tozzer Library collection, Harvard University.

174. Schmidt, "Towards a History of the Department of Social Relations," 100.

175. Ibid., 100–101; Minutes from Faculty of Arts and Sciences Meeting, May 16, 1971, Harvard University, E. L. Pattullo files, Center for the Behavioral Sciences, Department of Psychology and Social Relations, Harvard University.

176. Ibid.
177. Ibid.
178. Ibid.

CHAPTER 8

1. Patrick L. Schmidt, "Towards a History of the Department of Social Relations, Harvard University, 1946–1972" (undergraduate honors thesis, Harvard University, 1978), HUA, 102.
2. Gordon W. Allport, *The Person in Psychology: Selected Essays* (Boston: Beacon, 1968), 399.
3. Ibid.
4. Robert Reinhold, "A Mentor of Sociologists Retires after 42 Years at Harvard Post," *New York Times*, June 14, 1973.
5. Ibid.
6. Ibid.
7. Ibid.
8. Schmidt, "Towards a History of the Department of Social Relations," 102–4.
9. Howard Gardner, "A Requiem for 'Soc Rel': Here's to Synthesizing Social Science" (blog of Howard Gardner, Hobbs Professor of Cognition and Education, Harvard Graduate School of Education, October 4, 2018), https://www.thereal worldofcollege.com/blog/a-requiem-for-soc-rel-heres-to-synthesizing-social -science.
10. Schmidt, "Towards a History of the Department of Social Relations," 102.
11. Lawrence T. Nichols, "Social Relations Undone: Disciplinary Divergence and Departmental Politics at Harvard, 1946–1970," *American Sociologist*, 29, no. 2 (Summer 1998): 105.
12. Seymour Martin Lipset and David Riesman, *Education and Politics at Harvard* (New York: McGraw-Hill, 1975), 349.
13. Ibid.
14. Ibid.
15. Ibid.
16. George Caspar Homans, *Coming to My Senses: The Autobiography of a Sociologist* (New Brunswick, NJ: Transaction, 1984), 307–8.
17. Ibid.
18. Ibid.
19. Allport, *The Person in Psychology*, 398.
20. Ibid., 399.
21. Schmidt, "Towards a History of the Department of Social Relations," 103.
22. Ibid.
23. David Riesman, *Constraint and Variety in American Education* (Garden City, NY: Doubleday, 1958), 107.
24. Schmidt, "Towards a History of the Department of Social Relations," 103.
25. Ibid.
26. Ibid.

27. Ibid., 103–4.

28. Ibid., 104.

29. Ibid., 104.

30. Ibid. For an analysis of the system of rewards and norms of an analogous profession (that of scientist), see Norman W. Storer, *The Social System of Science* (New York: Holt, Rinehart & Winston, 1966).

31. Gardner, "A Requiem for 'Soc Rel.'"

32. Ibid.

33. Schmidt, "Towards a History of the Department of Social Relations," 104.

34. Riesman, *Constraint and Variety in American Education*, 96.

35. Ibid., 99.

36. Ibid.

37. Ibid.

38. David Riesman to Patrick L. Schmidt, May 23, 1978 (author's files).

39. Ibid., 2.

40. Ibid.

41. Ibid.

42. Ibid.

43. Ibid.

44. "I came to Patrick Schmidt's thesis just after having been called in as referee in my own Department to judge between two undergraduate theses which were tied for the prize our Department offers for the best undergraduate thesis. It might interest you to know that neither of these theses seemed to me to be work of quality, although they were works of serious and studious effort. They are not in a class with the work of Patrick Schmidt. They are not in a class with other undergraduate theses I have read either in Social Relations or Social Studies. Each in its own way indicates the narrowness of our Department at present, and I cannot criticize the students because, as I pointed out to Dick Madsen in commenting on the dissertations, it is hard for a river to rise higher than its source." David Riesman to E. L. Pattullo, May 23, 1978 (author's files).

45. Norman Birnbaum, interview by Patrick L. Schmidt, August 10, 2015, Washington, DC.

46. Riesman to Schmidt, May 23, 1978, 3.

47. Ibid.

48. Ibid.

49. "Soc Rel Criticized at Adams Forum," *Harvard Crimson*, March 22, 1950.

50. Schmidt, "Towards a History of the Department of Social Relations," 105.

51. Ibid.

52. Ibid.

53. Donald T. Campbell, "The Ethnocentrism of the Disciplines and the Fish-Scale Model of Omniscience," cited in Muzafer Sherif and Carolyn Sherif, *Interdisciplinary Relationships in the Social Sciences* (Chicago: Aldine, 1969).

54. Schmidt, "Towards a History of the Department of Social Relations," 105–6.

55. Ibid., 106.

56. Campbell, "The Ethnocentrism of the Disciplines," 338–39.

57. Ibid.

58. Ibid.

59. Ibid.

60. Ibid., 339.

61. Ibid.

62. Michael D. Nolan, "PSR Simplifies Moniker, Forsakes SR to Become P," *Harvard Crimson*, February 7, 1986; E. L. Pattullo, "About," Department of Psychology, Harvard University, https://psychology.fas.harvard.edu/about.

63. Nolan, "PSR Simplifies Moniker."

64. Ibid.

65. Ibid.

66. Ibid.

67. Ibid.

68. Ibid.

69. Alston Chase, *A Mind for Murder: The Education of the Unabomber and the Origins of Modern Terrorism* (New York: Norton, 2003), 228–29.

70. Ibid., 229.

71. Ibid., 235–36.

72. Ibid., 238.

73. Ibid., 228.

74. David Kaczynski, *Every Last Tie: The Story of the Unabomber and His Family* (Durham, NC: Duke University Press, 2016), 11.

75. Chase, *A Mind for Murder*, 240.

76. Kaczynski, *Every Last Tie*, 12.

77. Ibid., 12.

78. Chase, *A Mind for Murder*, 292.

79. Ibid.

80. Kaczynski, *Every Last Tie*, 10.

81. Chase, *A Mind for Murder*, 236.

82. Ibid., 238.

83. Kristen G. Studlien, "Murray Center Seals Kaczynski Data," *Harvard Crimson*, July 14, 2000, https://www.thecrimson.com/article/2000/7/14/murray-center-seals-kaczynski-data-plondon-buried/?page=3.

84. Ibid.

85. Alston Chase, "Harvard and the Making of the Unabomber," *Atlantic*, June 2000, https://www.theatlantic.com/magazine/archive/2000/06/harvard-and-the-making-of-the-unabomber/378239.

86. David Kaczynski, "Ted and the CIA, Part 1," *Times Union*, December 19, 2010, https://blog.timesunion.com/kaczynski/ted-and-the-cia-part-1/271.

87. Forrest G. Robinson, *Love's Story Told: A Life of Henry A. Murray* (Cambridge, MA: Harvard University Press, 1992).

88. Anna Fels, "Hello, Jung Lovers," *New York Times*, February 21, 1993.

89. Ibid.

90. Alston Chase, *A Mind for Murder*, 243.

91. Fels, "Hello, Jung Lovers."

92. Mark C. Taylor, "End the University as We Know It," *New York Times*, May 26, 2009.

93. Ibid.

94. Jerry A. Jacobs, "Interdisciplinary Hype," *Chronicle of Higher Education,* November 22, 2009.

95. Ibid.

96. Schmidt, "Towards a History of the Department of Social Relations," 107; Campbell, "The Ethnocentrism of the Disciplines," 339.

97. Schmidt, "Towards a History of the Department of Social Relations," 107.

98. Ibid.

99. William Sims Bainbridge, "The Harvard Department of Social Relations," in *Leadership in Science and Technology: A Reference Handbook* (Thousand Oaks, CA: Sage Publications, 2012), 502.

100. Corydon Ireland, "Howard Gardner: 'A Blessing of Influences,'" *Harvard Gazette,* October 17, 2013.

101. Ibid.

102. Ibid.

103. Ibid.

104. Gardner, "A Requiem for 'Soc Rel.'"

105. Ibid.

106. Howard Gardner, *A Synthesizing Mind: A Memoir from the Creator of Multiple Intelligences Theory* (Cambridge, MA: MIT Press, 2020), 51.

107. Ibid.

108. Ibid.

109. Ibid.

110. Schmidt, "Towards a History of the Department of Social Relations," 107.

Bibliography

ABBREVIATION

HUA   Harvard University Archives

Adelson, Joseph. "Against Scientism." Review of *Endeavors in Psychology: Selections from the Personology of Henry A. Murray,* edited by Edwin. S. Shneidman. *New York Times,* August 9, 1981. https://www.nytimes.com/1981/08/09/books/against-scientism.html.

Ad hoc committee letter to Dean Franklin Ford. October 1, 1968. Department of Psychology and Social Relations files, Harvard University.

Allport, G. W., C. K. M. Kluckhohn, O. H. Mowrer, H. A. Murray, and T. Parsons. "Confidential Memorandum on the Reorganization of the Social Sciences at Harvard." September 1, 1943. HUA.

Allport, Gordon, to Edwin G. Boring, March 23, 1944. HUA.

Allport, Gordon, to Jerome Bruner, October 29, 1951. HUA.

Allport, Gordon, and Edwin G. Boring. "Psychology and Social Relations at Harvard University." *American Psychologist* 1, no. 4 (April 1946): 119–22.

Allport, Gordon, Crane Britton, Clyde Kluckhohn, Edward Mason, Talcott Parsons, and Payson Wild to President Conant, October 16, 1945. HUA.

Allport, Gordon W., to Edwin G. Boring, September 27, 1944. HUA.

Allport, Gordon W., to Paul Buck, July 24, 1944. Files of E. L. Pattullo, director, Center of Behavioral Sciences, Harvard University. Author's files.

Allport, Gordon W., to Paul H. Buck, November 16, 1945. HUA.

Allport, Gordon W., to James B. Conant, January 6, 1937. HUA.

Allport, Gordon W. *The Person in Psychology: Selected Essays.* Boston: Beacon, 1968.

———. "The Psychologist's Frame of Reference." Presidential address delivered at the Forty-Seventh Annual Meeting of the American Psychological Association,

Berkeley, California, September 7, 1939. *Psychological Bulletin* 37, no. 1 (1940): 1–28. https://www.sapili.org/subir-depois/en/ps000009.pdf.

———. "William James and the Behavioral Sciences—Remarks at the Installation of the Ellen Emmet Rand Portrait of William James in William James Hall, Harvard University, November 5, 1965," *Journal of the History of the Behavioral Sciences* 2, no. 2 (April 1966): 145–47.

Allport, Gordon W., Clyde Kluckhohn, O. H. Mowrer, H. A. Murray, and Talcott Parsons to Paul H. Buck, June 10, 1943. HUA.

Alper, Thelma. Interview by Patrick L. Schmidt and Julia Moore, October 10, 1977. Tape recording. HUA.

Anderson, James William. "An Interview with Henry Murray on His Meeting with Freud." *Psychoanalytic Psychology* 34, no. 3 (2017): 325–26.

"Annual Report of the Center for Cognitive Study, 1961." Harvard University.

"Are You Unhappy?" *Harvard Crimson*, March 24, 1969. https://www.thecrimson.com/article/1969/3/24/are-you-unhappy-with-the-education.

Bainbridge, William Sims. "The Harvard Department of Social Relations." In *Leadership in Science and Technology: A Reference Handbook*. Thousand Oaks, CA: Sage Publications, 2012.

Bales, R. Freed. "Graduate Training of Social Psychologist at Harvard University." As cited in *Higher Education in Social Psychology*, by Sven Lundstedt. Cleveland, OH: Press of Case Western Reserve University, 1968.

Bales, Robert Freed. Interview by Patrick L. Schmidt and Julia Moore, December 9, 1977. Tape recording. HUA.

Barnouw, Victor. *Culture and Personality*. Homewood, IL: Dorsey Press, 1973.

Beebe-Center, J. G., to Dean Paul H. Buck, November 26, 1945. HUA.

Bell, Daniel. "Talcott Parsons: Nobody's Theories Were Bigger." *New York Times*, May 13, 1979, E9.

Birnbaum, Norman. Interview by Patrick L. Schmidt, August 10, 2015, Washington, DC.

Birnbaum, Norman. *From the Bronx to Oxford and Not Quite Back*. Washington, DC: New Academia, 2017.

Blass, Thomas. *The Man Who Shocked the World: The Life and Legacy of Stanley Milgram*. New York: Basic Books, 2004.

Bonder, Saniel B. "Social Relations Department Meeting Yields No Conclusion on Reorganization." *Harvard Crimson*, February 28, 1970.

———. "Sociology Faculty Wants Independent Department; Committee to Lay Plans." *Harvard Crimson*, December 8, 1969.

Boring, E. G., to Jerome Bruner, May 21, 1951. HUA.

Boring, E. G., to Paul H. Buck, November 19, 1945. HUA.

Boring, E. G. "Social Anthropology, Comment by E. G. Boring," November 19, 1945. HUA.

Boring, Edwin G. *Psychologist at Large: An Autobiography and Selected Essays*. New York: Basic Books, 1961.

Boring, Edwin G., and Gardner Lindzey, eds. *A History of Psychology in Autobiography*. Vol. 5. New York: Appleton-Century-Crofts, 1967.

Briker, Gregory A. "B. F. Skinner at Harvard." *Harvard Crimson*, October 16, 2014.

Brown, J. F. "The Position of Psychoanalysis in the Science of Psychology." *Journal of Abnormal and Social Psychology* 35 (1940).

Brown, Roger. Interview by Patrick L. Schmidt and Julia Moore, October 20, 1977. Tape recording. HUA.

Brown, Roger. "Social Relations 148–149, Report to the Faculty." June 9, 1969. Department of Psychology and Social Relations files, Harvard University.

Brown, Roger, and Richard Herrnstein. "Reorganization Plan." N.d. Department of Psychology and Social Relations files, Harvard University.

Brotzen, Franz. "Social Sciences Marks 30th Anniversary." *Rice University News & Media*, March 19, 2010.

Bruner, Jerome, to Gordon Allport, April 11, 1950. HUA.

Bruner, Jerome, to Gordon Allport, December 23, 1951. HUA.

Bruner, Jerome, to E. G. Boring, May 10, 1951 (marked "letter never sent"). HUA.

Bruner, Jerome, to James C. Miller, November 1, 1948. HUA.

Bruner, Jerome. *In Search of Mind: Essays in Autobiography*. New York: Harper & Row, 1983.

Buck, Paul H., to G. W. Allport, C. K. M. Kluckhohn, O. H. Mowrer, H. A. Murray, and Talcott Parsons, June 11, 1943 (copy to Dean Jones, July 6, 1943). HUA.

Buck, Paul H., to E. G. Boring, 1944. Quoted in Lawrence T. Nichols, "Social Relations Undone: Disciplinary Divergence and Departmental Politics at Harvard, 1946–70," *American Sociologist* 29, no. 2 (Summer 1998): 87.

Buck, Paul H., to E. G. Boring, November 20, 1945. HUA.

Buck, Paul H., to Talcott Parsons, October 16, 1945. HUA.

Buck, Paul H., to Payson S. Wild et al., November 14, 1945. HUA.

Buck, Paul H., ed. *Social Sciences at Harvard, 1860–1920: From Inculcation to the Open Mind*. Cambridge, MA: Harvard University Press, 1965.

Buhle, Paul. "David Riesman: Radical American Sociologist Whose Landmark Book, *The Lonely Crowd*, First Challenged the Values of the Consumer Society." *Guardian*, May 13, 2002.

Campbell, Donald T. "The Ethnocentrism of the Disciplines and the Fish-Scale Model of Omniscience." As cited in *Interdisciplinary Relationships in the Social Sciences*, by Muzafer Sherif and Carolyn Sherif. Chicago: Aldine, 1969.

Carey, Benedict. "Jerome Bruner, Who Shaped Understanding of the Young Mind, Dies at 100." *New York Times*, June 9, 2016.

Chase, Alston. "Harvard and the Making of the Unabomber." *Atlantic*, June 2000. https://www.theatlantic.com/magazine/archive/2000/06/harvard-and-the-making-of-the-unabomber/378239.

———. *A Mind for Murder: The Education of the Unabomber and the Origins of Modern Terrorism*. New York: Norton, 2003.

Christoffel, Tom, David Finkelhor, and Dan Gilbarg, eds. *Up Against the American Myth: A Radical Critique of Corporate Capitalism Based upon the Controversial Harvard College Course, Social Relations 148–149*. New York: Holt, Rinehart & Winston, 1970.

Church, Robert L. "The Economists Study Society: Sociology at Harvard, 1891–1902." In *Social Sciences at Harvard: From Inculcation to the Open Mind*, edited by Paul H. Buck. Cambridge, MA: Harvard University Press, 1965.

Cohen-Cole, Jamie. *The Open Mind: Cold War Politics and the Sciences of Human Nature*. Chicago: University of Chicago Press, 2014.

Colt, George Howe. *The Game: Harvard, Yale, and America in 1968*. New York: Scribner, 2018.

"David Clarence McClelland, Faculty of Arts and Sciences." Memorial Minute. *Harvard Gazette*, November 8, 2007. https://news.harvard.edu/gazette/story /2007/11/david-clarence-mcclelland.

"David Riesman, Author of *The Lonely Crowd*." Memorial Minute. *Harvard Gazette*, November 13, 2003. https://news.harvard.edu/gazette/story/2003/11 /memorial-minute-david-riesman-author-of-the-lonely-crowd.

Davis, James A., to Franklin Ford, October 1, 1968. HUA.

Department of Psychology, Harvard University. "History." Accessed October 31, 2021. https://psychology.fas.harvard.edu/about.

Diamond, Sigmund. *Compromised Campus: The Collaboration of Universities with the Intelligence Community, 1945–1955*. New York: Oxford University Press, 1992.

Dunlop, J. T., et al. "Toward a Common Language for the Area of Social Science." Unpublished memorandum, Harvard University, 1941. Tozzer Library, Harvard University.

Elliott, Clark A., and Margaret W. Rossiter, eds. *Science at Harvard University: Historical Perspectives*. Cranbury, NJ: Associated University Press, 1992.

Engerman, David C. "The Rise and Fall of Wartime Social Science: Harvard's Refugee Interview Project, 1950–1954." In *Cold War Social Science: Knowledge Production, Liberal Democracy, and Human Nature*, edited by Mark Solovey and Hamilton Cravens. New York: Palgrave Macmillan, 2012.

———. "Social Science in the Cold War." *Isis* 101, no. 2 (June 2010): 393–400.

"Erik Erikson, 91, Psychoanalyst Who Reshaped Views of Human Growth, Dies." *New York Times*, May 13, 1994.

Evans, Richard I. *Gordon Allport: The Man and His Ideas*. New York: E. P. Dutton, 1971.

Fels, Anna. "Hello, Jung Lovers." *New York Times*, February 21, 1993.

Fine, Gary. "The Dissolution of Social Relations at Harvard: A Social History." Unpublished paper, n.d., 5–6.

Gardner, Howard. "A Requiem for 'Soc Rel: Here's to Synthesizing Social Science." Blog of Howard Gardner, Hobbs Professor of Cognition and Education, Harvard Graduate School of Education, October 4, 2018. https://howardgardner .com/2018/04/10/a-requiem-for-soc-rel-heres-to-synthesizing-social-science.

———. *A Synthesizing Mind: A Memoir from the Creator of Multiple Intelligence Theory*. Cambridge, MA: MIT Press, 2020.

"Garmezy Attacks Soc Rel Dept." *Harvard Crimson*, April 15, 1967.

Geertz, Clifford. *After the Fact: Two Countries, Four Decades, One Anthropologist*. Cambridge, MA: Harvard University Press, 1995.

———. *Available Light: Anthropological Reflections on Philosophical Topics*. Princeton, NJ: Princeton University Press, 2000.

Gerhardt, Uta. *Talcott Parsons: An Intellectual Biography*. Cambridge, UK: Cambridge University Press, 2002.

———. "A World from Brave to New: Talcott Parsons and the War Effort at Harvard University." *Journal of the History of the Behavioral Sciences* 35, no. 3 (Summer 1999): 263–64.

Getz, Marshall J. "Henry Murray: Brief Life of a Personality Psychologist, 1893–1988." *Harvard Magazine*, March–April 2014. https://harvardmagazine.com/2014/03/henry-a-murray.

Gilman, Nils. *Mandarins of the Future: Modernization Theory in Cold War America.* Baltimore, MD: Johns Hopkins University Press, 2003.

Goethals, George. "Memorandum Containing Plans Submitted by Messrs: Pattullo, Bales, DeVore, Whiting, Newman, Homans and Lamberg-Karlovsky." November 18, 1970. Department of Psychology and Social Relations files, Harvard University.

Gordon, Noah. "The Hallucinogenic Drug Cult." *The Reporter*, August 15, 1963, 36. https://bibliography.maps.org/bibliography/default/resource/13433.

Greenfield, Robert. *Timothy Leary: A Biography.* Orlando, FL: Harcourt, 2006.

Greiger, Roger. *American Higher Education after World War II.* Princeton, NJ: Princeton University Press, 2019.

Gyure, Dale Allen. *Minoru Yamasaki: Humanist Architecture for a Modernist World.* New Haven, CT: Yale University Press, 2017.

Handler, Richard. "An Interview with Clifford Geertz." *Current Anthropology* 32, no. 5 (December 1991): 603–13.

"Harvard Conspiracy Seeks New Education." *Harvard Crimson*, March 20, 1969. https://www.thecrimson.com/article/1969/3/20/harvard-conspiracy-seeks-new-education-pa.

"Harvard Ousting Aide in Drug Case." *New York Times*, May 27, 1963, 41.

Harvard University. *The Behavioral Sciences at Harvard.* Faculty committee report. Cambridge, MA: Harvard University Press, 1954.

Hechinger, Fred. "Use of 'Mind-Distorting' Drugs Rising at Harvard, Dean Says." *New York Times*, December 11, 1962, 1, 3.

Hechinger, Fred M. "Harvard Debates Mind-Drug Peril, Psychologists Say Dean Errs on 'Danger' of Stimulants." *New York Times*, December 14, 1962, 7.

Herman, Ellen. *The Romance of American Psychology: Political Culture in the Age of Experts.* Oakland: University of California Press, 1995.

"Historical Faculty, B. F. Skinner." Department of Psychology, Harvard University. Accessed October 31, 2021. https://psychology.fas.harvard.edu/historical-faculty.

Homans, George C. Interview by Patrick L. Schmidt and Julia Moore, October 20, 1977. Tape recording. HUA.

Homans, George C. "Bringing Men Back In." *American Sociological Review* 25, no. 5 (December 1964): 809.

Homans, George Caspar. *Coming to My Senses: The Autobiography of a Sociologist.* New Brunswick, NJ: Transaction, 1984.

Inkeles, Alex. "Clyde Kluckhohn's Contribution to Studies of Russia and the Soviet Union." In *Culture and Life: Essays in Memory of Clyde Kluckhohn*, edited by W. Taylor, J. Fischer, and E. Vogt. Carbondale: Southern Illinois University Press, 1973.

Ireland, Corydon. "Howard Gardner: A Blessing of Influences." *Harvard Gazette*, October 17, 2013. http://news.harvard.edu/gazette/story/2013/10/the-mentors-of-howard-gardner.

Isaac, Joel. "Theorist at Work: Talcott Parsons and the Carnegie Project on Theory, 1949–1951." *Journal of the History of Ideas* 71, no. 2 (April 2010): 300–301.

———. *Working Knowledge: Making the Human Sciences from Parsons to Kuhn.* Cambridge, MA: Harvard University Press, 2012.

Jacobs, Jerry A. "Interdisciplinary Hype," *Chronicle of Higher Education*, November 22, 2009.

James, William. *The Will to Believe: And Other Essays in Popular Philosophy.* New York: Longmans Green, 1907.

Johnson, Benton, and Miriam Johnson. "The Integrating of the Social Sciences: Theoretical and Empirical Research and Training in the Department of Social Relations at Harvard." In *The Nationalization of the Social Sciences*, edited by Samuel Z. Klausner and Victor M. Lidz. Philadelphia: University of Pennsylvania Press, 1986.

Johnston, Barry V. "The Contemporary Crisis and the Social Relations Department at Harvard: A Case Study in Hegemony and Disintegration." *American Sociologist* 29, no. 3 (Fall 1998).

———. *Pitirim A. Sorokin: An Intellectual Biography.* Lawrence: University of Kansas Press, 1995.

Kaczynski, David. *Every Last Tie: The Story of the Unabomber and His Family.* Durham, NC: Duke University Press, 2016.

———. "Ted and the CIA, Part 1." *Times Union*, December 19, 2010. https://blog.timesunion.com/kaczynski/ted-and-the-cia-part-1/271.

Kahn, E. J., Jr. *Harvard: Through Change and Through Storm.* New York: Norton, 1969.

Keller, Morton, and Phyllis Keller. *Making Harvard Modern: The Rise of America's University.* New York: Oxford University Press, 2001.

Kelman, Herbert. Interview by Patrick L. Schmidt and Julia Moore, January 27, 1978. Tape recording. HUA.

Klausner, Samuel Z., and Victor M. Lidz, eds. *The Nationalization of the Social Sciences.* Philadelphia: University of Pennsylvania Press, 1986.

Kluckhohn, Clyde, to Paul H. Buck, November 18, 1945. HUA.

Kluckhohn, Clyde, and Henry Murray, eds. *Personality in Nature, Society, and Culture.* New York: Knopf, 1948.

Kutik, William M. "Black Leader Plans Lecture Here Monday." *Harvard Crimson*, September 24, 1968.

Lagemann, Ellen Condliffe. *The Politics of Knowledge: The Carnegie Corporation, Philanthropy and Public Policy.* Chicago: University of Chicago Press, 1989.

Lashley, Karl S., to Edwin G. Boring, January 6, 1937. HUA.

Lattin, Don. *The Harvard Psychedelic Club: How Timothy Leary, Ram Dass, Huston Smith, and Andrew Weil Killed the Fifties and Ushered in a New Age for America.* New York: HarperCollins, 2010.

Leary, Timothy. *Flashbacks: An Autobiography.* Los Angeles: J. P. Tarcher, 1983.

Leary, Timothy, and Richard Alpert. Letter to the editor. *Harvard Crimson*, December 13, 1962.

Lee, Joseph. "Report of Committee to Visit the Department of Philosophy and Psychology, in Reports of the Visiting Committee of the Board of Overseers of Harvard College: For the Academic Year 1932–33." Harvard University.

Leighton, Alexander. *Human Relations in a Changing World.* New York: E. P. Dutton, 1949.

Leonard, John. "Rent a Liberal Technologue, Cheap." Books of the Times. *New York Times,* June 3, 1970. https://www.nytimes.com/1970/06/03/archives/books-of-the-times-sociology-2-rent-a-liberal-technologue-cheap.html.

Lindzey, Gardner. Interview by Patrick L. Schmidt and Julia Moore, December 10, 1977. Tape recording. HUA.

Lipset, Seymour Martin, and David Riesman. *Education and Politics at Harvard.* New York: McGraw-Hill, 1971.

Lundstedt, Sven. *Higher Education in Social Psychology.* Cleveland, OH: Press of Case Western Reserve University, 1968.

Lyons, Gene M. *The Uneasy Partnership: Social Science and the Federal Government in the Twentieth Century.* New York: Russell Sage Foundation, 1969.

Magalif, Jeff. "Professors Seek Autonomy for Social Psychologists." *Harvard Crimson,* April 6, 1970.

Maher, Brendan A. Interview by Patrick L. Schmidt and Julia Moore, December 1, 1977. Tape recording. HUA.

McClelland, David C. Interviews by Patrick L. Schmidt and Julia Moore, November 8 and 16, 1977. Tape recording. HUA.

McClelland, David C. "Final Report to Dean Ford from David C. McClelland, Chairman, Dean's *Ad Hoc* Committee on the Future of the Behavioral Sciences at Harvard." May 1963. HUA.

McCown, James. "For a Time, Jose Lluís Sert's Brawny Buildings Defined Modern Boston." *Metropolis,* September 23, 2019.

McGrath, Charles. "The Lives They Lived; Big Thinkster." *New York Times Magazine,* December 29, 2002. https://www.nytimes.com/2002/12/29/magazine/the-lives-they-lived-big-thinkster.html.

Mead, Margaret, and Rhoda Metraux, eds. *The Study of Western Cultures.* Vol. 1, *The Study of Culture at a Distance.* Chicago: University of Chicago Press, 1953.

Minutes from Faculty of Arts and Sciences Meeting, January 29, 1946, Harvard University. HUA.

Minutes from Faculty of Arts and Sciences Meeting, May 16, 1971, Harvard University. E. L. Pattullo files, Center for the Behavioral Sciences, Department of Psychology and Social Relations, Harvard University.

"Modern Monday: William James Hall." Cambridge Historical Commission, December 11, 2018.

Morrison, Samuel Eliot. *The Development of Harvard University, 1869–1929.* Cambridge, MA: Harvard University Press, 1930.

Mowrer, O. Hobart, to Paul H. Buck, November 16, 1945. HUA.

Murray, Henry. "What Should Psychologists Do about Psychoanalysis?" *Journal of Abnormal and Social Psychology* 35 (1940): 154.

Murray, Henry A. Interviews by Patrick L. Schmidt and Julia Moore, September 28 and November 30, 1977. Tape recordings. HUA.

Murray, Henry A. "Professor Murray Describes Department of Abnormal Psychology." *Harvard Crimson,* January 12, 1929, 1.

Newman, Edwin B. Interviews by Patrick L. Schmidt and Julia Moore, October 21 and November 4, 1977. Tape recordings. HUA.

Nichols, Lawrence T. "Social Relations Undone: Disciplinary Divergence and Departmental Politics at Harvard, 1946–70." *American Sociologist* 29, no. 2 (Summer 1998): 83–107.

Nolan, Michael D. "PSR Simplifies Moniker, Forsakes SR to Become P." *Harvard Crimson,* February 7, 1986.

Nossiter, Bernard D. "Radicalism Course Splits Harvard." *Washington Post,* May 29, 1969, A8.

———. "Student-Led Course Shatters Tradition at Harvard." *Washington Post,* May 30, 1969, A6.

Official Register of Harvard University, Department of Social Relations. Cambridge, MA: Harvard University Press, 1946. HUA.

"Ousted Educator Rebuts Harvard." *New York Times,* May 28, 1963, 13.

Owens, B. Robert. "Producing Parsons' Reputation: Early Critiques of Talcott Parsons Social Theory and the Making of a Caricature." *Journal of the History of the Behavioral Sciences* 46, no. 2 (2010): 174.

Parsons, Talcott, to Paul H. Buck, April 3, 1944. HUA.

Parsons, Talcott, to Paul H. Buck, November 16, 1945. HUA.

Parsons, Talcott, to McGeorge Bundy, November 8, 1955. HUA.

Parsons, Talcott. Interviews by Patrick L. Schmidt and Julia Moore, October 17, 1977; November 1 and 15, 1977. Tape recordings. HUA.

Parsons, Talcott. "Clyde Kluckhohn and the Integration of Social Science." In *Culture and Life: Essays in Memory of Clyde Kluckhohn,* edited by W. Taylor, J. Fischer, and E. Vogt. Carbondale: Southern Illinois University Press, 1973.

Parsons, Talcott. *Department and Laboratory of Social Relations: The First Decade, 1946–1956.* Chairman's report, 1956. HUA.

Parsons, Talcott. *Essays in Sociological Theory.* Glencoe, IL: Free Press, 1949.

Parsons, Talcott. "On Building Social Systems Theory: A Personal History." *Daedalus* 99, no. 4 (1970): 826–81.

Parsons, Talcott, and Edward Shils, eds. *Toward a General Theory of Action.* Cambridge, MA: Harvard University Press, 1951.

Patterson, Orlando. "The Last Sociologist." *New York Times,* May 19, 2002.

Pattullo, E. L. Interview by Patrick L. Schmidt and Julia Moore, October 28, 1977. Tape recording. HUA.

Pattullo, E. L. Director of the Center for Behavioral Sciences, Harvard University. Personal communication, November 1977.

Pattullo, E. L. "About." Department of Psychology, Harvard University. Accessed October 31, 2021. https://psychology.fas.harvard.edu/about.

Pattullo, E. L. Note to file, n.d. Department of Psychology and Social Relations, Harvard University.

Penner, James ed. *Timothy Leary: The Harvard Years.* Rochester, VT: Park Street Press, 2014.

Perry, Ralph B. *The Thought and Character of William James.* Boston: Little, Brown, 1936.

"Personality and Its Functions; Personality in Nature, Society and Culture." *New York Times*, November 21, 1948.

Peters, John Durham, and Peter Simonson, eds. *Mass Communication and American Social Thought: Key Texts, 1919–1968*. Lanham, MD: Rowman & Littlefield, 2004.

Pettigrew, Thomas F. Interview by Patrick L. Schmidt and Julia Moore, November 6, 1977. Tape recording. HUA.

"The Place of Psychology in an Ideal University: The Report of the University Commission on the Future of Psychology at Harvard." Harvard University, 1947.

Potts, David B. "Social Ethics at Harvard, 1881–1931: A Study in Activism." In *Social Sciences at Harvard, 1860–1920: From Inculcation to the Open Mind*, edited by Paul H. Buck. Cambridge, MA: Harvard University Press, 1965.

Price, David H. *Anthropological Intelligence: The Deployment and Neglect of American Anthropology in the Second World War*. Durham, NC: Duke University Press, 2008.

———. *Cold War Anthropology: The CIA, the Pentagon, and the Growth of Dual Use Anthropology*. Durham, NC: Duke University Press, 2016.

Reinhold, Robert. "Harvard Changes Sociology's Role." *New York Times*, June 1, 1970. https://www.nytimes.com/1970/06/01/archives/harvard-changes -sociologys-role-reestablishes-department-after.html.

———. "A Mentor of Sociologists Retires after 42 Years at Harvard Post." *New York Times*, June 14, 1973.

Riesman, David, to E. L. Pattullo, May 23, 1978. Author's files.

Riesman, David, to Patrick L. Schmidt, May 23, 1978. Author's files.

Riesman, David. *Constraint and Variety in American Education*. Garden City, NY: Doubleday, 1958.

Riesman, David, with Reuel Denney and Nathan Glazer. "Storytellers as Tutors in Technique: From *The Lonely Crowd*." In *Mass Communication and American Social Thought: Key Texts, 1919–1968*, edited by John Durham Peters and Peter Simonson, 293–308. Lanham, MD: Rowman & Littlefield, 2004.

Robinson, Forrest G. *Love's Story Told: A Life of Henry A. Murray*. Cambridge, MA: Harvard University Press, 1992.

Russin, Joseph M., and Andrew T. Weil. "The *Crimson* Takes Leary, Alpert to Task: 'Roles' & 'Games' in William James." *Harvard Crimson*, May 28, 1963. https:// www.thecrimson.com/article/1973/1/24/the-crimson-takes-leary-alpert-to.

Sahakian, W. S. *History and Systems of Psychology*. New York: Wiley, 1975.

Schmidt, Patrick L. "Towards a History of the Department of Social Relations, Harvard University, 1946–1972." Undergraduate honors thesis, Harvard University, 1978.

Schneider, David M. *Schneider on Schneider: The Conversion of the Jews and Other Anthropological Stories*. Edited by Richard Handler. Durham, NC: Duke University Press, 1995.

Sendor, Benjamin. "Clinical Psychology at Harvard: Case History of In [*sic*] Institutional Identity Crisis." *Harvard Crimson*, May 23, 1973. https://www .thecrimson.com/article/1973/5/23/clinical-psychology-at-harvard-pbabt-the.

Sherif, Muzafer, and Carolyn Sherif. *Interdisciplinary Relationships in the Social Sciences*. Chicago: Aldine, 1969.

Skinner, B. F. Interview by Patrick L. Schmidt and Julia Moore, October 28, 1977. Tape recording. HUA.

Smith, M. B. Review of *Toward a General Theory of Action*, edited by T. Parsons, E. A. Shils, E. C. Tolman, G. W. Allport, C. Kluckhohn, H. A. Murray, R. R. Sears, R. C. Sheldon, and S. A. Stouffer. *Journal of Abnormal and Social Psychology* 48, no. 2 (1953): 315–18.

"Soc Rel Criticized at Adams Forum." *Harvard Crimson*, March 22, 1950.

"Soc Rel Votes to Drop Clinical Psychology." *Harvard Crimson*, March 2, 1967.

"Social Relations 'Correction.'" *Harvard Crimson*, May 3, 1949.

"Social Relations Dep. Will Study Its Program." *Harvard Crimson*, October 18, 1949.

Solovey, Mark. "Cold War Social Science: Specter, Reality, or Useful Concept?" In *Cold War Science: Knowledge, Liberal Democracy, and Human Nature*, edited by Mark Solovey and Hamilton Cravens. New York: Palgrave Macmillan, 2012.

Solovey, Mark, and Hamilton Cravens, eds. *Cold War Social Science: Knowledge Production, Liberal Democracy, and Human Nature*. New York: Palgrave Macmillan 2012.

Spiegel, John. Interview by Patrick L. Schmidt and Julia Moore, November 17, 1977. Tape recording. HUA.

Stern, Sheldon M. "William James and the New Psychology." In *Social Sciences at Harvard, 1860–1920: From Inculcation to the Open Mind*, edited by Paul H. Buck. Cambridge, MA: Harvard University Press, 1965.

Storer, Norman W. *The Social System of Science*. New York: Holt, Rinehart & Winston, 1966.

Stouffer, Samuel. *The American Soldier*. Vol. 1, *Adjustment during Army Life*. Vol. 2, *Combat and Its Aftermath*. Princeton, NJ: Princeton University Press, 1949.

———. *Social Research to Test Ideas*. Glencoe, IL: Free Press, 1962.

Studlien, Kristen G. "Murray Center Seals Kaczynski Data." *Harvard Crimson*, July 14, 2000. https://www.thecrimson.com/article/2000/7/14/murray-center-seals-kaczynski-data-plondon-buried/?page=3.

"Survey of Harvard Ph.D.'s from Department of Social Relations 1950–54." Department of Social Relations file, Harvard University. HUA.

Taylor, Mark C. "End the University as We Know It." *New York Times*, May 26, 2009.

Taylor, Walter W., John L. Fischer, and Evon Z. Vogt, eds. *Culture and Life: Essays in Memory of Clyde Kluckhohn*. Carbondale: Southern Illinois University Press, 1973.

Triplet, Rodney G. "Harvard Psychology, the Psychological Clinic, and Henry A. Murray: A Case Study in the Establishment of Disciplinary Boundaries." In *Science at Harvard University: Historical Perspectives*, edited by Clark A. Elliott and Margaret W. Rossiter. Cranbury, NJ: Associated University Press, 1992.

Triplet, Rodney G. "Henry A. Murray: The Making of a Psychologist?" *American Psychologist* 47, no. 2 (February 1992): 299–307.

"Un Original," *Harvard Magazine*, March 1, 2000.

United States Office of Strategic Services Assessment Staff. *Assessment of Men; Selection of Personnel for the Office of Strategic Services*. New York: Rhinehart, 1948.

University News Office, 1946–71. Friday Afternoon Papers, Harvard University, February 1, 1946. HUA.

Vidich, Arthur J. *With a Critical Eye: An Intellectual and His Times.* Knoxville, TN: Newfound Press, 2009.

Weil, Andrew. *Dying to Know: Ram Dass & Timothy Leary—Extras.* Directed by Gay Dillingham. August 26, 2016.

Weil, Andrew T. "Social Relations at Harvard after Seventeen Years: Problems, Successes and a Highly Uncertain Future." *Harvard Crimson*, June 13, 1963.

———. "The Strange Case of the Harvard Drug Scandal." *Look*, November 5, 1963. https://bibliography.maps.org/bibliography/default/resource/15046.

White, Harrison. Interview by Patrick L. Schmidt and Julia Moore, October 19, 1977. Tape recording. HUA.

White, Harrison. "Directions for Sociology." April 21, 1970. Unpublished memorandum in E. L. Pattullo files, Center for the Behavioral Sciences, Department of Psychology and Social Relations, Harvard University.

White, Robert W. Interview by Patrick L. Schmidt and Julia Moore, December 1, 1977. Tape recording. HUA.

White, Sheldon. Interview by Patrick L. Schmidt and Julia Moore, November 14, 1977. Tape recording. HUA.

Whiting, John. Interview by Patrick L. Schmidt and Julia Moore, November 27, 1977. Tape recording. HUA.

Wylie, Laurence. Interview by Patrick L. Schmidt and Julia Moore, October 20, 1977. Tape recording. HUA.

Yarrow, Andrew L. "Nathan Pusey, Harvard President through Growth and Turmoil Alike, Dies at 94." *New York Times*, October 15, 2001. http://mobile.ny times.com/2001/11/15/us/nathan-pusey-harvard-president-through-growth -and-turmoil-dies-at-94.html.

Index

Aberle, David, 64

The Achieving Society (McClelland), 118

Adams, Henry, 12

affectivity–affective neutrality, 78

Air Force, U.S., Human Relations Research Institute (HRRI) of, 89, 91

Allport, Gordon, 2, 4, *16*, 25, 26, 57, 59–61, 64, 171; on animal psychology, 22; Boring and, 15, 20–23, 36–37, 55; Bruner and, 96, 99–100; Buck and, 37–38, 39, 40, 41–42, 53; Center for the Behavioral Sciences and, 132–33; death of, 137; Emerson Hall and, 132; experimental psychology and, 20–23; Freud and, 14–15, 21, 29; interdisciplinary research and, 29, 36–38; James, W., and, 21; lines of inquiry of, 84; Murray and, 14–16, 18, 29, 36; on operationism, 20–21, 133; as possible Soc Rel leadership successor, 103; psychoanalysis and, 29; "Psychological Service for Civilian Morale" by, 44; Psychology Department and, 42; Sociology Department and, 39; on Soc Rel decline, 95, 99; on Soc Rel end and

value, 162; on Soc Rel prematurity, 101; temporary departure of, 24; in *Toward a General Theory of Action,* 76, 80; on veterans in Soc Rel, 69; William James Hall and, 136; World War II and, 44

Alper, Thelma, 64

Alpert, Richard (Ram Dass), 2, 117–31, 161; *Be Here Now* by, 119; dismissal of, 125; at Fourteenth International Congress of Applied Psychology, 128; IFIF and, 124; Pusey and, 125

"American Character and Social Structure" (Harvard course), 109

The American Soldier (Research Branch of War Department), 48

"Analysis of the Personality of Adolph Hitler" (Murray), 47

animal psychology, 22

anthropology: FMAD and, 47. *See also* cultural anthropology; social anthropology

Anthropology and Modern Life, 65

Anthropology Department, 1; Human Relations Department and, 32, 35; Parsons on, 39–40; Riesman on, 116–17; social anthropology in, 3,

"Toward a Common Language for the Area of Social Science" (Parsons, Kluckhohn, C., Dunlop, Gilmore, and Taylor, O.), 31, 34–36, 160

Toward a General Theory of Action (Parsons and Shils), 76–81, 105–6, 139, 159; Bruner on, 100; White, R., and, 104; as "Yellow Book," 80

Tozzer, Alfred M., 26, 54–55, 57

Unabomber. *See* Kaczynski, Ted

"Values, Motives, and Systems of Action" (Parsons and Shils), 76–77, 80

veterans of WWII, 69

Vidich, Arthur, 82–84

Village in the Vaucluse (Wylie), 111

Vogel, Ezra F., 152, 172

Vogt, Evon Z., 103, 131, 171

War Department, Research Branch of, 3, 44–45, 48, 65

Warner, Lloyd, 5

Watson, John, 177n67

Weber, Max, 26, 27, 29, 41

Weil, Andrew, 125–26, 131–32, 210n120

Wellman, Barry, 172

White, Andrew Tredway, 23, 24

White, Harrison C., 149, 152–53, 172

White, Robert, 14, 64, 100; as possible Soc Rel leadership successor, 103, 104

Whiting, Beatrice, 172

Whiting, John, 172

Whitney, E. A., 25

Wild, Payson S., 35–36

William James Hall, 132–37, 161

The Will to Believe (James, W.), 136

Winston, Harry, 125

Winston, Ronnie, 125–26

Working Knowledge (Isaac), 195n128

Working Papers in the Theory of Action (Parsons and Bales), 102

World War II: interdisciplinary research and, 44–50; veterans of, 69. *See also specific offices and departments*

Wylie, Laurence, 171; as Soc Rel faculty member, 108, 111

Yale, Institute of Human Relations at, 2, 49, 60, 160, 167

Yamasaki, Minoru, 134–35

"Yellow Book," 80

Yerkes, R. M., 7

Young Man Luther (Erikson), 110

Zimmerman, Carle C., 26, 57, 64; Parsons on, 39

About the Author

Patrick L. Schmidt is an attorney in Washington, DC. He received a BA, magna cum laude, from Harvard College, a JD from Georgetown University Law Center, and an MIPP from the Johns Hopkins University School of Advanced International Studies. He also completed graduate studies in international law in the PhD program at the University of Madrid (Complutense) Law School pursuant to a Rotary Foundation Fellowship.

Made in United States
North Haven, CT
26 February 2023